MW01699659

MORE ADVA

Prepare To Prosper, Taking Your Business to a HIGHER LEVEL

By Kathleen D. Mailer

Kathleen has a true desire to help other people around her succeed, which I believe is one of the main themes in this valuable book. Her no-nonsense approach and perseverance are what makes her one of the greatest leaders and influencers of our time. The book is for the business owner who wants to walk and prosper in authority in the very industry to which God has called them.

Brad Fisher, Speaker/ **CEO of Solid Financial Solutions Inc.**

Kathleen offers great coaching and enthusiasm for the work that she does. Her pursuit of living every day with great hope and inspiration is a vital aspect in an otherwise trying task of bringing your dreams to reality. Every bit of this is evident in this book. I respectfully endorse and encourage you to devour every morsel. The value of doing so will become abundantly clear and the outcome is as real as she suggests in her teachings.

Richard G. Hobbs, Senior Financial Consultant/Speaker/Author of *When Money Hurts: 10 Prescriptions for Long-Term Financial Health*

This is a must read book for marketplace ministry. Jesus was a “marketplace minister.” Most of His ministry was with the people in the market, not in the synagogues. There seems to be a “poverty spirit” within the church, and we need to recognize that the real “church” is outside the four walls of the sanctuary. Christians need to take their rightful place as leaders in business, media and government. Why would the world want to follow someone who has a mentality of poverty? This book will show you how to move in your gifts and is written by someone who has “walked the walk.”

Reverend Ellen Campbell, CEO and Founder of **Canadian Centre for Abuse Awareness/**Author of *‘Put Your Therapist Out Of Work’*

Kathleen has been in the trenches of business and knows what it takes to succeed. She is dedicated to helping others grow and build their dreams. In this book you will discover the fundamental truth; in order to be successful all of the success elements must line up or there will be constant struggle. You will learn to align your purpose, gifts and talents; and merge them with experience, knowledge and perseverance. Let this powerful book guide you down your own success path.

Colleen Hierath, CEO of Customer Recruiting Academy/ Author of *Breath*/Speaker/ Trainer/**Executive Managing Director**, Lethbridge Chapter, **eWomenNetwork**

Kathleen Mailer is definitely someone who has touched my life with her teachings in so many ways. When she says, "A book is never a book, it is a ministry," THAT without a doubt is the truth. This is the truth with this book! The wisdom and insight you will gain will take you to a level you never dreamed of. Thought provoking tools, inside and out! Marketing starts in your heart. As she says, "success comes within — where Jesus lives." If your purpose is PURE PURPOSE, then you need this book to pursue your passion.

Laura Streicher, Speaker/Author/Trainer.

Kathleen's ability and willingness to transfer this profound knowledge and these deep insights are astounding. This is definitely the way we should all be doing business. Those who are unable to evolve or modify their businesses quickly enough to start following these core principles will be left in the dust, wondering what happened. If I would have had this reference manual 20 years ago when I started creating and running many of my own businesses, I would be in a completely different and far better place today **guaranteed**! Since applying these principles, I now can create abundance for myself (and in return advance the Kingdom) in many more ways than just financial.

Paul Larsen, CEO, Founder of Ground Zero Recovery Group/Speaker/Author of *Too Afraid to Live, Too Scared to Die*

Running a business can be your opportunity to showcase your expertise and position yourself as an authority. But — it can also get complicated FAST. Without a mentor to share a proven strategy, the whole process can simply end up in disappointment and financial failure. To make it a success, you'll need an adviser to pilot you past the pitfalls and an advocate to make sure your business makes the positive impact it was meant to have in the world. Kathleen D. Mailer is that mentor and her new book *Prepare to Prosper; Taking Your Business To a Higher Level* will light your path to prosperity and include you in the inner circle of triumph. See you at the top!

Cheryl Scoffield, The Follow Up Specialist, **CEO of Kickstart Your Company**/Speaker/ Trainer/Author

I have worked with Kathleen for two years now and I don't believe I've ever met such a creative, focused, faith-filled business owner before. Kathleen gets a vision, then just goes out and makes it happen. She is fearless, wide-thinking, encouraging, supportive and delightfully fun to work with. I watch and listen carefully to everything she does and says, and my business is better because of it. Remarkably all of that is transferred within the pages of this magnificent book. Grab it, read it, and apply it. You'll be glad you did!

Darlene Hull, Founder of **HotSpot Promotion**/Author/Speaker/Trainer

There are a lot of very good well-known speakers ministering the Word of God, and there are a few very good Christian TV journalists who are unashamedly faith oriented in their points of view. I enjoy hearing and reading their works... With Kathleen you get both and more. With the combination of being a prophetic speaker for 'situation', a strong practical business sense, and the passion to see others succeed in dreams once held, she has a voice that speaks directly to the sense of the common man or women. Just hearing Kathleen's voice one feels energized to consider lost initiatives and dreams again, both men and women. She is a voice for common sense, a voice that accesses a knowledge we sense is right, but without a reason to believe it, we lack the courage to start. Kathleen gives such an anointing that one feels they can start to pursue personal hopes and dreams again.

Patrick L. Kilpatrick, Former Pastor/ Blog Writer/Author/**Christian TV Studio Manager and Producer**

Kathleen D. Mailer is a woman of her word that stands firmly on the Word of God! She truly delivers the keys for you to successfully accomplish what she teaches. I fully expect that Kingdom Business Owners (K.B.O's) will uncover the essential elements necessary to blaze a trail to entrepreneurial success in this exciting and greatly anticipated new book Look out business world .....here we come!

Barb Needham, Author of *Fear Knot*/Coach

"Prepare to Prosper" is not just another book on being a Christian in the marketplace. It is a manifesto on having the right mind-set as a prosperous Kingdom Business Owner (KBO) as well as a seminal guide on how to be the hands and feet of Jesus in a lost world. If you are truly committed to being fired up and sold-out to Jesus as a KBO, read this book, practice its principles and prepare to prosper!

Leslie J. Smith, **B.A., LL.B./** Author of, *Legal Ease-Essential Legal Strategies to Protect Canadian Non-Union Employees* /**Of the Ontario Bar**, 1988

Although I have only known Kathleen a brief time, I sensed an instant bond. It quickly became evident that Kathleen works with those who are serious about making a difference for the Kingdom. She not only models the principles and has experienced the rise and fall of leadership; she has a deep heart for each one she works with. Kathleen transforms from the inside out. Just like her program, A Book is Never a Book, it is so much more; so is the training she offers to Kingdom Business Owners. She is the real deal and comes with a complete package. Kathleen is the pilot who will help you soar to levels you never dreamed possible.

Linda A Olson, Founder of **Made for Something More/** Author of *Uncovering the Champion Within; 101 Truths to a Powerful You/*Trainer/Speaker

I am very excited to be learning and applying the system Kathleen has put in place under the leadership of the Holy Spirit. We ARE meant to create wealth so that we can fund Kingdom purposes through our business ministries – just as Kathleen teaches. We do that by sharing our gifts talents and abilities with each other and FOR each other. Prepare to Prosper speaks the Truth about who our God is in relationship to our businesses and how satan is really just a "has been" who has NO business being in OUR business. It is time for K.B.O.'s to stand tall and take hold of the victory that is ours! This reference guide will expertly navigate you to ultimate success.

Margie McIntyre – Financial Advisor/Speaker/Author of *MIND MATTERS – Change Your Mind, Change Your Life*

Has Kathleen Mailer chosen a 'Big Mission' to help eradicate poverty? You bet she has! Is she up for the challenge? I know she is! This girl is on fire with both her Love of God and a desire to help entrepreneurs serve the world with their gifts. She knows AND applies the ultimate TRUTH: "Having the gifts differing according to the grace that is given to us, let us use them." (Romans 12:6 – New Kings James Bible). A big part of her Life Mission is to ensure people don't hide their gifts under a bush – but instead allow them to shine brightly in the world. She wants us to make a positive difference. She has poured everything into this one-stop reference guide…to that, I say, "Amen."

Janine L. Moore, Career Counsellor/Speaker/Trainer/Author of *Work On Your Own Terms In Midlife & Beyond.*

What a delight to walk side by side with Kathleen in marketplace ministry! I love her book and the truth that is spoken in the chapters. We must prosper in business and the power of our testimony can be the platform that sets us free. I know that I have experienced this full force by telling my story. Thank you Kathleen for paving the way for so many!

Diane Cunningham, M.Ed., Founder and President National Association of Christian Women Entrepreneurs

Grab a coffee and sit down with the best business book you will ever read! Kathleen D. Mailer is a highly successful entrepreneur, writer, speaker and business partner to many. She is brilliant, encouraging, and Spirit-filled. This exceptional woman shares openly the keys to living an abundant life. She provides concrete answers to the important question: "As a Christian, how should I run my business both to be very successful, and to honour God?" Learn from someone that actually lives the principles they outline and that excels in business and in life herself. Have time for your family, to travel, and to do good works WHILE having a very prosperous ongoing business. Prepare to Prosper will take your business, and your life, to a completely new level.

Coralie Banks, Fellow Certified Management Consultant, President of Leaping Cowgirl™ Productions and Braum Consulting Ltd., investor, entrepreneur, and strategist.

PREPARE TO PROSPER,

TAKING YOUR BUSINESS

TO A HIGHER LEVEL

By Kathleen D. Mailer

Published by **Aurora Publishing**
(a division of Doing Business God's Way International Inc.)

Aurora Publishing offers that this title may be purchased in bulk for any form of education, business, fundraising, or sales promotion use. For more information please contact our office at: 403-230-5946 x 2 **OR** email: aurorapublishing@shaw.ca

Unless otherwise noted, Scripture quoted in this book is from the NLT Version.

Library of Canada
Mailer, Kathleen D.
Prepare To Prosper, Taking Your Business To A Higher Level/Kathleen D. Mailer
Includes references and interviews
ISBN #1-897054-59-9; 978-1-8970545-9-8

1. Christian Business 2. Market Place Ministry 3. Entrepreneurship I. Title

Manufactured in Canada

Aurora Publishing, 44 Bernard Way NW, Calgary, AB T3K 2E9

<u>THIS BOOK IS DEDICATED</u>

My Deepest Thoughts

To all of the wonderful Christian Business owners, (aka: Kingdom Business owners), pastors, authors and trainers I have met through the years who have been struggling to be the 'Wealth Creators' they are called to be. This book is for you!

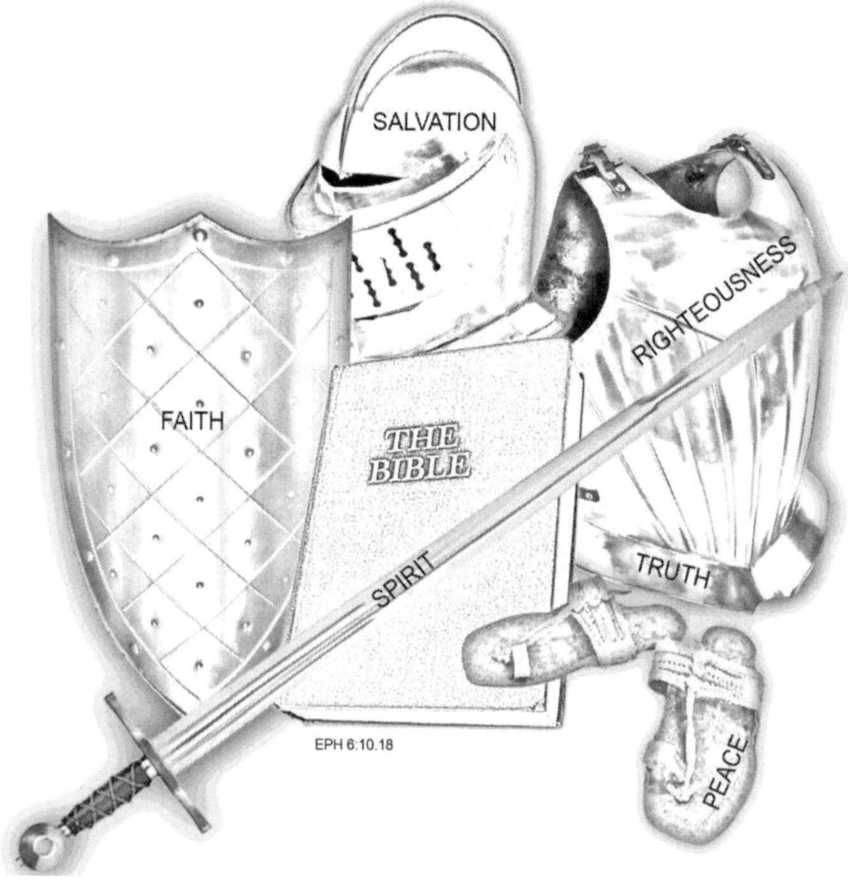
SALVATION
RIGHTEOUSNESS
FAITH
THE BIBLE
SPIRIT
TRUTH
EPH 6:10.18
PEACE

ACKNOWLEDGEMENT

Before Moving Forward

This book would not be sitting in your hands right now if it wasn't for wonderful, **dedicated men and women** who walk my path with me.

Their loyal dedication and push for excellence in all that they do reflect positively on me by default. Know, as you read through the pages, that there were many behind me who tirelessly poured over every aspect of this book – to make sure you have the reference material you have today.

People like, Mario Kaun, my God-given editor. Your help to make my scribbles understandable and coherent is more than a gift to me. It is truly a 'marvel'. Because you used this talent, I feel confident and proud of this book we accomplished. I feel like we can really go to the next level in a way I could never reach before. I don't know what I would do without you… a simple thank you seems so much less than I want to express in my heart.

My **Creative Design team**! You really packed a punch! Not only could you 'see' what I desperately wanted to express visually, you were able to 'show me'. The vision of what was in my heart came to life on these pages because of you. Thank you.

My cousin by blood and friend by choice, **Michelle**, thank you so much for your willingness to share your talents with me and help me stay on track. You helped me by-pass hours of work and let me focus on writing my message. Thanks for helping me and bailing me out when I needed an expert.

Pastor Mel and Heather Mullen, what can I say? You are my spiritual parents. You have helped us through so much. If I was to write everything down I could fill volumes of books. That being said, you believed in us as we grew and made our transition from the worldly business realm into full-fledged, head on doing business God's way. You lovingly guided us through the heart ache and pain of so much loss in our life. You encouraged us to step out and be who God has called us to be. You prayed for us when we thought we could not get up one more time. You positioned us as worthy through God's eyes of taking on this platform of purpose. My eyes swell with tears as I write this, because truly - no one could put into words the depth of gratitude I feel for both you. Thank you.

There is a **whole other 'category' of men and wome**n I would like to acknowledge here. I pray that the Holy Spirit awakens your heart when you read this, and tells you Himself that this acknowledgement was written with YOU in mind. You are friend, family and a partner - in business and in life. I pray that you KNOW I am talking directly to you - and just because I didn't list your name here… doesn't mean you are NOT just as special. Thank you for standing by me. Thank you for caring for me (and my family). Thank you that no matter what, I can come to you should I need a shoulder and support.

Dan Mailer, my best friend, lover, partner in life and in business. Even after 23 years of being married to you, I still feel the intensifying in my heart that God gave you to me! He made you ahead of time so that you could be ready for me, when I was ready. Working alongside of you all of these years has been a privilege and an honour. Merging our gifts and talents together to do the will of God has been one of the most incredible great decisions of my life. I look forward to our ministry and having it grow beyond our wildest dreams. God has been faithful and so have you.

May God bless each of you that I have mentioned above beyond anything you could ever imagine. May your life be filled with His love through many others. May you prosper, as your soul prospers. May you be forever sheltered by the storms of life. May you be lifted on wings, like eagles, and live the rest of your days in true blissful harmony. I pray an anointing of ease upon your life now as we grow together, even stronger, because together - we are leaving a legacy.

Last, but first in my life, I acknowledge **Jesus.** You are my Lord and Saviour. I owe you my life! I once was in such a horrible place. I was guilt ridden; debt ridden, at times, bed ridden – but you freed me from all of that. I was a workaholic; you delivered me. I am a shadow, now, of my former self – because you took it upon yourself to change my life for 'good'. How can one say thank you for that? I can only give you what I have, and that is my hands and my feet. I am honoured to serve you and even more determined than ever to shout out to the world… 'Better is one day in your courts than 1000 elsewhere!'

Holy Spirit, my business partner, friend, protector, counsellor, provider… and so much more! Through the process of writing a book, you have healed me from so many toxic pieces in my life. You have prepared me to take on the enormity of my calling. You have positioned me to prosper in ways that far exceed any monetary value. As I tell my students, when writing a book, you learn more about yourself and others than you would if you just lived a day-to-day existence. This book was no exception. I feel that I have come to know you better than ever. You have shown me open doors I never even knew existed. You have shown me fundamental truths that will take Dan and me to the far corners of the earth – to make an impact in the nations. You have truly opened my eyes to see and my ears to hear what lies beneath the snow-capped mountain tops.

You wrote this book, and you gave it to me to share… I am in awe that YOU personally asked ME to help you eradicate poverty in the nations – one business at a time. I still feel so unqualified. I still need your grace MORE than ever before. I WILL move forward – saying 'YES and AMEN' to the whispers you have placed on my heart.

Father God, your guidance, love and support mean everything to me. This book has felt like a long time in coming, but I know it is because you were making sure I was ready to take this to the level in which it has been received. You have shown me that you, are not like earthly fathers, you ARE the FATHER of us all. The healthy, strong, loving, guiding, disciplining, caring parent that wants His child to grow up and be the 'apple' of His eye.

Thank you Father for your never-ending patience with me. Thank you for making the 'crooked' places straight in my life. Thank you for continuing to lovingly correct my inadequacies. Thank you for reminding me of who I truly am. Thank you for forgiving me when I fall short even when I know better. THEN, only by your grace and mercy, you make it 'right' again. I love you…

Oh yes, I minister to those He has called me to minister…because of His GREAT love. I do it not because I have to but because I want you, my dear friend (who is reading this book now) to know the truth about your limitations, to break free of any obstacle in your way, and to have the tools you need to get to where you need to go.

We are in this thing together. We are NOT alone! Hallelujah! We are messengers in God's great army. God is asking for our help to reach the far corners of the earth by helping to advance the Kingdom. It is time for us to RISE to the challenge and let us take a stand! Thank you for trusting in me. I pray you enjoy the journey. May we all prosper just as God has intended us to. I speak this in Jesus mighty name. *Amen.*

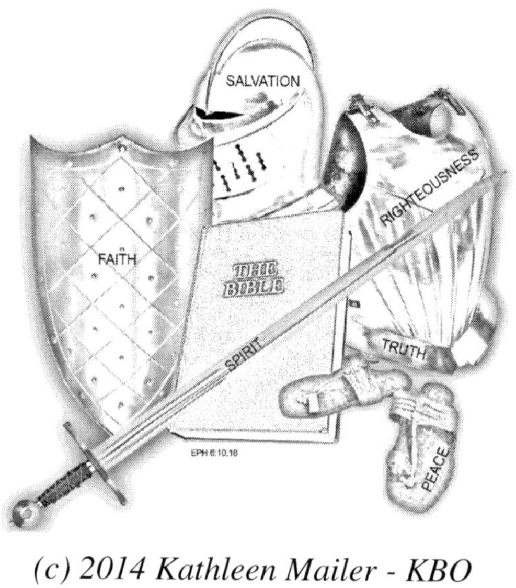
SALVATION
RIGHTEOUSNESS
FAITH
THE BIBLE
SPIRIT
TRUTH
EPH 6:10,18
PEACE

FORWARD

Pastor Mel Mullen

Kathleen's "Prepare to Prosper" will inspire you to believe for the bigger, the better and the greater in your life, family and business.

Kathleen understands the battles that you could face as an entrepreneur as you step into the arena of business. As a friend of Kathleen, I have watched her challenge the odds and come out on the other side with positive truths and a life experience that will strengthen you as you prepare for a more prosperous life.

Kathleen believes that every business needs a good Biblical foundation upon which to be successful. *"Prepare to Prosper"* provides you an excellent balance between spiritual truths and marketing strategies. She believes that the end result of owning a business that flourishes is the ability to contribute, and to meet the needs of people in our world.

By reading this book, you will become a better business leader, prosperity will come to you in every area of life, and you will have good success. Prosperity is not only the way you think, it is also the actions you take. This book will help you to gain the bountiful future God has ordained for his children.

Mel C. Mullen

Founding Pastor Word of Life Centre Church and Ministries/ Author of *Be A Man*/ Trainer/Speaker

TABLE OF CONTENTS

PREFACE

A note from Kathleen

15 Years ago I wrote the best-selling book, *Breaking Through Your Business Barriers, An Entrepreneurial Handbook.* I didn't know it then, but that book altered the course of my life - for the better.

It marked the season of my life where I could finally grow and prosper in my destiny. I found a passion in teaching people about business. I found the passion in encouraging others to find their voice and bringing their uniqueness to the masses. *'A Book is NEVER a Book Boot Camp, How to Write, Publish & Market Your OWN How To Book Now!'*

Unlike the years before, when I built businesses that would hit up against the proverbial glass ceiling – leaving my life in a shattered mess, my life took on a new direction. It was almost as if it was on a mission of its own design. I would not only shatter the glass ceiling when I came up against it, I would launch into a spiritual promotion that was WAY better than I could have expected. What I found was, with each advancement God would position me to stand face to face with a new challenge. The Holy Spirit and I would have to find new ways to succeed in business, in life, and in relationships.

Today I stand before you, 37 books later, retiring a 'good friend' (*Breaking Through Your Business Barriers*) and replacing it with a book that will surpass the success of every former book I have ever written. I believe it will catapult some entrepreneurs to explore creative business opportunities, blast others victoriously through their glass ceiling moments, and even promote others to prosper and live the life they are destined to live.

Business is but a metaphor to living a life of purpose… and I am determined to get that message out. If you do business God's way, you will not only forge a path and live a life of significance; you will impact and influence others to make the necessary changes they need to navigate through the course set before them. This is your business AND it IS a ministry!

I am looking for Christ-centered business owners who truly understand that inside of us lives the only HOPE for this world. As Kingdom Business Owners (throughout this book I will now call you a K.B.O.), we are meant to create wealth so that we can fund the purposes that are set before us and advance our church and our community. This may even mean GLOBAL community.

The truth is we are called to fund Kingdom purposes through our business ministry. My prayer is that this book will equip you with K.B.O Mentorship – for you and your team.

God gave me a vision of every church around the world embracing the K.B.O Mentorship Model and building up this ministry as a KEY element of their outreach to the world. Someone has to pay for the God sized ministry that every church should hunger for. It is time for business owners to step up to the platform and say, YES to a life of giving.

We are CALLED to use our gifts, talents and abilities and make a difference.

If this sounds like you, please read on… let's link arms and 'eradicate poverty in the nations!'

Glory to God!

Kathleen D. Mailer

PS: As a side note, you will notice that we have not spelled the name, satan with a capital 's'. This is not a grammatical mistake, or a typeset issue. Many years ago, I decided that satan doesn't deserve to be acknowledged as anything but a 'little s'… that's all I am saying on this subject. Shall we begin?....

SECTION ONE

BUILDING YOUR BUSINESS UPON THE ROCK

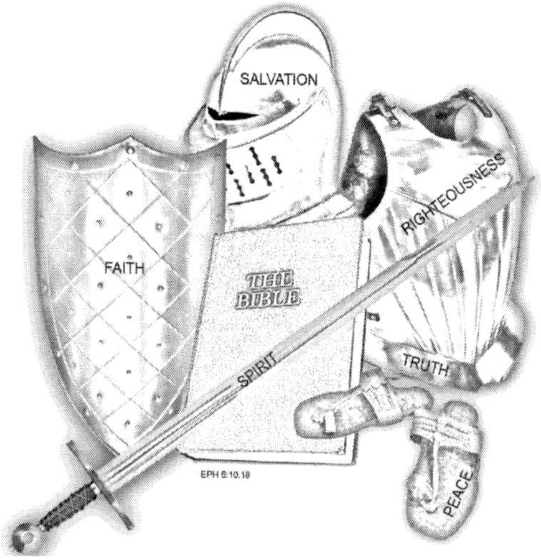

(c) 2014 Kathleen Mailer - KBO

CHAPTER ONE

Answering the 'Call'

Looking out from my vantage point at the top of a thread bare, worn out, dry hill, I could see for what seemed like hundreds of miles. Looking around me, I watched men and women being pummelled by their enemy. Some are tied up, and strapped down, unable to move. The bondage is extreme.

Although their nemesis never actually physically touched them, they seemed so hammered down, face planted into the filth of grime and mud - they are unable to stand up.

Oddly, although this was a desolate wasteland now, I could sense that it was once a rich, fertile, lush land. I could tell that horizon to horizon, in its prime, it was once alive with an illumination of green grass, rolling hills, wildflowers, bountiful farm land and happy flocks of livestock. I could almost taste and feel a strong remembrance of the smooth warmth of milk and honey covering my tongue.

Now tears spilled down my cheeks as the reality of this moment set in. I held my chest as the searing pain of a broken heart came to the surface. My knees buckled under the weight of this monumental burden. Thousands of my brothers and sisters lay defeated, in fear and frustration. They believed that this enemy had a strong hold on them. They believed 'the curse' that was spoken over them – about the reality of poverty. The smell of defeat assaulted my nostrils. The overpowering sense of hopelessness filled the air. I could hear the chilling, desperate cries of the people, “HELP LORD! HELP!”

A sob caught in my throat as my body broke out in goose-bumps. I fell to my knees, lifted my head toward the Heavens and wailed, “WHY LORD? What is happening here? What’s going on? This is NOT the way YOU said we should live!”

I was startled by the audible, powerful words that shook me clean through to the bone. Just as immediate, a peace came over me from the top of my head to the bottom of my feet. I turned to find Jesus holding his hand out to me, motioning me to stand with him.

Although his voice was silky smooth and soft, I could not be prepared for the blow to my heart as his words sank in. “I have done my part – by defeating satan thousands of years ago. Now it is up to you and your sisters and brothers to do their part and begin to ACT like it is done!”

My mind rumbled as I tried to wrap it around what little brainpower I had left. The enormity of what He had just revealed was almost too much for me to contain. How true it is. We are in bondage. This is not by some Devine design because Jesus settled that score so long ago with the work He did on the cross. We are in bondage because we believe somewhere deep inside, consciously and unconsciously that satan has some sort of right to treat us like this. We open the door to him in our everyday life. WE choose by our words, thoughts and actions to live a life of poverty and lack. My mind was going a million miles an hour. Walking WITH the Lord has a way of changing me, moulding me, melding me to his heart, body, and mentality.

Jesus continued to disclose the truth as we strolled around the battlefield. Although we were surrounded by chaos, we seemed to be invisible to the beings around us. "These soldiers are Christian business owners who know their business is their ministry. They can do so much to make an impact on the lives of those I have positioned them to serve. They are great shepherds, as I was, and their flocks await their leadership. Right now, those lost, hurting, scared sheep are up against a cliff crying out into the valley below for food, water, and shelter.

"As you can see,' his hand gracefully swept the air from the left to the right as if to say, 'look around!' "Although they are positioned in perfect alignment with Almighty God's purposes, they are not walking in this alignment in their everyday life. They must begin to take ownership of their calling to the Kingdom and take care of the sheep they have forsaken."

Coming to a soft halt, Jesus turned me to face him eye to eye. The depth of my spirit and soul were lifted as if we were on wings like Eagles. "I want your help. The Father and I want you to help Kingdom Business Owners to understand that their position in life is not only important to the body of Christ, but it is VITAL to the body of Christ. If this were not so, Father would have not called the WISE MEN and the

SHEPHERDS to my side when I was born in a manger to help me to fulfill the salvation promised for all of mankind.

Your mission is to help them understand that I went to the cross so that they can come boldly before my Father, in my name, and form a relationship with the God of the entire Universe. Remind them that I have commissioned them to spread the good news around the world.

They are to feed the hungry, clothe the poor and take care of widows and orphans.

I have sent the Holy Spirit to be a partner and give them the grace they need to accomplish every dream in their heart which, as a true believer, is a dream in my heart.

A Kingdom entrepreneur is to live a life of generosity and be a light in the darkness. The call of 'financial stewardship' on their life is a gifting. The enemy will often bring poverty and lack to the table to keep them from ever seeing the promises I have given them.

The truth is their biggest challenge will be overcoming a strong hold of lack mentality. This doesn't have to deal JUST with the tool called money. Money or lack thereof, is just a symptom. It is not the cause of their trouble.

The time has come for you and Daniel to confront the enemy head on. You are ready. Your preparation time has come to a close. You are promoted in my mighty name. Be released, dear one."

Feeling invincible, standing in front of Christ himself, he dressed me for the battle. He placed firmly on my head the Helmet of Salvation. I began to supernaturally understand, at the deepest level I have ever experienced before, His incredible work on the cross: what that selfless act truly meant for me, for my family, and for humanity as a whole. Tenderly he spoke, "I have already given you the key to victory over every battle with the enemy."

He strapped on my Breastplate of Righteousness. This was followed quickly by my Belt of Truth which he firmly secured. When both were locked into place, he handed me an exquisite object that glistened in the sun.

My OWN Sword of the Spirit - although as a Christian I knew how important it was to read the Word of God (bible), my breath caught in the back of my throat as I received the profound unveiling of a colossal truth. The bible is not only filled with tools for living with vivacity, joy, peace and abundance; it is The LIVING WORD that does not come back void. This is the most powerful weapon we have. As I started to declare His Word out loud I noticed the shift on the battlefield around me. THE ENEMY STOPPED! This evil army was seemingly agitated and maybe a little frightened. It began to retreat. Excitement built inside of me and started to consume every fibre of my being. I felt a fierce sense of hope and faith that far surpassed any understanding, unlike anything I could relate to in any experience in my previous life.

With a loving smile that would melt even the hardest of hearts, Jesus bowed before me and slipped on my feet the Sandals of Peace. I am not sure if he actually spoke these words out loud, or if I was starting to hear his voice internally, 'You will always know that your walk was my walk and these sandals will keep your feet from slipping and falling. I will not let your feet stumble. My peace is with you always."

Then, as if it had always been there, my Shield of Faith appeared before me. It was breathtaking. It was beautiful. It was magnificent. It was laced with gold and silver. It was shellacked with crushed gems that could blind the enemy when the 'light' hit and reflected it intense rays. I felt a breath of fresh air wash over me and I immediately straightened my back. I stood what seemed like 7 feet tall. I knew I was equipped. I knew I was ready.

Just then a whistle blew. It sounded more like a siren calling in the wind, "RESIST THE DEVIL AND HE WILL FLEE!"

Without warning, all of the soldiers were dressed and on their feet. K.B.O's from all over this land stood on each side of me, making a straight and unified line of defense. We were clean, equipped and fully engaged.

In front of us, standing all alone, an arrogant smirking devil didn't seem to realize that his 'minions' were gone with the wind. He screamed, spoke nasty, vile and foul things to individuals. He was the king of the bullies.

Together we locked arms. We lifted our Shields in an overlapping position. We then raised our swords simultaneously, as I roared, 'AS ONE!'

We took one step forward, then another. With each stride, the evil one matched us, only he was receding. Each soldier using the tools that Jesus armed us with began to take on a momentum that no man, nor beast, nor malicious spiritual entity could stop.

satan started to stumble. His slurs began to get weaker, less convincing, and less effective. He started to bleed black blood. It oozed out like molten lava or toxic tar. He started to shrink.

Relentless, we kept moving. This incredible army of messengers have found solace, strength, and freedom by banding together against the common enemy instead of trying to 'go it alone'.

The next thing I knew this once "self-proclaimed god" stood before us as this tiny little pipsqueak. (I now will shout 'Pipsqueak Alert' when I hear lies of the enemy coming out of anyone's mouth!). He was jumping up and down, throwing a temper tantrum because we weren't listening to him. It was so comical. I laughed out loud. It was just like a cartoon with the voice over being influenced by ingesting a helium filled balloon.

One final step and POOF! He was gone! We resisted the devil and he did, indeed, flee. We did it together! We did it!

Rejoicing, we PRAISED GOD! For He had gone before us, therefore this battle was already ours. Now, we can take the land he has given us and receive the promises in his word.

To this day, I still don't know if this was a vivid dream or a powerful vision. What I am sure of is it was the 'CALL' for all of us to take ownership of our kingdom. It was confirmation from God himself that Dan and I were done with this season, done with our learning curve on this subject, and done with the cleaning out (physically, mentally, emotionally, spiritually AND relationally) of our life.

Here I am today, humbly before you, pouring out the Holy Spirit's training and teaching. I take no credit for the words on these pages; I am merely a scribe. I am sitting in wonderment as He teaches me, shares with me, and guides me each and every day.

The passion to give you what was freely given to me burns deeply within my belly. I am praying now that the directions you read will inspire you to take action. With direction from the Holy Spirit comes the call to be obedient. With this obedience comes the call to action. With action comes the success in our business we are called to just as God intended it to be.

CHAPTER TWO

God is calling you, how will you respond?

What does it mean to be a K.B.O?

K.B.O's know that his/her business is their ministry. I am often quoted when I say, "God gives us a business so we can go out and DO God's business!"

We are every bit as important as every other ministry in the body of Christ including children's ministry, pastoral care, missions work, and the like. As a matter of fact we are meant to powerfully PARTNER with ministries like this to fulfill humanities purpose – and prepare ourselves for the glorious day when Jesus comes back.

Once we understood this calling clearly my husband and I started the '*Christian Collation of K.B.O's'(C.C.K.B.O).* Our mandate is to FUND Kingdom purposes with business ministry. This is a network that we are starting to build, to provide support, guidance, education, intercession, and encouragement for business owners who recognize that a business isn't really a business – it is a vehicle to fulfill the purpose of our true identity and help those in need.

We will partner with charities, missions and most importantly the local church that is fully equipped in faith and based on the principles of the bible.

We believe that Jesus Christ is the only-begotten Son of God. There is no grey area in this. It is black and white. In the paraphrased words of Rice Brooks, Author of *"God's Not Dead"*

We believe he lived the life we should have lived. He was pure, holy, compassionate, giving, and loving.

We believe he died the death we should have died.

We believe he was raised on the third day, proving once and for all to the world that HE IS THE SON OF GOD!

As a K.B.O., we also believe in paying our tithes to our church in accordance to his word so that we can, by his grace, live in proper stewardship and the promises he has given us if we do so. Let's face it, we need all of the supernatural help we can get from God to multiply that which He has given us so that it can be used even more greatly and powerfully. When we start to live in that truth everyone in the world can see that we are called to be a blessing and therefore we are blessed. Hey! I don't know how God does it. I just know tithing works!

It shows up for K.B.O's as we make money, leverage money, share money, give money, and grow money for the purposes of God – more comes to us who are faithful.

Another thing to remember, as a K.B.O we are a ***Master Relationship Builder.*** In all we do, this is first and foremost in our mind. I coined this phrase because it is so very true.

God is never very interested in a project or business for the product or business. He is interested in the 'people' we serve.

A great example is our Today's Businesswoman Magazine. This international platform is to give quality, affordable mentorship every quarter for Christian businesswomen around the world. God isn't interested in the magazine itself, he is interested in the women (and men too) who read it, who write articles for it, who are debuted in it, and who work on it.

It isn't the magazine (or the business) it is about who YOU become in the process and how YOU shepherd the flock he has entrusted you to. Does this make sense? I get into this in great length through this book, and my prayer now is that the Holy Spirit will bring this revelation to life in ways you never dreamed of.

The problems many of us face, as K.B.O's.

Many of us grew up in situations or circumstances that fight against the call of God on our life. This isn't new is it? However, the one thing that I have always shared on my platform is, *"The Hell you have been through is the platform to your purpose."*

What this translates to, for many, is that even though you truly know you are called to make millions (or billions and maybe trillions), you struggle with defeat so you can't even seem to feed your own family! OR, maybe you CAN make a lot of money, but your health, family, relationship seem to suffer.

As a leader, so many of us feel alone. We feel like we are the ones that are always doing everything. Even if we are blessed with great people in our life, we take 'soul' responsibility for our business. This causes an open door for the enemy to walk in. satan sends REAL spiritual warfare over you and your business. This is what can keep us in bondage, and it seems like there is nowhere to turn. Every time you want to get ahead, something comes and crushes us down.

We are entrepreneurs; we have a natural ability to see 'hope' in every situation. But as the bible says, *"Hope deferred makes the heart sick, but a dream fulfilled is a tree of life."* **Proverbs 13:12.**

Many K.B.O's are sick at heart and don't know if they should give up, move on, or run away. They want the pain to end at all costs. Some wrestle with dilemma, 'Should I just go get a job? OR Should I keep fighting what seems like an uphill battle.' For most entrepreneurs getting a J.O.B. (just·over broke) is like a death sentence. They would rather chew crushed glass than to do that. Why? They are called to lead, to provide, to grow and to prosper.

I want to go on record right now, stating very clearly: I am not saying you shouldn't work to take care of your family. What I am saying is: it is hard not to SEE your God given dream taken through to completion. Am I right?

The Lord put on my heart a very powerful revelation, *"Resist the devil and he shall flee. The more you resist him; the more you strike him with your Sword of the Spirit; the more aware you are of your full armour and how it protects you – the more you already know that I have equipped you."*

This is as good of time to add another truth that haunts many entrepreneurs all over the world that causes sickness and disease to creep into their lives.

This state of being actually is celebrated by the world and also by many in Christian leadership. It is called, "work-a-holism". Believe me this is not a blessing it is a 'curse' and we should grow in greater understanding by the grace of God. We need to really do a study for ourselves and answer the many questions that arise. What is this addiction? What is it doing to us individually, physically, relationally, corporately, and spiritually? I will touch more on this later.

Counteract the enemy's attempt to thwart you from your God given purpose.

1. You do that by **finding others** who have the same vision, heart, and passion as I have put on your heart. (That is why we have started the C.C.K.B.O).
2. **Form a positive partnership** by blending your gifts talents and abilities with theirs to form an affiliation to ultimately glorify God.
3. **Get real and pray for one another.** Prayer matters! It is a privilege to be able to have conversations with the Holy Spirit who gives us everything we need.

4. **Envision** what your life would be like when your God ordained dream comes to fruition.
5. **Write down your plans and purposes**, asking God to direct your steps.
6. **Get crackin'** – Do what God has told you to do. One step at a time. I have found that obedience is the blood flow in your business and your life.
7. Remember to also set into action what you can to **acquire the knowledge, skill, habits you do not currently possess.** The Holy Spirit will bring you the right leadership or guide your path when there seems to be no genuine leaders around.
   "I can do all things through Christ who strengthens me." **(Philippians 4:3)**

It's now time to take control!

By the grace of God I have been healed from being a workaholic. This sickness in my life caused countless problems to my health, my family, my finances, and most detrimentally - my purpose and relationship with God.

Workaholism is a direct symptom of the Spirit of Poverty. It causes us to be so busy being busy that we let the most important things escape us. We end up sick, financially strapped, with discord in our home and in our hearts.

We let ourselves become a victim instead of a victor.

If you feel that I am talking directly to you at this moment, I want to encourage you. As you work through this book you will find the tools you need to break free from this spiritual bondage. You have got to come face to face with this demon so that you can be ALL God called you to be.

Taking control of our Kingdom is a completely different thing than being controlling in your life.

Back in my early days of business, I was out to prove to the world that I, Kathleen, can be in control of my business and make myself powerful in order to help people around the world.

I pushed my way into the financial services industry that was more a 'good ol' boys club' than a business. Females in the industry were few and far between at that time. I actually worked 9-16 hour days (no joke). I also went 7 days a week. I made excuses to my husband that I had to do it because I was starting a business. I enjoyed the financial success that started (slowly) coming. I had a new car, new house, new marriage, and new business. I had approval from my up line and all of the guys in the office. I caught the attention of the companies 'corporate leadership' and went on to teach internationally at an education seminar they had for thousands of people. To the world, I was the epitome of success.

My husband and I were ecstatic when the news of my pregnancy came. We were going to have a baby! Yes, life certainly was perfect wasn't it? I did remember to thank God because I had always wanted to be a Mom and prayed for a baby to complete me. I say 'remember to thank God' because in those days, I was too busy most of the time to even think of stopping and say, 'thanks'.

Oh yes, I enjoyed (NOT) the morning sickness that had me in the bathroom instead of the boardroom. The guys in the office lovingly teased me about my numbers dropping and that they were going to 'trounce' on my #1 Salesperson status. They were over joyed at knocking me off my pedestal. Even though I laughed with them, fear started to kick in.

I felt that my husband, my father, my up line, and my down line would lose respect for me if I dropped off in my numbers. They would call me lazy and tell me that I was using my pregnancy as an excuse. This was NOT the truth by the way. It was what I perceived as the truth. satan kept whispering in my ear so many lies and unfortunately for me, I believed him.

I decided I could do ALL things and that means I could do my business at my current pace AND have a baby. I knew I would make it happen somehow!

The problem was I pushed even harder now. One morning my morning sickness took on a whole new level. I had to stay in bed. I had to ask others to take over my meetings for the day. I had 4 appointments to 'close' and 2 new ones.

By mid - morning, I had to call my husband home from work to take me to the Doctor. "Something just isn't right, Dan, please come and get me." What happened next crushed me.

"After reviewing your test results Kathy," Dr. Martin said, "I am sorry, but you have lost your baby. Due to the situation there isn't a great chance you will ever have children." I was devastated.

I was very sick after that, bed ridden as a matter of fact. That forced me to evaluate what was important to me. The longing in my heart as far back as I could remember was to be married and have many children. This dream shattered into a million slivers all around me. Here I am childless because of my childish behaviour.

For the record, I did lose my #1 spot. I lost my business. I lost my car. I lost my home. What I gained was two valuable lessons.

a) **WHY GOD? Why me? Why did this happen?** I think when I asked this question I didn't want the answer, I just wanted to complain. But God in his mercy and graciousness answered. I didn't like what I heard.

   "How does working 7 days a week, 24 hours a day with no rest affect your health? Whose fault is it that you got sick? Even I, God of the universe, took my 7th day to rest. It isn't because I needed to rest. It is because you need to see how to celebrate your success. I give you a living example of how to live your life. If you read your Bible, and talk to me through the process you will know the truth of building a thriving, life producing leveraged business."

b) **Doing things on my own will, power, and steam-never work**. It may look like it works for a while but long term you are setting yourself for disaster.

It is not by force nor by strength, but by my Spirit, says the Lord of Heaven's Armies.
Zechariah 4:6

I wish I could say I stopped doing the things that derailed me right then and there, but God had to remind me over and over until I finally 'got it'. However, after being delivered if I even remotely start to feel myself STRIVING, I hear the Holy Spirit quietly tinkle his bell of warning. I drop to my knees and repent. I get things right and put God first. Oh how blessed we are that we have a God that loves us that much!

Taking control of your Kingdom for God is allowing God to be with you and making you the powerful one. We don't have to strive to become powerful. If we walk with the Lord and do it His way we will find the foundation of our businesses will be built upon a rock. Then, nothing can blow it over, burn it down, or destroy it.

Taking control of your Kingdom for God is simply this... take control of your thoughts, habits and mindset. THAT is where your Kingdom exists. It isn't land or physical possessions. Those things are the physical manifestations of God's favour and love.

Seek the Kingdom of God above all else, and live righteously, and he will give you everything you need. Matthew 6:33

Get a new belief system based on the word of God. By being consistent, persistent, and having focused on your growth, the Holy Spirit will reveal how much you can do, and what our glorious God will do!

Use this scripture as your foundation as you move forward in your business today. Write it out every morning until it gets ingrained deep within. Put it up on your desk or your wall. Replace Solomon's name as your own. Understand, GOD is the one who can take you further, faster because of the work that Jesus did on the cross for us.

Solomon son of David established himself firmly over his kingdom, for the Lord his God was with him and made him exceedingly great. ***2nd Chronicles: 1***

Let's put the word into action,

1. Write down what you think about the 'vision' of a K.B.O?
2. Is this how you feel? Why? Or Why not?
3. How many of the K.B.O beliefs do you share? Are there some you have already solidly affirmed in your life? Are there some you need to work on in order to get there?

4. Do you see yourself in any of the problems a K.B.O is faced with? If so, which ones? If not, did these issues used to be in your past? How did you move past these obstacles?
5. Do you currently have anyone you can positively partner with help you with: prayer covering, accountability, mentorship, vision planning, executing the vision God gave you? If not, write down a plan of how you are going to put this into action today.
6. Do you need to be delivered from workaholism? Drop everything and get on your knees now! Ask Jesus to heal you. Get real with him right now and let him know that the world's view of lack and platform around money needs to be removed at your core. Ask the Holy Spirit to begin a work in you, to take control of your Kingdom for God's glory and leave all of the B.S. behind! (B.S. = belief system).
7. Make a decision that today is the day you will take control of your Kingdom as King Solomon did.

Let me pray with you,

Oh Lord, my God, my King… I pray for blinders to come off. I pray Lord that you would allow me to see the truth of your word. I pray that you can show me clearly if I have tendencies to put work above you and/or above my family. I pray Lord that you show me, deep in my core, the issue I have. Show me that the time is right for me to stand firm. Yes, I need to take control of my Kingdom and not let satan rule and reign in my life. I am learning to be a *Master Relationship Builder*, but first - I have to develop my relationship with you. Through you, I will build a relationship with myself. In Jesus name, Amen

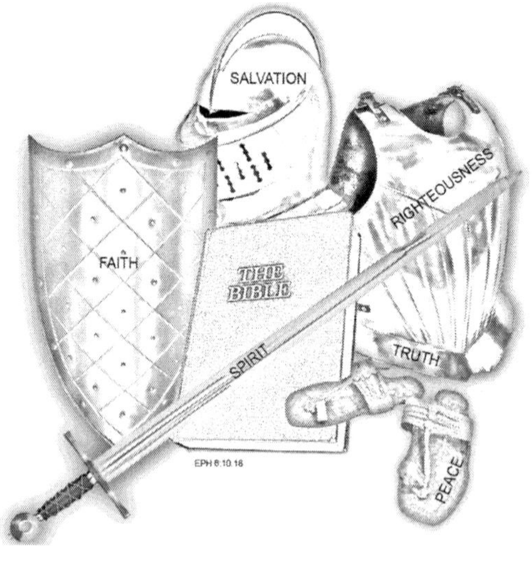

(c) 2014 Kathleen Mailer - KBO

CHAPTER THREE

Deliverance, Finding Freedom in Christ

I know it is sometimes hard to believe that there is a driving force created to kill, steal and destroy the work of God in your life. For many reading this, this concept is bizarre and out of the scope of their understanding.

I invite you to open your mind and your heart as we walk through this section. Prayerfully consider the truth of the word. Dig deep within the Word. The Bible will confirm that what I am saying is truth. I will give you true-to-life examples of how Christ can set us free.

Take your time; this is not a race. This is a deep look within to find those blockages and destroy them so that you can finally release the bondage that has you wrapped up in addictions, habits, mind-sets, choices that don't serve you OR the King.

This is by NO means an in-depth study. This is simply to help you be aware of some of the 'spirits' or demons or tactics that satan uses to keep control over your life, your health, your business, your family and your pure walk with God.

However, before we begin to uncover some of these deceptions of the enemy… let me tell you how to be set free.

Knowing that you can overcome anything that the devil tries to throw at you is an exciting journey.

The 'R' Factor – Live a Revolutionized Life With A Breakthrough Mentality.

What does it mean to live a revolutionized life? It is a life that has been transformed, reformed, altered, updated, changed, and modernised (efficient). It sounds like the life that we can have through Christ Jesus Who loved us so very much that He gave up everything so we can be set free.

Understand that freedom is necessary for us to make an impact in our business.

I want you to seriously work through these steps over the next few chapters. It is time we live 'Breakthrough-Minded'. It is time we learn how to push through the bondage that keeps us stuck in life.

I encourage you to make a list of the things you can't seem to break free from in each chapter as we uncover how the enemy 'curses' us. We need to clean up any messes from our lives and that of the generations passed. Press in to the Lord, and he will reveal what you need to work on. He, above all, wants your heart pure and fully focused on your relationship and the work at hand.

Set your sights on the Holy Spirit and begin each process daily for the next 30 days. I do mean one chapter at a time. This book isn't a 'get rich quick' book. It is a fully systemized, fully developed journey to walk with Christ. Will your financial outlook grow? OH YES! The marketing section can be used and put into practice at any time. However, freedom takes time to learn, understand, change and grow.

I pray that you fully participate in every section of this book – and that the results stop at nothing short of a miracle. Then, give HIM the glory as you share your testimony of success with others.

Keep very clear notes, and review them often. Living breakthrough-minded helps you to be KINGDOM-minded as you walk on the earth.

Right now, I am going to join you in faith - as we prepare to go through these clear steps.

Go ahead, reach your hands to the heavens right now and declare:

"As God is my witness, I WILL find my faith! GOD, you are THE God of perfection! YOU and YOU alone will supply my every need according to your riches in glory! You will see me THROUGH this situation. Even though right now, it seems as though all things are falling apart, I am NOT seeing the FULL truth! Please Lord, give me perspective. Give me FRESH NEW EYES to see, NEW EARS to hear what the answers are. What are those answers that I need to succeed? In Jesus' name, AMEN!"

One more thought before we begin this process:

I can honestly say, through experience, that the enemy will not like the fact you are making this stand! He will try to send obstacles to stop you from being here and receiving what God has for you. PUSH THROUGH, do not be distracted, do not procrastinate, the time has come RIGHT NOW for FREEDOM.

Let's put the word into action:

Here are the 13 steps to a relevant life.

1. **Realization**: You've got to admit that something isn't working for you. Seriously, do you have a goal that you have on your goal list month after month, year after year, prayer after prayer that you are not attaining? When are you going to admit that your way is NOT working? You don't see fruit in things like weight loss, making money or relationships flourishing. It is time to realize that 'something has got to give'? Get real about this and get tough. It is time for freedom.

2. **Reveal:** Ask the Lord to make it abundantly clear what the problem is. Learning the truth about your B.S. in this situation is sometimes the very catalyst that sets you free even without the other steps.

3. **Rebel**: Many people get a little crabby at this point because they want to be a victim in their circumstance. They want to say, "it isn't my fault that…" They want to say "I had

problems. I had life experiences. I can't help that this thing happened to me!" While it is true, life experiences do happen, that isn't the relevant issue here. The issue here is that you have had 'stuff' happen over and over and over and the same result comes up. Frustration and defeat turns to guilt and shame. Let's get real here and know that God is there to break you through, but rebelling isn't the answer – it just may be the cause of what keeps this problem unresolved.

4. **Resolve:** Simply get real about saying YES to God. Obey His commands, His directions, His desires, and HIS word on the subject. Even if it doesn't make sense at the time, that is ok. Just have faith that He knows what He is talking about.

5. **Repent:** Ask God for forgiveness because you have allowed His transformation power to be blocked. Maybe you didn't do it on purpose, but you nevertheless have allowed this, for whatever reason, to be a part of your reality.

6. **Review:** What things have you done in the past to resolve this issue? What worked for you before? What didn't work for you before? Where are you now with this issue compared to last year, 2 years ago, and 5 years ago? When did this issue start? What did you learn from it? What are the benefits of it (oh yes, if we have it in our life on some level it benefited us to have it). What are the disadvantages of it? How has it held you back? What things have you done in spite of it? Really take time to review each question. Pray for the Holy Spirit to reveal truth to you.

7. **Re-align:** Make a decision and pull out scripture verses that pertain to the issue at hand. What does God's word say about it? Write these scriptures, read them over, and meditate on them. I find it helpful to find one scripture that really speaks to me about it and re-write it every morning for 30 days. It is the best way for me to start to realize God knows me intimately. I ask the question: "If I am created in His image, does my current situation reflect my impression of who God is?" Oh, I can feel someone out there getting hit with a Holy Spirit nudge. That is great! You are right on track to gain your freedom.

8. **Release:** Time to go through this situation and take stock of what you need to give up. Do you need to part with sin, friends, habits, B.S., or all of the above? These things have a tendency to block you from the healing that is your birthright. Is it hard? Well, like anything that is worth the work, it won't likely be easy. The truth is it is harder to make the decision to do it, than it is to actually do it when God gets first place in your heart. He will help you make the crooked places straight in your life. He understands what you are going through and what you need to do to let go.

9. **Responsibility**: Remember too, that resolving this situation is not just for you. I know you must get tired of hearing me say, *"It's NOT about you!"* However, I am going to keep drilling this point home. Take a minute to write down how you will be responsible for this gift of freedom as this problem is solved. How will you steward your new gift? How will you share it? How will it affect your family, friends, clients, colleagues, business, health, finances etc.?

10. **Revive**: God will now start to breathe new life into you. Stay consistent and believe that God can make a way even if it seems impossible. He is a good God and will make everything work together for good.

11. **Restore:** He will start to restore broken dreams. Time and time again, He will bring to mind a dream He had given you in the past. Often He will want to bring it up (even if it failed miserably), dust it off, tweak it ever so slightly and set you on the path to success. The key to remember, it is time to give up the fear, pain and suffering associated with this past. With God, it is never the actual fulfilment of the dreams and desires He has placed on your heart; it is WHO you become in the process. Amen?

12. **Relevant:** You will find yourself living a life of legacy. Generations to come will benefit from what you have done and are doing. They will receive from where you are now going and who you now are. Even now, people around you will be inspired, motivated, and set free by your example. There is power in your testimony and you need to go through the 'tests' to get it. The key is going through it, not setting up camp and living in it forever. Thanks be to God you are on the other side! Thank you Lord. That brings me to the next point.

13. **Rejoice!** Praise God for what he has done. Write this down and remember it when times get tough. When you start this process over for another issue you are facing in your life – pray a prayer of thanksgiving.

Let me pray with you,

"Lord, you got me through. It seemed impossible, but here we are! I want to thank you, Jesus, for your ever present help in my times of need. I pray now, Holy Spirit, for your guidance and steps to help me break free of the next issue – so I can be all you have called me to be. Now, my serving is greater than ever before.

I pray this in Jesus precious name, Amen!"

CHAPTER FOUR

The Spirit of Poverty
The Control Tower of Hell

As Christians, this is the one spirit that is easy to see running rampant in our churches today. This by far is the easiest spirit to detect and discern. It is designed to keep us stuck because satan knows that a Christian with money is a very REAL threat to his goals.

It stands to reason that the devil will want to control every aspect of this earthly tool. He will make what God intended for good into something evil, scarce, and put an element of an uncontrollable appetite upon it that gets in the way of our relationship with Christ.

As K.B.O.'s we are called to fund Kingdom purposes through our business ministry. That means the widows and orphans are taken care of. That means meeting the needs of the people. That means our churches will walk in their full-on purpose preaching the gospel and then - as satan fears – Jesus will come for his bride!

He starts out with the scripture so often misquoted,

For the love of money is a root of all kinds of evil. Some people, eager for money, have wandered from the faith and pierced themselves with many griefs. **1 Timothy 6:10**

In my own life, I grew up thinking you had to be broke in order to be humble. You had to opt for love over money. I heard more than once a declaration of how un-important money was in our lives and therefore we lived a life of knowing how much we were loved - but not having the fullness of what Christ died on the cross for us to have.

The truth is the bible says 'the LOVE of money is the root of all evil'. THAT is the truth. Putting money ahead of God is wrong. Worshiping money is wrong. Striving to never have enough is wrong. Working to gain more money at the expense of your family? Now that, my dear friend, is wrong.

But money is not evil nor is it good. It is a tool that is at the mercy of the shepherd that stewards it. This tool is designed to help us go further on earth to see that His Kingdom come and His will be done on earth as it is in Heaven.

Here is what I see. If money was truly evil, the devil would be delivering boat loads to our bank accounts. He would make sure we all had it no matter what. He would see to it that you and I wouldn't even have to work for it at all. Am I right?

The very fact that he is not doing this should be enough to tell you if you struggle now with lack, where you never having enough to make ends meet OR if you always end up having just enough but your hands are tied to give more… you most likely are struggling with the Spirit of Poverty.

I could go on and on. Actually, I could write a whole book that helps you take a look deep inside about your money blueprint. But for now, having you aware of it is a great start.

I am going to list only 3 statements that you may speak out loud now, or perhaps have heard your parents say in the past. Ask yourself how true this is for you? Write down any revelations you have as you read this. Begin to pray for Jesus to heal you. Apply the "R-Factor" to this process – it is a great start to begin to fast track and clean up the messes around your life.

Remember, this is a work in progress and not at all a final destination. We must continue to challenge our belief system as we grow in the Lord. I don't think it ever ends, but it does make for a wonderful and exciting life!

1. **"I am sick and tired of not having any money."** This is a self-fulfilling prophecy. Poverty begets sickness and disease (dis-ease). Is this what you want in your life?

2. **"Everything cost too much money!** I pay the electric bill, gas bill, those guys in the 'big fancy offices' have no idea what it is to have to pay this crap every month. They don't need to charge so much!"

   Careful! You are now cursing other businesses. They deserve to make money just as you deserve to prosper. The devil will catch your words and rejoice! Why? This is classic biblical law, what you sow you will reap. You are sowing curses to another business owner, and therefore - by your OWN design (not the devil's doing) you are pushing away your inheritance. Something you need to think about!

3. **"I can't tithe because I don't have any money right now!** When I have more, I will start to give a tenth of my income to God." The bible clearly states that God wants us to give a tenth of what we receive back to the house of God.

Right now, I do not want to get into a theological debate with you. I think I have heard all of the excuses to NOT tithe that I can handle. Heck, in the past I have used some of them myself. We begin to justify… there is not enough money, the New Testament doesn't tell us to tithe, I give to a charity and that is my tithe.

The bottom line: God's word says to give a tenth of everything we make to his house. It also says that all of the gold, silver, etc. is HIS. It also talks about the fact that HE has given us the ability to create wealth.

So, based on this truth, it is easy to visualize the following: Your Father gives you a dollar to use on whatever you need. He says first, 'Could you break this dollar into 10 dimes? I would very much like you to give one to the church this Sunday but you can have the rest. If you would like, I can show you how to multiply the rest – but never the less - just give a dime to the church and you can keep the change."

It is a simple concept, but very hard for many people to do. Even in impoverished countries K.B.O's can grasp this concept and be blessed by God himself. If they can do it, you can do it too. I want to encourage you, over the next little while together; you will find yourself breaking free of the bondage of poverty.

One more thought before I show you how you can put this word into action. Poverty shows up in every area of life: in your health, relationships and spiritual life as WELL as your financial portfolio. The Spirit of Poverty is an issue of the mind that infects the heart. I challenge you to study this deeply.

I believe as K.B.O's – we all have limiting beliefs that are attached to such a spirit. Wealth or not, we can't totally be free from its existence. As Jesus said,

There will always be some in the land who are poor. That is why I am commanding you to share freely with the poor and with other Israelites in need. **Duet. 15:11**

However, we can destroy its hold over and in us. Once we truly understand it, we can use its strength to combat in a spiritual war which will, in the end, bring Jesus back and send us home! OH how glorious that day will be!

When we went to India, I introduced a concept new to the women there. I had the privilege to speak to incredible women of God who came to find Jesus in their circumstances.

I used what I call the 'Dial 10' Method to teach them about finances and money. As a result MANY are being blessed by God, prospering and growing.

Let's have a look to see how this works.

The 'Dial 10' Method: Starting a "Dial 10" Success Group

- I start with 10 women who have given their life to Christ. They believe he died on the cross to deliver them from poverty. They believe in his mighty word. They want and are hungry for change.

- They are taught that the tithe is important, so is giving, so is building relationships, so is eating for today, and so is building a storehouse for tomorrow. They know that 'God supplies ALL of our needs." Every piece of currency they get – they plug it in to the 'dial' system.

- **Position 1** – is the beneficiary of a collective effort via a micro-loan (from the rest of the group or from an outside 'gift'). Those in position 2-10 focus their efforts as described.

  10% of their currency goes to tithe – we don't steal from a bank to get what we want, we don't steal from God either!

  10% goes into a storehouse - a savings for the future, something God can help to multiply and create even more money for the His glory.

10% is given to the woman in the 'FOCUSED' position to help build a thriving business.

10% is given to advance the Kingdom of God.

60% - they use for their daily needs – with careful stewardship.

In other words, if she gets $1.00 – she would break it up in dimes. 1 dime would go to church in form of a tithe. The second dime would be put into a savings account (leveraging it, growing it and compounding it). The third dime would go into a pot to help another woman, such as herself (using this dial method), to get/manage/grow a business. The fourth dime would go to advance the Kingdom of God. The other 6 dimes are hers to pay her bills, feed, clothe and shelter her own family – she will steward it well.

- Once we get this woman set, we 'dial over' to the next position and begin again.

- When we are finished all 10 positions… each woman who has received this micro-loan will go out and start their own "**Dial 10 Success Group!**"

Just for the record, I want to tell you Jessie's story, as told to me by the Pastor who had invited my husband and I to speak in India.

Pastor David was on his mission trip, preaching the good news to the poor around the interior of India around 1 month after Dan and I had left. He came across a roadside palm juice stand and decided it was time for a break from the heat.

In his usual way, his conversation began over a cup of refreshing juice with the woman who had supplied him with a smile and a glass. Her name was Jessie and she had a sparkle in her eye.

David asked her if she knew who Jesus was. He marvelled at the sovereign God who stood in the midst as she told her story. She had come to a conference about a month before when a woman of God from another country spoke about God's plan and purpose for her life. It was to save her from a life of eternal damnation. It was also to 'prosper' her now, not to condemn her. (*That woman was me! She was at the very conference Pastor David had set up.*)

She went on to tell him how she gave her life to Jesus that day and she felt so light. She began to think about the rest of the message, "We all have what we need to sow at our fingertips," this lady said. What did she have? She had a quarter of a cup of rice to feed her and her children.

She portioned it out into 10 bundles. She thought, 'How could a few kernels of rice benefit the work of God?' Then she remembered how many billions of people on the planet there were – and she, like a rice kernel, was destined for greatness.

When she went to her 'church' (an outreach post of Pastor David's where he had yet to meet all the people) – she spoke to the leader of the conference. They knew and heard the message that day.

Together, she and the minister prayed for God to bless her offering – a few kernels to give to her church, a few to help another woman, and the rest – she would make tonight for her and her family to eat.

Not knowing how, she felt the faith build inside of her on her walk home. She told the story of Jesus to her children as she began to cook the rice. Tonight they would savour every morsel they had and give God thanks that he would supply more in the hours to come.

As they sat at the table, there was a knock on her wall. Her spirit leapt with joy and she listened to how much Jesus loved her.

The lady at the door was also at the conference, although they never met. God had been speaking to this lady about giving $25.00 to start a palm juice business to help her feed her, her family and God's growing family. The gift was given and the rest is history.

As far as I know, she is doing well – and has helped many women get their start in business. This is our God! This is his multiplication. This is his way of doing business.

When we whip the spirit of poverty in the butt, and trust the TRUTH in the word of God we can know all things are possible! Amen?

Let's put the word into action,

1. Write down the aha's you got from reading this chapter. What are your own limiting beliefs?
2. Does your belief or choices match with the word of God?
3. Go through the steps of the "R- Factor" to bust through the enemy's stronghold on your life.
4. Are you are in a position to start a 'Dial of 10 Success Group' – it will work for you. OR perhaps, God is even speaking to you about investing in microloans to help women in need. Either way, just get started! Let's join arms to 'eradicate poverty in the nations'! In the back of the book we will show you how you can be a part of an exciting project *Today's Businesswoman Magazine* & *Home of Hope* have put together to eradicate poverty in the nations.

No matter how you look at it, the 'spirit of poverty' is nasty business. Isn't it time we took a stand to say "NO MORE!" to satan and his minions!

Let me pray with you,

Holy Spirit, I thank you for wisdom, discernment, strategies, open doors, health and healing. Today I ask that your hand come upon my dear reader. Lift him/her to the throne of grace where he/she can break free from the bondage of poverty.

Speak clearly over the next 30 days where this evil lurks. What words are spoken and what needs to be accomplished can demolish under our feet this work of the enemy.

I also ask Lord God, that you seal this work in the Holy Spirit. I pray that you protect it by the blood of Christ. That no weapon formed against any of us shall prosper in Jesus' name. I pray that you go before us, behind us and on each side of us as we delve into the work of deliverance. Any fiery darts of the enemy will ricochet off of us and right back in his own hind end! It is done! In the mighty name of Jesus! Amen!

CHAPTER FIVE

The Spirit of Jealousy
The Root of All Evil

So many people look at the title of this chapter in passing and decide it isn't for them. They know they are not the jealous type therefore it doesn't apply. The truth is, there may be elements of jealousy that we carry within us (unknowingly), OR we may have been cursed by another with a jealous spirit that blocks us from God's bounty of blessings.

Have you ever looked at your life and wondered why you are not further along in your goals and dreams?

In your search for answers you find yourself making declarations followed by 'but I am not'.

- I should be healed by now, but I am not.
- I should be a millionaire, but I am not.
- I should be married (happily) and have a family of my own, but it just hasn't materialized yet.

We believe that God has a purpose and a plan to prosper us, but it just doesn't seem to be happening. As I mentioned the bible talks about the fact that hope deferred makes a heart sick and that totally seems like a statement about your life right now.

Before we delve deeper into this subject, I want to go on record. I am NOT talking to the people who don't take action in their life OR to those that don't want to learn or pray. I am talking directly to those of you who have tried everything you can to succeed and see these things come to pass in life.

You have really been trying to follow God. You know deep inside God's call on your life. I am talking about you, with gifts, talents and abilities – but you never seem to get anywhere with it.

When I was younger and starting out in the business world – I would work so hard at proving myself in every business I ever had. I would build it really BIG. I would do all of the right things. Everything seemed to work until one day, it would be like I was hitting a glass ceiling and it would tumble down around me.

I had the mentors. I had the strategies and I had the tools. I also had highs, but when I hit the low, it was really low. So low, I would lose it all.

The truth is we can't really completely blame the devil. We have already had victory in Christ Jesus, now we have to ACT like it.

If this is the case, then WHY, WHY? Are we still under the influence of a life that isn't under God's complete blessing?

The bottom line is there are two things that we, as good-hearted people, unknowingly do that make the devil delight in his evil schemes. It ultimately positions us to make satan our God.

This leaves us under a veil where the blessings of our Father cannot completely and fully connect with us. His promises for our life of complete victory can't be fully measured unto us, the way God intended it.

As a matter of fact, I am going to be so bold as to say that this particular curse over your life is about to be lifted as you work diligently to seek the Holy Spirit in the next 30 days. Deeper revelations are coming even now as you read this.

Let's ask the Holy Spirit to take our blinders off so that we can see. "Lord let us see clearly, hear like we have never heard before, and open our heart to have you cleanse it, message it, and soften it for use in your Kingdom, Amen!"

This curse started right from the beginning of time, the stories of the bible clearly show you this particular curse form and pass on generation after generation.

This curse is the ROOT of all evil. I sincerely mean that. I want to illustrate my point by asking you a question. 'Why did God cast satan from Heaven?' The bottom line, he was jealous of God and wanted everything to be about him, the all-encompassing (in his own egotistical head), Lucifer. True? Or True?

Since that time, satan spends his time whispering into the hearts and minds of men how much they 'deserve' to be the one that has everything. He teaches us to compare, to covet, to lust, to desire things our neighbour has. If we let it, it opens the door to a greater, bigger problem – the **Unloving Spirit.** (There is more on this later in the book. I suggest you work through this one before you work through the chapter on the Unloving Spirit).

While I don't have enough room in this book to really devolve deeply into this subject, believe me, there is SO much to uncover, I will give you some of the basics.

There are two ways this curse works.

Jealous of someone else: Maybe it drives you crazy when you see someone else's success and want so badly for that to be you. You focus on it. You meditate on it. You complain to God about it. "Why Lord, does everyone else around me has this and I don't?" You become a voluntary victim by focusing on the problem, day in and day out. What happens is, this 'covet-ness' gets in the way of you succeeding.

You are in comparison mode instead of action mode. You want another's gifts, talents and abilities instead of developing your own special and unique that the Creator has given to you.

I want to give you an example of how this shows up in our words without our thinking about it. When I shared this concept with a Christian Business Owner, she sent me a note the day after. The Holy Spirit revealed a pattern to her in her life – which was inside of her and needed to be destroyed.

She told me how the Lord showed her a comment she made on Facebook. When she made it, it was – in her mind - a compliment. Now, she could see that she was PLACING a curse upon them and her as a result. This helped her to see that she too most likely had this curse on her life and it was time for deliverance.

Her friends were on vacation in a hot, tropical place and they were posting how much fun they were having. Without skipping a beat she typed in, "I am SO jealous! I wish it was me!"

Now think about it? If you have ever thought that or said that – ask yourself what were you thinking? Our words have power! They have the power to curse and to bless! This is SO important we mind our hearts and our words. I am not telling you this so you can feel condemned because most people have done this or something similar. I am telling you this, so that you can have victory over something you may not have seen before.

When we declare such things, we come into alignment with the father of all lies himself: satan. That means, we make satan our God! That means that we put him in the forefront ahead of Jesus.

If most Christians knew that this is what they were doing, they would be mortified! Let's not let satan take Jesus' place in our hearts. Let's truly understand how this operates in our lives so we can release this demon once and for all.

Someone has been jealous of you and has put a curse over you.

This is the second way this operates in our life. Take a stroll back through your life with new eyes today. Think back to your childhood. Go way back as far as you can remember. Were there any situations that occurred where you can clearly see how someone else was jealous of you? Perhaps you heard, 'You are so lucky that…' or maybe even, 'I wish I could be you!'

Or maybe, no words were exactly spoken it was just actions.

At a K.B.O. round table discussion, one business owner who is extremely gifted and talented explained her situation. She can sing and dance. She can make friends easily and gather people around her. She is pretty, funny and has a heart of gold. When she reviewed her childhood she had to admit she had these qualities and that she was smart and carefree. Now realize, that these gifts and talents (like all of us who are gifted) took time to hone and perfect. She worked very hard at everything she accomplished. She realized she was always looking for approval from her Mom. She was met with the words, "Good job sweetie", but her Mother's actions were one of venom, seething – then the competition began.

Every time she would try something new like acting in a play, her Mom decided she would act in a play – but not just act in play. She would make sure she excelled and then set up situations where she could be 'better' than her daughter. She even joined a church talent competition that her daughter had signed up for the year before. She took home the trophy and my friend took home a broken, betrayed heart.

This made her entire life an impossible to please situation. Because of her Mother's jealousy a hole in my friend's heart was formed. This hole was called the unloving spirit - and opened the door for addictions, cursing others, perfectionism, never getting ahead, unworthiness and so more.

Something to remember, those that curse have been cursed. This isn't a licence for you to begin dredging things up from the past and putting blame on another. This is about lovingly correcting yourself. Once you understand the how and the why you think, say and do the things you find yourself doing you can find freedom in the knowledge.

I want to state this one more time. I find that often, both scenarios are prevalent in our lives. After all, those that are cursed end up cursing another unless they: identify it, eliminate it and refuse to let it come back.

Some of the feelings one has that are associated with this spirit? You may feel: displaced, like giving up, feel insignificant, despair, and feel a victim. You find yourself being disobedient to God's word. You start to turn to overspending, working, drinking, or drugs… to be better than someone else OR to fill the hole in your heart.

How do you combat this?

The simple counter-active measure to take is by applying honour to every situation and circumstance in your life.

Let's take a deeper look at the story of David and Saul. David showed amazing strength with Saul in many different interactions.

David knew he was to be God's chosen King, yet he didn't throw Saul off his thrown he waited on God's divine timing.

David could have killed Saul, and no one would have blamed him. Yet, he still stayed honourable and waited.

The devil hates it when we honour one another, even if someone has treated you with disdain or disrespect. If you keep honour at the forefront of all that you do the foundation of your business will gain a fortress of integrity and strength. This in turn, will attract right standing with future relationships ensuring God's will be done on earth as it is in Heaven.

Honour all men. Love the brotherhood. Fear God. Honour the king. **1 Peter 2:17 (KJB)**

Let's put the word into action:

1. Make sure you put a pen to paper as these revelations come to pass.
2. Ask the Holy Spirit for guidance.
3. Begin to study stories in the bible. A few examples would be the story of Cain and Abel; David and Saul, Sarah and Hagar, and Joseph and his brothers.
4. How does the 'spirit of jealousy' play out in this? Notice that it usually ends in death (murder) of a physical life or relationship! What does it do their descendants and other people in their family? Community? Kingdom?
5. In this story, can I see characteristics or circumstances of this showing up in my own life? How? Why? When?
6. Now that your eyes are open. Are you being blessing or a curse?
7. Have you been cursed? IF so, when, where and how?
8. Use the "R-Factor" steps to get things right, clean it up and totally release yourself from the shackles of the enemy. It is time to RISE and SHINE!

Let me pray with you,

Jesus, you are so good to me. You paid the ultimate price for the hardened hearts mankind has received due to envy, resentment, distrust and spite. I don't want the work you did on the cross to go unnoticed or to be in vain. I want freedom from this curse in and through my life today. Please cleanse me Lord. Please forgive me for cursing another and putting satan's mandate ahead of yours in my life. Help me to change the force of this once ingrained habit, and now become a blessing and an encouragement. Help me to go deeper every day to ensure that this curse does not and will not be passed down to my future generations in Jesus' name!

I also ask Lord God, that you seal this work in the Holy Spirit. That it be protected by the blood of Christ. That no weapon formed against any of us shall prosper in Jesus' name. I pray that you go before us, behind us and on each side of us as we delve into the work of deliverance. Any fiery darts of the enemy will ricochet off of us and right back in his own hind end! It is done! In the mighty name of Jesus! Amen.

CHAPTER SIX

The Spirit of Apathy
The Devil's Disciple

This is a killer business practice! Apathy shows up and business slows down. It's isn't just a crawl, but may sometimes be an actual gridlock filled to the brim with inactivity, cash flow decline, and hopelessness.

Your passions and desires blaze to nothing and you feel confused, defeated, like giving up.

Yes, apathy is a business killer. However, we are blessed by the Almighty. He has overcome the whole world for us. Apathy is one thing we can cast out spiritually and get back to the work at hand, building a thriving business.

One of my K.B.O. students came to me complaining of procrastination.

"I know what I am supposed to do Kathleen, but I keep finding shiny new objects to fill my attention. At the end of the day, I wasn't productive and I carry a mountain of guilt and shame."

I asked him why he thought that was. Here is his answer, " I knew what I should be doing and didn't do it. If I work through the system I have in place, I make money. I have proven it. I could do it in the past. I have seen others do it. Heck, I have even taught others to do it. When they put the plan into action it works for them too. The system always brings in cash for me, and lately I find myself purposefully avoiding it. It is like taking food out of my family's mouth and I can't seem to stop myself. The last thought I have on this is the fact that I promised a partner I would get it done, and I broke my promise. It's at this junction I turn back to MORE guilt, shame, pain and frustration? Breaking promises is NOT Christian like and it really isn't me."

OH YUCK! Can you relate? Can you see where the enemy rejoices? He wants you to walk in this place and be oblivious to the fact that you are under a curse. He wants you to think this is entirely your fault, you are not good enough, not smart enough, and basically a 'lazy, good for nothing so and so'. Does that sound like something God would say? NO! You can always tell when the enemy is speaking because his words are always about stealing, killing and destroying aren't they?

Knowing what God says about you helps you to overcome the spirit of apathy. It will help you break free and have breakthrough in every area of your life.

The Merriam-Webster dictionary defines apathy as: lack of feeling or emotion – impassiveness; lack of interest or concern - indifference.

If you have been delivered from an addiction and didn't fill that hole in your heart with the word of God, apathy loves to rush to fill in that place. This is especially true if you have been released from being a workaholic.

One of the characteristics of this demon when it shows up in our lives is often described as a numbness, or lack of desire or passion. A general feeling comes over you where you believe there is no use in trying anymore. It wants you to withdraw or play weak so that you don't get hurt. When you begin to experience these thoughts all you can see are limitations. All you can feel is futility and a like a big fat failure. It physically shows up in your life by having little or NO energy to act on the things you want to do. You feel pulled in so many different directions. You can feel, desolate, bored, careless, defeated, depressed, indecisive, indifferent, lazy, listless, hardened, forgetful, drained and so much more.

What are my words to describe it? *"Apathy shows up in avoidance and creates a deep annoyance in your life and in the life of others you walk with in your journey."* ***Kathleen D. Mailer***

Before you move ahead and apply the 'R-Factor' to this chapter, let me ask you some questions.

1. **How much time in this last month did you waste avoiding what you needed to do?** Did you avoid income-generating activity? (This is a big reason why we are called to business my friend!)
2. **Where did you spend most of your inactive time?** Facebook or other social media platforms? Did you go shopping? Eat? Clean up other messes that could be scheduled in a different time and place?

Did you lie to someone about what you are doing? A fellow K.B.O. was moved to tears when I asked this question. He said, 'Yes, I lie to my wife and say I am going to the office to work. Then, I find myself playing computer games and getting more and more frustrated. At the end of the month, we struggle and she looks at me with disdain. Her silent question is, "Why so little output to all your input?"

The counter to apathy is action:

Once you go through the "R-Factor" start taking small-bite sized action steps to regain your trust. It is like learning to walk again. When your legs have given out from underneath you and you haven't been able to do it on your own for a long period of time – you need to step up and step out. Slowly at first hanging on to something for support (thank you Jesus!), then with each step you find yourself stronger and stronger. Pretty soon you can go the distance. God is good!

Let's put the words into action:

1. If you truly believe that this business is God's business, I would like you to think about this for a moment. If God is the C.E.O. – that means you are managing the company, right? Now put yourself in the C.E.O's shoes. Look at the bottom line of dollars and cents in the business. Look at the activity of management.

- What does this management do with their time during their work hours?
- What are they contributing to the business?
- What are they contributing to society?

Here is the million dollar question,

- Would you fire you?

2. This scenario was not to condemn you but to convince you to take charge over this evil spirit. Our God is merciful! Thank you Jesus! I am going to say this again he is not interested in the business for the sake of the business. He is interested in who you become in the process of managing a great company for God.

3. When you answer the following questions, make them your small-steps. Learn and refresh your mind. Get a book, watch a DVD, get some mentorship. Anything like this is better than sitting. In active thoughts and hands, bring in active results.

   - What can you do to make habitual changes and to get your fire back?
   - What skills are needs do you have in able to turn things around?
   - Who do you need on your team?

- What are your top 3 reasons for being in your company?
- How and to whom can you delegate the rest of the day to day activities?

4. Go ahead and delve deep into this subject over the next 30 Days with the "R-Factor'. You will see changes quickly.

Let me pray with you,

Lord give me the strength to release apathy from my life. Help me to look at every action I take. (Remember inaction is ALSO an action!) Help me to see how it serves or does not serve my life and the purpose and plan you have for it. Show me what I need to do, in the flesh, to conquer and emancipate myself from such a heavy burden.

I cast away apathy from my life, and the life of my future generations! I cut off any ties from the past, present and future in regards to apathy.

I also ask Lord God, that you seal this work in the Holy Spirit. That it is protected by the blood of Christ. That no weapon formed against any of us shall prosper in Jesus name. I pray that you go before us, behind us and on each side of us as we delve into the work of deliverance. Any fiery darts of the enemy will ricochet off of us and right back in his own hind end! It is done! In the mighty name of Jesus! Amen!"

CHAPTER SEVEN

The Spirit of Offence satan's Best Defence

Have you ever met someone whom you can see that God has clearly marked as truly gifted? They are unbelievably talented, brilliant and skilled. You lovingly see that you are a fit in partnership (perhaps as your partner/client, joint-venture, friend, or as a team member). Then one day, it seems like it was out of the blue, you find them lashing out, retreating, or acting way off base!

A great example of this is a situation I found myself in. As the Editor-in-Chief of Today's Businesswoman Magazine I have found myself partnering with many people over the years. I came to understand that this magazine is God's magazine, and not Kathleen Mailer's magazine. It truly takes team effort to put out even one issue of quality. That means that the columnists, cover girls (and some men), editors, layout and design, sponsors and readers are really brought to the table by God's choosing, not by my own choice. I am careful to speak to the Holy Spirit on every aspect of the magazine. He has plans, purpose and reasons for each decision he orchestrates and I get the privilege to see some of the outcomes.

All of these outcomes are very positive. Sometimes he wants me to interview people so that they themselves can see who they are in his eyes and set them on their journey. Sometimes he wants columnists to gain expert status to be able to take their own journey to the next level. He always wants all of us to glean knowledge and understanding.

Of course the devil has other plans. He wants to kill, steal and destroy the works of God in our lives so that we don't accomplish the intended target that our lives are positioned to take.

In this one case, I was working with a few of our columnists to nudge them to the next level in business and in life. I wanted to motivate and inspire them. A few of them, wanted to burst forward and be on the stage teaching with their books and programs designed to help others shatter the bondage of abuse and oppression.

The Lord spoke to me, 'Ask them what would set them apart from any other columnist in their genre out in the world." In other words, anyone could write an article on the benefits of exercise right? (This was not the column by the way - I am just protecting the columnist's identity right now by not referring directly to the exact column). The truth is, you and I both could do it. All we would need to do is some research on the internet and then write it as a fact based column. Even someone who has not exercised a day in their life could write this article and it would be good enough. However, 'good enough isn't God enough'. He wants us to be the head and not the tail. Can I get an Amen?

God wanted these ladies to go immerse themselves in the communion they had with him. He wanted to uncover the spirit of offence in their lives in a safe and wonderful environment. Right under the wing of this anointed, God-centered magazine is the perfect place where we all can learn about ourselves without judgement.

God wanted to take these powerful women to a more profound level of influence. He wanted them to see past mediocrity and walk boldly into the promotion he had in store for them. This promotion would help many in communities all over the world occupy the nations just as God had ordained and anointed them to possess.

There was only one lady that didn't 'hear' God's question fully. She did seem to understand the question as we were talking about going to the next rung on the ladder with our magazine. However, not long after she had left for home I received an email with her formal resignation.

In the letter she directly stated she talked to her counselor and they both had agreed that she should not and would not deal with abusers like me. She took offence to what I was saying. What she 'heard' was, "You are not good enough. Anyone else can do that job better than you. You are lazy and good for nothing."

Now, was that what I said? Of course not! I WANTED her to be on the magazine and cared deeply for her and her family. The spirt of offence was alive and well. Even when I tried to talk to her she refused to listen. We had known each other for years and this one little situation – working for God`s glory - abruptly ended it. I still have not been able to totally mend this relationship to this day.

I did, however, send her a note of explanation. I did try and phone her. I did stop by and she wouldn't answer her door. You can't always get through to the person who is offended. Can you see why the devil loves this strategy?

It is now years later and I have heard from mutual friends she is in the same place she was **prior** to starting with the magazine. She still complains to them about how God never promotes her. She grumps about the fact that she has written her books, programs, and workshops for nothing. This makes my heart break. She is lonely and frustrated and feeling like an 'old maid' with no purpose. At this junction, I have to go on record and say, "I hate the devil!"

I didn't understand the spirit of offence back then. I sure the heck do now! Now when situations arise like this, I cast out this demon once and for all. I have a team of intercessors who work with me. I call the devil out and demand he take his hands off of my team member/family/friend/partner. Then, I lovingly ask that person to work with me. I ask them to sit down with me and **look for some perspective in the situation.** He/she is usually now open to hearing the word of God and we can then walk through some painful situations that arise from his/her past.

This curse is caused by wrong thinking, past experiences, and of course whispers of lies pulsating into our mainstream thinking by satan. The truth is this curse is dangerous because it is easily spread from person to person. It will destroy relationships, self-esteem, confidence, and trust.

What usually happens, and I think you will know what I am talking about, is the spirit of offence rises like a stallion forging forward into battle. It rears up on its hind legs and then sets its sites on the other party to make them take offence at the offence!

I hope I didn't lose you there. Stay with me for a bit. If I use the same scenario above, except I react to the spirit offence with offence, the curse lands directly on me. If I lash out at her for not hearing me right; if I come swinging and say things I should never say, I could open up doors to the curse fully manifesting it`s ugliness.

This ungodly re-action could cause a rift so big that the amount of damage could spread further, faster. Many times the offended will talk to others about the situation in context of explaining. It spreads in the gossip mill faster than a wild-fire on the back of a field of dry, 100-day, sun-baked grass. She did try to bad mouth me and spread the lies that I was an abusive tyrant. I know that at the time she did believe that satan`s lies were true. I also believe that it did actually die down quickly because I didn't engage in the same activity and spread the curse further.

I want to interject a point on that subject,

"Say it once to someone who can give you proper perspective is explaining. Saying it over and over again to anyone who is listening is complaining." **Kathleen D. Mailer**

Perspective is the counter measure to the spirit of offence and the spirit of rebellion (more on that later).

When the spirit of offence rears its ugly head, lovingly insert the following sentence into the conversation. **"(*Insert person's name here*), why don't we ask God to help us put this into perspective?"** This will cause the demon to stand in confusion long enough to make way for the Holy Spirit to enter the heart of the other person. It works! Try it!

When you are carrying the 'spirit of offence' – go on the defence.

If it is you who is easily offended, this is a day ordained by God. Once you see what it is like to live offence-free, you will crave a life where this drama doesn't exist. You will have to go through the chapter on the 'R-Factor' and take a good look at your situation. Before you do that, let me tell you what happens when you do NOT carry that spirit of offence and what you can accomplish for God.

I was getting ready for a large conference that we were putting together. There were so many attacks of the enemy while my intercessors and I pushing through obstacles every day. This event would definitely see captives set free and the consequences of destruction to the enemy camp was evident.

I was tired, stressed, on edge, fighting what seemed an uphill battle. This one particular day I felt something 'snap' in me. That was my first clue that the situation at hand was not being run by my heart for Jesus. I immediately took it to the Holy Spirit.

Let me tell you what happened.

I had put in a substantial order with a new supplier that we needed to have delivered at least 3 weeks prior to the event we had put on. It seemed like every time I tried to connect with this person she would forget about our meeting, call and cancel, or send me the wrong price quote. Over and over she would 'blow me off'. When I tried to call, there was always something of an excuse as to why she was late or couldn't attend to the order. Every time I asked the Holy Spirit to send me someone else to fulfill the order, he would say, "No, I have already sent you the right person."

On this particular day, I had truly had enough. There wasn't time now to get the order and have it come through in time to help us with the conference. We had a set time and place for a phone conversation to see if the order had arrived. Again, there was no answer. Twice I phoned and twice she didn't pick up. I was VERY upset! My thoughts went to a very bad place, "What is wrong with her? I give her an order and she can't follow it through? She doesn't respect me, my time or what I am trying to do. How dare she treat me with such disrespect?" Do you follow me? It's not pretty, I grant you that.

The first thing I thought about was getting in touch with guy who had recommended her to me and giving him a 'piece of my mind'. Thank God, the Holy Spirit had been revealing to me on my current 30 day fast, about the spirit of offence. With that 'snap' I immediately took it to God and repented.

I begged God, "I don't know what this is Lord, but I know it isn't you! You would NEVER want me to behave in this matter. You have never showed this kind of behavior. There must be something that the enemy is up to and I need some perspective please!"

It was then our faithful Jesus put my heart at peace. He forgave me and removed my sin and then revealed this evil spirit. He showed me into this woman's life. It was falling apart. She was deep into the throws of divorce, depression, homelessness, frustration and defeat. The enemy pummeled her every day with the thoughts of how stupid she is. He lied to her about the fact that she will never make it in business OR in life. He told her that she should just walk off a cliff somewhere and put her pain in the ground.

I felt sick! What could I do? How could I help? I phoned and left another message, "This is Kathleen. I want to first say to you that I am sorry I sounded so frustrated on the phone in my last few messages. I shouldn't have done that. I also want you to know that I am not mad at you. I don't care about the lateness of this order or that it isn't even coming in. That is the truth! What I do want is for you to call me as soon as you can. I realize, even though we don't know each other well yet, that this situation is not really you. Are you ok? Please call me so we can chat. I WANT to help you. I feel I can do something, although I don't know what at this point."

Did she call? YES, she did. I gave her a word from God. As a direct result of this conversation she confirmed everything the Lord spoke to me about. She gave her life to Christ on that call. She started coming to church. She released the hold the devil had on her life and she is moving forward, getting better and better every day!

THAT is our God! THAT is the business of ministry! THAT is one of the reasons we all live and breathe. Just for the record? **It turned out we didn't need those supplies after all. God didn't want them, he wanted the supplier!**

For those that receive the brunt of the spirit of offence, remind yourself that this isn't the child of God you see, it is truly a demon that wants to shut down any communication and have you stop this union.

The devil knows that two are always more powerful than one. Don't receive the curse of offence by reacting to the venom poured on you. Build relationships that foster honesty, trust and truth above all things. Soon you find yourself growing exponentially and living the adventures of life with joy.

Let's put the word into action,

1. Where have you acted out of offence in the past and realized that you were actually in the wrong?
2. In what situations do you get easily offended? Why do you think that is? What is the reason behind it? Many times we can see a pattern in our life once we understand the root of the problem.
3. Have there been times in the past, when you can now recognize the spirit of offence coming after you? How could you handle it differently now?
4. Are there any situations or concerns, where you could use the 'perspective technique' to repair relationships with partnerships in your life (client/partners, team members, church family, authority figures, children, spouse etc.?)
5. How does this effect, affect and infect your business?
6. Go ahead and delve deep into this subject over the next 30 Days with the "R-Factor'. You will see changes quickly.

Let me pray with you,

Lord God I thank you for the revelation of this nasty, vile spirit. I pray that you help all of us go deeper with you and a greater understanding that could never come from our own flesh or even from another person's thoughts. I pray, Jesus that you give all of us perspective and a vast level of discernment when it comes to the spirt of offence. Let us not 'jump into bed' with it and be a host in which it spreads.

I also ask Lord God, that you seal this work in the Holy Spirit. That it is protected by the blood of Christ. That no weapon formed against any of us shall prosper in Jesus name. I pray that you go before us, behind us and on each side of us as we delve into the work of deliverance. Any fiery darts of the enemy will ricochet off of us and right back in his own hind end! It is done! In the mighty name of Jesus! Amen!

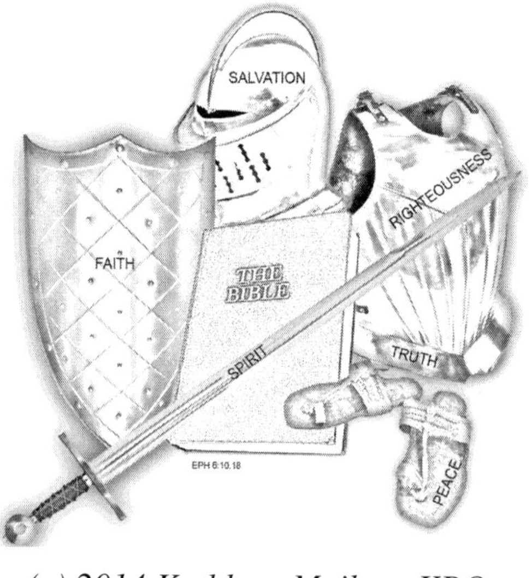

(c) 2014 Kathleen Mailer - KBO

CHAPTER EIGHT

The Spirit of Fear
satan's Wicked Web of Defeat

There are so many phobias and fears that exist in our world today. Some of them are so unbelievable that the average person can't conceive of the notions.

The truth is ALL fear comes from the enemy not from the All Mighty.

For God has not given us a spirit of fear and timidity, but of power, love, and self-discipline. **2 Timothy, 1:7**

I don't have a lot to share with you in this chapter, except to bring your attention to a few things.

1. Fear feels like a real thing to people.
2. Fears are really just a part of our belief system (B.S.) that comes from our perception to our life experiences in the past.
3. A counter attack to fear is to walk in faith.
4. Get to know God's heart on the subject.
5. Declare as many times as you need, "Today, I will choose faith over fear!"
6. Fear generally dissipates once one takes repetitive action to walk through it.
7. Fear has you imagining the outcome of circumstances that haven't even happened yet. Therefore, we begin

> making a series of small choices that result in actions that will actually bring what we fear into reality. It is a self-fulfilling prophecy for us. Why not use that same great imagination and imagine it turning out fantastic? Just sayin'.

Fear is actually a 'gift'. It is like a double-edged sword. It can be used for a curse or a blessing. Let's find the gifts of fear and use it to give the glory to God!

I want to share with you some fears I have conquered over the years of building my business. Are they all totally conquered and I am never bothered by them now? No, the devil isn't anything much but he is persistent. As believers, if we learned how to be as persistent as the devil is, we would be so very powerful wouldn't we?

He often tries to re-install the wrong inner software programs that can easily run under my radar without me knowing it. However, the good news is, God's word has us covered. If you declare the truth it will render the devil completely useless. Now that is a reason to shout 'Halleluiah"!

Fear of Success: You most likely have heard this before. Some of us think we have this fear so we go into 'counter' mode to ensure it doesn't block us. The question that we try to answer, that starts the proverbial ball rolling is, "What will happen if I succeed?"

This is a justifiable question. In the past I have seen some great success in business. The consequences of said success were devastating to me in my early years.

First, I had jealous people surface and curse me. I didn`t know anything about curses back then and I received their insecurities, negativity, and venom straight into my heart. Seriously, I actually succumbed to the lies and received the curse on my life. It took me a long time to identify this issue and ask God to cut off the curse so that I could once again receive His blessing over my health, family and business.

Second, I had team members spread their venom from the spirit of offence that operated in their lives and consequently caused huge upheaval in my organization.

Third, and I am being very honest, I was crushed under God`s blessings. I grew too fast, too soon and didn`t have the foundation in my life, habits, and character to expand gracefully.

As a result, I even had people who were close to me make rude and crude remarks because they had the belief that in order to make a lot of money you must be a 'scammer'.

This, in a small part, is one of the reasons I am writing this book today. This does not have to be your reality. If it has been your reality in the past, it is time to let that go and let God guide you.

I am not saying that these things will not come up for you, because they will. Sorry if I am not being an encouragement with this statement. It is just the way of the enemy.

Let's focus on the good news though. You will be totally equipped to handle it now! You will know what you are fighting and you won't have to dwell in the valley of death, you can walk right though with your head held high.

Fear only exists in the past, not your future. Focus on the work of the cross – really understand that it is more than the wonderful gift of salvation when one passes here and moves home to Heaven. It is about the grace: the knowledge, help, provision, protection, focus, clarity, time stretcher, and blueprint maker that God freely gives us. This grace will help us to discern these things, learn about these things, change these things, embrace these things, prepare for these things, and understand these things. Wow, that excites me how about you?

Fear of Failure: "What happens if I fail? I can't go through this again!" This stops so many of us from even trying. The truth is we are supposed to fail. I learned that failure isn't actually a FAIL.

I like to define failure as this: *Failure is a success marker that marks the graduation line of one season and the start line to your new promotion.*

The sooner we understand that failure is in our future we can stop looking at it as a bad thing. We can see it as an actual gift. Once that happens we will move quickly to reach our own definition of success.

I would like to come against the fear of failure right now and pray over you,

"I am on to you fear! I know you are meaning to harm this person reading this book right now. You want to render them motionless. You want them to run from the action steps they need to succeed. You want them to hide, stay back, stop, cease and desist!

Well, not today! NOT on my watch! The truth is they are learning right now that failure is a natural part of success. They are learning right now this gift from God is a part of the grace that is imparted into their lives. They are learning right now that they must fail forward fast to get to where they want to go!

They understand that when they were learning to tie their shoes, they failed over and over. They can see that they had enough encouragement to keep trying then and finally they had success!

They receive the knowledge now, that the only reason they didn`t have success immediately is that they didn`t know how to do something, YET. That is it! That is all! It wasn`t bad or good or in between. It just was.

By the POWER of grace they can learn to do each step to success the right way. From now on, satan, every time you try to call something an epic fail it will actually turn into an epic stepping stone of success!

Praise GOD for his mighty and wonderful ways. Thank you Jesus for showing us, what seems to be a failure (not working out) is actually PROOF it is working! In Jesus name."

This is exactly my point. When Jesus' ministry began it was exciting. Many people received miracles, healings, and prosperity. Oh there is so much we can learn from this.

Jesus had the devil on his butt sending religious nuts, judgemental, jealous, slanderous, physical and emotional abusers. He had members of his team betraying him. Heck family and friends heckled him! You name it, it all came against him.

If we didn`t know the story and it was unfolding in front of us now, it looked like an epic fail. How? This guy named Jesus? He sure doesn't look like the King of the World right now. By the looks of the way things were going, it looks like he failed big time! I mean, they caught him, persecuted him, and hung him on the cross to die beside all of the other 'bad guys'. He was supposed to live forever? Yeah, I don't think so!

We are blessed though, because we all know what happened don't we? God proved that, that seemingly disappointing, big fat-failure was actually a gift of grace. Jesus conquered that grave and then gave us the power to do the same thing. This piece of the work of the cross is so that we can overcome any situation, any storm, and any problem. Why do you think you are in business? It is to solve people's problems for them. If you don't believe that, then maybe you are in the wrong vocation!

Fear of Finishing: "What?" you say, "there is such a thing?" Yes! There is! I didn't realize it myself until the Lord spoke to me about the amount of 'projects' I had on the go. I really needed to finish what I start.

Do you want to know how he showed me that this is something I had inside of me? He asked me a few simple questions that I will now ask you, "How many almost empty or half empty bottles of hand-lotion, shampoo etc. do you have in your cupboard? How many ½ done books, projects, ideas have you sitting around? How many marketing systems have you started to implement only to go ¾ of the way and not completely see it into fruition? Why don't you finish them?"

That was the million dollar question right there. What about you? Do you have piles of things here there and everywhere? Why don't you finish them?

Note to self: Now when you can see it, you can work at creating a success habit of being able to finish what you start.

Plan of attack to counteract the fear of finishing:

1. **Make a list** today of messes you have in your office, projects, partners/client check in's, orders sitting on the shelf, presentations, marketing plans and the like. Don't judge them, don't react to them, and don't start to work on them yet.

2. Get serious about going through and deleting the things you thought you wanted to do and ask the question: “Is this still relevant? Important? Or mandatory?” If it isn’t release it. IMPORTANT: as you release it pray, “Lord Jesus I release this project (or whatever it is) in the name of Jesus and take it off of my list of choose to do’s. I ask that you help me with the grace I need to decipher and discern the rest of my list today to make my time more efficient and move quickly to my goals.”
3. Now go through the list and take a look at the priorities. List each project on your choose to do sheet in order of importance. To find the top 3, a good question to ask is, “What projects would be the most important to reaching all of my goals, dreams and desires?” **Find your #1 – and get to work.**
4. Ask the Holy Spirit to partner with you to write a list of everything that needs to be accomplished. If you seriously take the time to plan, you can achieve much more than you ever imagined.
5. From there, you want to go through and ask the question: **Delegation**? Who could do some of these steps in order for you to move forward. When you have that list complete write and email or make a phone call and clearly state what the project is and what you need from that person. Give them very clear instructions. Give them a clear deadline of when it needs to be completed. Give them encouragement. Give them a chance to ask questions now. Then, ask them to repeat back to you what they heard for

instructions. Make sure you are clear and focus will come into your life. When you are done that pray, "Lord, I thank you for this person in my life that you have given me to help me on my way to cleaning up this project. I pray that you help guide them, and me, so that it is done effortlessly, with focus and clarity in Jesus name. Amen."

6. Now the real fun begins! I mean it. Take the rest of the list now and see what you need to do. **Schedule in time** daily, weekly or monthly (depending on the size of the project).

Do it consistently and you will see that the fear of finishing will dissipate. It isn't that we have to 'get rid' of the fear of finishing; it means we replace it with the gift of finishing and embrace the wonderful consequences that this gift brings.

The next chapter will really help us to release all of these fears as we begin to uncover the real cause of our issues.

It isn't the fear that is the root, it is only a symptom. I believe the cause of all of our fears come from the unloving spirit. I think you will also agree.

Let's put the word into action:

Surrender Your B.S.

My prayer is that you are able to breath past your fear and develop and replace fear with a new belief and trust in yourself, in God and in others.

Here is what I sometimes need to do. I pray for the Holy Spirit to help me. Then, I answer the following questions:

1. What exactly am I afraid of?
2. Why am I afraid?
3. Does this fear serve me?
4. What would happen in this situation if I didn't have this fear?
5. What would I rather have what I have now and walk in fear? Or…
6. Would I rather conquer this fear and move forward?
7. What does the fact that Jesus conquered all of the works of satan have to do with your business today? This is a VERY good question to look at your belief systems and line up what your fears are to the truth of knowledge about Jesus' life and death.

Once I have answered these questions, I ask the Holy Spirit to help me to release the fear in this manner…let's pray this process through together shall we?

Let me pray with you,

Lord, I come to you today to release the fear that is stopping me from moving forward today.

I am ready to let go of the fear of _______________.

(Take a deep breath in and when you release it by blowing it out of your mouth say,)

I now let go of the fear of _____________ in the name of Jesus.

(Take a deep breath in and when you release it by blowing it out of your mouth say,)

I let go of the control it has over me and the feelings of safety and security it currently gives me. In Jesus name.

I pray Lord God now for help to take the action I need to take to prove to the devil once and for all I don't succumb to his trickery of putting 'fear' into my imagination. I believe in the promises of my God!

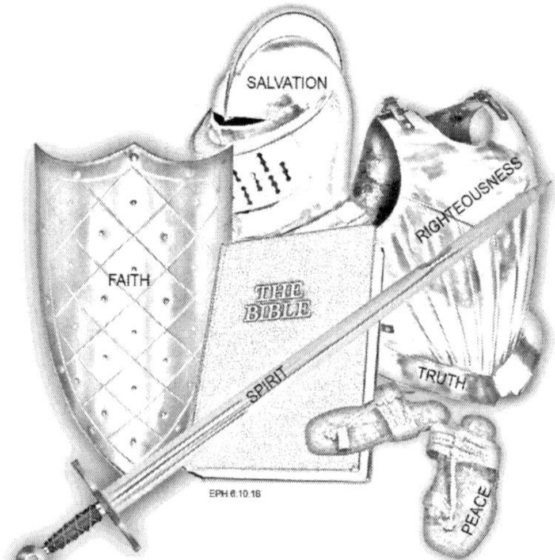

(c) 2014 Kathleen Mailer - KBO

CHAPTER NINE

The Unloving Spirit
satan's Instrument of Mass Destruction

While there are many other demonic spirits that plague us, I am afraid this book would not be able to contain them all. There is the 'spirit of witchcraft' which is alive and well today. It isn't some mystical thing that happens in movies. It is front and center in the business realm. K.B.O's need to be on alert and understand what is in the enemy's playbook in order to fully engage in everything we need to do for Christ Jesus.

There is the spirit of, suicide, addictions, death, un-deservedness... but in my opinion the worst principality is the battle with the Unloving Spirit!

This revolting, loathsome evil is one we truly need to conquer and be delivered from. It resides in the heart of every man and woman as they begin to take ground for Christ. It can show itself through characteristics of all of its little 'minions' and I think it is the closest thing to being the devil's actual heart.

Many of us walk on our journey with different degrees of manifesting this demon. Feeling unloved, uncared for, disrespected, never good enough, never smart enough, unworthy, like you are not relevant, or can't measure up. It can show up in your choices and in your mindset.

It can manifest into deceptive thoughts that in turn become people's realities. Thoughts of suicide, depression, disease, spouting lies, over-committing, judging others, self-sabotage, fear of anything and everything, victim, victimizer, under achieving, loneliness, retreating, pain, anger, frustration, unwarranted or unhealthy risk taking, procrastination, people pleasing, work holism, unhealthy choices, deadly secrets, poverty, apathy, jealousy, offence, giving yourself away, debt, destruction, disease, and so much more.

THE DEVIL IS A LIAR!

We won't listen to him! It's time to be set free once and for all from this overshadowing, over bearing sabotager.

Even as I write this, I am sensing that the Holy Spirit is doing a work in your right now. I can see that you are recognizing not only the symptoms but now the cause of a great deal of problems in your life, or in the lives of those you love.

For the record:

Don't pass over this chapter with the thought of, "I am the most loving person out there Kathleen. This can't be for me." No, if you are having that thought then you need to realize it is exactly for you! Change the word, 'unloving' to 'undeserving' or 'unworthy' to receive goodness, grace, love, peace and joy. Proof you have it? Look at the fruit in your life right now? Does your life show the bounty, healthy, abundant, prosperous life God promises in the bible? I didn't think so. Keep reading.

The very problems we are trying to solve as K.B.O's will have this disgusting demon rear his ugly head throughout our flock, team, and our very own existence.

This is something that I feel you should take your time to intricately examine, uncover layer by layer and when it is time to be delivered, be sure to stick to the "R-Factor" and the prayer in I say later in this chapter.

This is nothing to play with. Ask God to wholeheartedly give you the grace you need in order to triumph.

When we are released from this bondage, we will learn to love and respect one another. We will always be patient with people. We will be able to comfort, tell the truth for and pray for each other. As part of his family, we will begin to truly learn to serve, bring joy, honor, cherish, forgive, be generous, and be kind to each other. Then the devil won't have any platform in any area of our lives. The devil won't be able to deceive us. The devil won't have a hold on us anymore.

His weapon of mass destruction:

This curse is the easiest to receive because it is usually those we love the most or who are closest to us that curse us. Many don't realize they are even doing it because they too, have received the curse most likely, generation from generation.

When someone victimizes another, you can trace back to that very same abuser being horribly abused as well. (Remember, there are two ways this spirit manifests, in the victimizer AND in the victim.)

I want to tell you a story about a K.B.O we will name Darren. Here is how Darren explains the situation. I want you to ask the Holy Spirit to reveal any parallel truths to you - in your life, and in your business.

My Dad wasn't the type to be lovey dovey with us. He was a good man, but just didn't show his emotions well. I grew up thinking crying was weak. There was no room for emotion except for anger because anger got results. When my Dad got mad, everyone moved faster, they gave him what he wanted so not to upset him.

He often told me how stupid I was, and that I would never amount to anything especially if I keep hugging my 'mommy' like a 'pansy'. I needed to 'suck it up' when I got hurt and never let anyone see me at a weak moment. If I do show that side, they will see me for what I am 'stupid and dumb'. Oh yes, he also added, 'lazy and good for nothing'.

Once I started school I didn't have a lot of friends. I played by myself and ended up observing people around me. There was a new boy who came to our small school in grade two. He was scared, and was not at all comfortable in his new situation. I saw him cry in the parking lot and watched as the older boys pushed him around and calling him a pansy.

I gulped as I saw the fact that my father was right. I think at that point I was really hoping that there was a chance he was wrong. But the truth was staring me right in the face. These guys will see me for what I am, 'stupid and dumb'. I bought the whole lie, hook, line and sinker.

I felt so bad for this kid. Something came over me and I walked boldly (something I had never done before)... and yelled at him!

*All of the older boys were shocked. I yelled, 'you pansy *ss, lazy good for nothing, stupid dumb mommy's boy! Don't you know cry-babies don't get anywhere? Get out of my face you make me sick!' He turned and ran home.*

For a few still moments, my heart was beating so loud that I couldn't breathe. There was a war within me. The voices went back in forth in my head. "You helped him because you didn't want to see him hurt." - "This was not the way and not the truth Darren."

Then the silence was broken by laughing, praising, and yes... hugging! The older more-wiser kids, who didn't give me the time of day, decided I was going to be a part of their 'gang'. I was cool, and brave. This was beyond exciting. It was exhilarating and intoxicating at the same time.

Needless to say that translated into many issues in my own life, addictions, failed marriages, no relationship to speak of with any of my children. I forced my way to the top in sales – just to find out that you can only push and bully your way for so long and then no one wants to work with you, let alone be your client.

Jesus saved me from myself – knowledge and deliverance from this generational curse explained everything for me.

Now the next step is to work with the 'flesh' (as Kathleen says) to ensure I never open the door to the enemy again. Restoration is happening, Praise God!

What did you learn from this story? I can sense how many people will be affected by this story right now. That is the stirring of the Holy Spirit. Understanding this concept should not bring condemnation (that is the devil right there), it should bring conviction.

Let`s put the word into action:

1. Where in your life does the unloving spirit show up?
2. How many of the characteristics can you check as say, "yep, that is me!"
3. Do you see this in the lives of those whom you serve?
4. How will you react differently now that you are aware of this aspect?
5. Do you have a team of intercessors that pray for you and your business on a regular basis?
6. What would your life be like if you were released? Where has this stopped you from succeeding in the

past? Where would you be if you had more confidence, joy, and a greater understanding?

7. Go ahead and delve deep into this subject over the next 40 Days with the 'R-Factor'.
   This is serious business, and takes prayers and fasting to bring deliverance.

One day I may write a whole book on this subject. Once the Lord revealed this to me, and I was delivered – I can honestly say that I meet several people daily who walk under a curse and don't know it.

My husband and I pray for them and ask God to deliver them from this monumental issue that plagues them. K.B.O's are definitely stalked and tortured by this spirit because without this curse their mandate would multiply. We are called to fund Kingdom purposes through business ministry. Imagine the freedom to do what God has called us to when we are out from under the canopy of this curse and living in the fullness of the blessing of God.

Finding freedom from the unloving spirit will take you to a whole new level of compassion and truly help you to become the "Master Relationship Builder" that you are!

Let me pray with you,

Lord I ask that you walk with us every day and open our eyes and hearts to the wicked plans of the enemy. Don't let satan rule and reign in us, our business or our lives. Open up our ears to hear you with exact precision when this demon lurks in our midst. Let us get in the habit of casting him out and pushing him away.

Fill us with a spirit of patience, kindness, and encouragement that we spread instead. Let us stand with blessings in our mouth that comes out of an indwelling of you in our heart.

I also ask Lord God, that you seal this work in the Holy Spirit. That it is protected by the blood of Christ. That no weapon formed against any of us shall prosper in Jesus name. I pray that you go before us, behind us and on each side of us as we delve into the work of deliverance. Any fiery darts of the enemy will ricochet off of us and right back in his own hind end! It is done! In the mighty name of Jesus! Amen!"

CHAPTER TEN

The Spirit of Rebellion
The Flesh Wants What The Flesh Wants

The toughest nut to crack is the Spirit of Rebellion. All of the rest of the demons are conquerable because Christ already did the work for us on the cross. He took authority of satan that day so that we could have the same authority in the spiritual realm too.

Why then, do we hear so many who have been delivered from addictions, disease, spiritual infirmities start living in that devastation again after they have already been delivered?

I believe it is the spirit of rebellion at play. This particular spirit cannot be cast out by any of our friends, pastors, mentors or families authority. It is a matter of the flesh wanting what the flesh wants.

This is the final action of overcoming anything. The bible says,

Rebellion is as sinful as witchcraft, and stubbornness as bad as worshiping idols. So because you have rejected the command of the LORD, he has rejected you as king. **1 Samuel 15:23**

Once we are finally free of the spiritual issue, our flesh decides to take over in the form of habits, desires, and cultural behaviors. It isn't that we 'get' the sickness back, no it is more that we decide we want to act like we still are sick.

Rebellion manifests in forms of refusing to stop doing what you know to be wrong, but expecting that it won't hurt you because you have been set free by Jesus. It can also be very present when we put what we are addicted to before our walk with Jesus.

This belief will get you in a heap of trouble. The enemy lies in wait, stalking you and hopes you open this door. **WARNING**: that might be the very door uses to come back into your life with 7 of his 'little buddies'.

Understanding grace is a pivotal point to conquering the Spirit of Rebellion. Grace is truly God's empowerment, provision, peace, joy, knowledge and PERSPECTIVE to help you see life from a 'God's Eye View'.

Grace does not take the place of doing the 'work' you need to do. In another words, you can't just decide that you have been delivered by God's supernatural grace and then go back to the everyday habits and knee-jerk reactions that you had before.

Then think that all you need to do is flippantly repent because God will forgive us and we can start fresh. No, that isn't how grace works. This mentality becomes a form of 'wish-craft' and is a huge component of the rebellion that I am referring to.

After grace has been given, we need to receive it by having our heart and our flesh work toward the gift Jesus has freely given to us. We need to ensure that we encompass in our flesh what the God did in the spiritual realm. (Please don't mistake legalism and a 'works' mentality to 'buy' God's grace. That isn't what I am discussing here.)

However, grace does empower us to lovingly correct ourselves without condemnation, guilt or shame. He will give us what we need to insert self-discipline into our life to have true freedom over those things that bind us.

Self-discipline is not about inflicting pain, guilt and shame. It is a deep act of loving who God created you to be. When we can lovingly correct our steps and move on, we easily rise to the platform of excellence.

Through this gentle instruction we cultivate a stronger relationship with the All Mighty and we learn to nurture and grow it into something beautiful as we spend more and more time together.

It not only will birth a trust in God, but you will have a sense of faith in yourself like you have never had before. As a result this confidence (or God-fidence) you will reach new levels of relationship with others in the land God has given you.

It does prove beyond a shadow of a doubt what seems impossible for man, is possible for God.

This parable I wrote will beautifully illustrate what happens when we encounter the power of grace and it is followed with perspective from a God's Eye View.

###

The Caterpillar Who Thought He Was Nothing But A Disgusting Little Worm

By Kathleen D. Mailer

Today was almost the same as every other day for Georgie the caterpillar. It was hot. He was full of fear, and it was oh-so-sl-oo-ow going.

Danger was at every turn. For instance, he had to be especially on guard when he crossed the grass in the playground that he didn't get trampled and tromped on by the evil malicious giants that scream and run like they are half crazed. Everyone knows that these giants are a natural enemy of not only caterpillars but of crawling bugs everywhere.

Last week, Georgie stood helplessly by as he watched his friend meet with a brutal nasty end to his life. It was gut-wrenching to watch the enemy zero in on his pal. He shook in terror when the giant lifted his foot and splattered his chum all over the sidewalk. The war-cry he heard the monster yell just before the deed was done still rang in his ears and made him sick to his stomach. "You deserve to die you filthy, disgusting maggot! You are nothing but a worm!"

Depressed and full of apathy, Georgie's thoughts traveled back to this morning. It was way too easy to recall that big black bird who laughed uproariously, 'Caw! Caw!" (He heard Ha-Ha!)

It seemed to mock and heckle the entire populations of caterpillars. It had swooped down and scooped another one of his friends, David, in its beak and took him back to its nest for its babies to eat. It is a tragic shame. David was so young.

Georgie was so darn tired. He was tired of fighting the enemy at every turn; tired of feeling so alone and lonely; tired of being depressed because life held no purpose for a disgusting little worm like him. Seriously, what good would he be to anyone or anything? Heck he failed even the easiest task like moving one step on his journey forward. He would move ahead an inch and then wind would blow him back two. Life is unfair and it was truly more that he could bear.

"Where is God in all of this?" Georgie wondered. "Obviously he doesn't care about a little maggot who has no purpose in life. If he does, he certainly doesn't care about me. If he did I wouldn't be living in so much pain."

Just then, something stirred deep inside Georgie's heart. He felt the call of God. He wasn't sure if it was a whisper in the wind or an imaginary friend pulling him closer and asking him to surrender his will.

"Something's gotta change!" The little caterpillar cried out. "I am tired of doing it my way. God if you are listening and you care at all – then please help me!"

Exhausted, he flopped down, curled up in a ball and threw the covers over his head. (Take note, for caterpillars this is known as a cocoon). He could feel that this was the end of his existence. It is over. As his took what he was sure to be his last breath, the world scarcely heard his tiny voice whisper, "I surrender all."

As surrender came, God's grace appeared. The Father's compassionate and loving touch transformed what was surely and completely the end to young Georgie's life. In God's time, and due process, Georgie woke up to face a new day. He felt so different. He felt the peace of God that surpassed all understanding. He heard clearly, audibly, the voice of Jesus speak directly into his heart.

The smile on Jesus face lit up the tight dark room that he found himself in. Jesus spoke so softly that only Georgie's spirit could hear. It was something about the trials and tribulations that he had previously faced. The Holy Spirit was unveiling truth from a 'God's Eye View'.

"My darling child, I never left you nor did I forsake you. I was always there. I protected you through every turn, every situation and every incident.

Do you remember the delightful little red-headed girl? She is the one with the smattering of freckles on her cheeks and the eyes that sparked like giant sapphires. Remember the day she picked you up with that minute tree branch. For the record, it was the very twig I instructed the wind to break from my tree that I created to protect all of the little creatures in the park.

That morning you were so full of fear. You were sure you were not going to make it. You thought she had picked you up so she could shove you in a jar and suffocate you. You thought for sure she would squish you like the 'bug' that you think you are.

But the truth is she didn't do those things at all. She and I had talked about your destiny, your purpose, and your future. She desperately wanted to help me, just like an angel, to see that any and all of my creation finds the freedom I have promised them. This is actually part of her purpose and calling.

Together we brought you to the tree and put you under the loving covering of a leaf where the birds of prey could not find you. This is where we find you on this day.

Yes it is true, you felt that you couldn't endure anymore, but by my grace and design, you did overcome. You made it through the 'test' so you could have a testimony to share with the world.

And today my little friend, I set you free to be who you are called to be. Now you have a 'God perspective' on, your past; who you truly are; and your future, it is time. It is time to break you free from the bondage you are in. It's time to fly, Georgie. It is time to fly."

Georgie could feel himself getting stronger and stronger. He began to fight the physical shackles that bound him, because he knew Jesus had set him free. As the last shards of covering were removed he noticed he not only felt different but he looked different too. He was a new creation in Christ!

The little butterfly stretched his wings and took flight! He rose to heights he had never ever dreamed he could. He danced and sang praises to the God of all creation. His gem-like colors glistened in the sun's rays. He swooped, and swished all around the park. He looked down at his once 'giant enemies' and noticed they were not evil at all. They were delightful little children who seem to be mesmerized by the splendour of his wings.

His eyes locked on the little red head and her mother. His tiny little heart swelled with so much gratitude. He flittered around her head and shouted, "Thank you, oh tiny one, for being a part of my journey. May God bless you and keep you."

Laughing he landed on her mother's shoulder. Katherine was even more beautiful than her daughter. She too had the same auburn hair and a smattering of freckles that ran across her nose.

His soft wings scarcely and ever so softly touched her cheek. The Lord began to speak to Katherine's heart through that one butterfly kiss.

"Oh Pure of Heart" he said, "like this butterfly had once felt, you too are in a cocoon. This spirit of cancer that you now carry seems like it is the end of the road to you. My child, allow me to give you a fresh perspective. Look back through the tests and trials you have been through. I have always been faithful. I never left you nor did I forsake you. This is no exception. Do you remember when?..... Remember who you are….." His voice faded out and was replaced by a knowing that was placed somewhere deep within her.

The little butterfly, who once thought of himself as a disgusting little worm – felt larger than life in that moment. He had the privilege to be God's hands and feet. Just before a tear of healing fell from the woman's cheek and reached the tip of his wing, he flew off to be a part of another miracle for his God - In Jesus name!

###

Now that's God's perspective!

I do have an important question for you.

Did the butterfly still have the same threats to enemy attacks as he did before?

Are there still dangers all around him for a butterfly? There are still monsters in amidst the delightful little people. There are still birds of prey that have to feed their young.

The truth is his circumstances didn't change did they? No, but he sure changed by the power and grace of Christ.

A little perspective goes a long way in changing our mind and changing our life.

Counter measure for rebellion:

It is all wrapped up in getting a new perspective.

Perspective: *viewpoint, outlook, perception, take, evaluation, assessment, take on things.*

When we are able to 'see' into the situation from a different angle, Holy Spirit can bypass the rebellion and go straight into the heart of the person who needs it.

Perspective is truly the key to success in everything we do. God can literally change our whole issue in a blink of an eye when he offers us a fresh perspective on things. Our situation doesn't necessarily change, but our reaction to it does.

When we change, everyone /everything around us will change. It is a fact.

Let's put the word into action,

1. Where in your life are you walking in rebellion?
2. Write down situations in the past where you thought for sure it was the end, and yet here you are today alive and well to talk about it.
3. Write down what new perspective you now have on your current situation you are facing.
4. What would happen if you didn't struggle with rebellion? (A by-product of rebellion is: wanting control, to people please and/or security.)

5. You may be in some sort of rebellion if you find yourself going around and around the same mountain – hoping and praying for different results.
8. Are you looking at life through 'worm' colored glasses?
9. Repent and ask for forgiveness, use the 'R-Factor' to walk you through the steps.
10. Release rebellion once and for all!

Here is a quick story from one of our K.B.O students.

"I had a mortgage to pay and no money left to pay it. I paid our tithes and trusted that God had a way of making this right. Of course, I thought his answer would be that he would provide me with the money on the day it was due but that day came and went.

I was upset and I heard the enemy go off in my head about not being able to trust God. Of course I had all of these visions of bill collectors, the rest of my bills not being paid. I had decided that I would lose my house and my children would not be able to eat. Of course, that wasn't true but it was where my mind was at and I believed it would happen.

Then, by God's grace your message on perspective came across my desk. I asked the Lord to give me a fresh viewpoint. I asked for forgiveness and for grace as you recommended.

I felt the peace of God come upon me and decided, "Either I believe God has this handled OR I don't. What would it be?"

I decided the bible was the ultimate authority no matter what this looks like or how I feel about it.

Do you know what happened? NOTHING! No bill collectors; no threats to my house or my family; no mark on my credit rating. Absolutely nothing! The following week everything broke free again and we paid the overdue mortgage with no negative consequences. (I know that was God!)

I learned I could trust God even if it isn't in my own understanding. Thank God, I didn't go into rebellion when the devil tried to goad me into it. I don't need or want that curse on my life, my family, my business or my finances.

Thank you for helping me understand.

Let me pray with you,

Lord I ask for supernatural revelation to the spirit of rebellion in this K.B.O's life. I pray God that you would be relentless to show the truth no matter what. I pray his/her heart is ready to receive the changes and that by your grace you help change habits and desires of the flesh so that this captive can be set free.

I also ask Lord God, that you seal this work in the Holy Spirit. That it is protected by the blood of Christ. That no weapon formed against any of us shall prosper in Jesus name. I pray that you go before us, behind us and on each side of us as we delve into the work of deliverance. Any fiery darts of the enemy will ricochet off of us and right back in his own hind end! It is done! In the mighty name of Jesus! Amen!"

CHAPTER ELEVEN

Your Spiritual Tool Kit

Every business owner knows that you need tools to help you not only function at your prime, but also to maintain your energy flow, staying connected to God who is our source. So many K.B.O's never see beyond their physical tool belt that helps them with marketing, time management, efficiency, effectiveness and more.

While these tangible aspects are very important they need to come as an asset or vehicle to express the fullness of these instruments from God. With each mechanism in place you will have a solid footing on the rock. Then your marketing, and time management tools will be much easier to implement, more effective and of course, much more joy-filled.

There are MANY more gifts our Lord has given us. I have just picked a few that have been vital for me in my business. I wish I could give each more attention, than I can on these pages. I invite you to explore each area. Sit with the Holy Spirit and the Word of God to find out how they fully function.

I love our K.B.O. Mentorship program because we do delve deeper into every subject. For now, I pray that revelations being as you start to read and implement these tools into your spiritual tool kit. May it bless your business beyond anything you can ever imagine?

1. **Put on the WHOLE armour of God**: I am so grateful that the Bible is so very clear about what we need to do to protect ourselves. It is surprising how few Christians actually know that they have power over the enemy, and they are fully equipped to stand strong against his attacks.

Almost every morning my husband and I 'suit up' with this scripture. Since I am very prophetic I find it easy to actually walk out the 'imaginary' actions as if they are real.

This tool is particularly helpful when you have difficult meetings. It is also imperative if you are going into battle on behalf of yourself or your partners. Remember, your business is your ministry! That means that at every turn, you walking in God's Kingdom. Every potential conversation, connection, and interaction is a ministry moment. It is a divine connection. Look for the ministry moments and you will find yourself excelling.

This action will help you keep your mind on God and the true purpose of your ministry. That is to be a **M**aster **R**elationship **B**uilder (MRB). It is time to get prepared!

(Bold words emphasized by the author only- to make a point.)

*10 A final word: **Be strong** in the Lord and in **his mighty power**. 11 Put on all of **God's armor** so that you will be able to **stand firm against all strategies of the devil**. 12 For **we** are **not fighting against flesh-and-blood** enemies, but **against***

***evil rulers** and authorities of the **unseen world**, against mighty powers in this dark world, and against evil spirits in the heavenly places.*

13 Therefore, put on every piece of God's armor so you will be able to ***resist the enemy*** *in the time of evil. Then after the battle you will still be standing firm. 14 Stand your ground, putting on the* ***belt of truth*** *and the* ***body armor of God's righteousness.*** *15 For* ***shoes,*** *put on the* ***peace*** *that comes from the Good News so that you will be* ***fully prepared.*** *16 In addition to all of these,* ***hold up the shield of faith*** *to* ***stop the fiery arrows of the devil.*** *17 Put on* ***salvation as your helmet,*** *and take the* ***sword of the Spirit, which is the word of God.*** *18* ***Pray in the Spirit*** *at all times and on every occasion. Stay alert and be persistent in your* ***prayers*** *for all believers everywhere.* ***Ephesians 6: 10-18***

2. **Walking in the Power of the Holy Spirit:**

8 But you will receive power when the Holy Spirit comes upon you. And you will be my witnesses, telling people about me everywhere - in Jerusalem, throughout Judea, in Samaria, and to the ends of the earth." **Acts 1:8**

49 "And now I will send the Holy Spirit, just as my Father promised. But stay here in the city until the Holy Spirit comes and fills you with power from heaven." **Luke 24:49**

There is so much to share about the power of the Holy Spirit! It is crucial you understand scripture when it comes to walking in your authority in the Kingdom. The Holy Spirit is your partner. He is wonderful, beautiful, and full of wisdom and discernment. He is the BEST teacher. He can help you pull back the curtain when you are looking at a business deal in order to 'see' what needs to be done. He whispers in your ear to make crucial decisions. He stands with you so you won't be shaken or moved, when you need to stand. He is your reason, your conscious, your intuition and so much more.

As K.B.O's, there is no one like the Holy Spirit. Your business ministry counts on the fact that you are not only saved by the wonderful work on the cross and the precious blood of Jesus, but also to be baptized in the Holy Spirit. It's essential to be empowered to do everything you are called to do.

The bible says, 'greater is HE that is in me, than in this world'. If we can wrap our mind around this concept, we truly will be unstoppable.

I will tell you what. Healings, salvations, signs, deliverances, wonders, provision, and miracles of all sorts will manifest all around you as you go about your daily business – which, of course, is the 'family business'.

No one is more surprised than my husband and me at the goodness of our God. Our business ministry took on a strange, yet wonderful, turn when we came out of our desolate wasteland. As I mentioned earlier, we had some tough years we had to go through. Among the multitude of life changing events, was that we had to lay aside and put down what seemed to be a successful business and business practices.

It wasn't that we were doing anything wrong. It was just that our hearts out-grew our current level of understanding. I now know when that happens, a promotion from God is in our future!

The closer we got to Jesus, the more we desired to do more for him. We had prayed for God to use us in a mighty way. I had NO idea what that looked like, I just knew in my heart I was hungry for him. I wanted to know him more. I wanted to see him more in my everyday life. I wanted to hear him more. In every way, shape and form I opened my heart to him. I wanted more! More of Jesus!

Now we are seeing what it means to know, feel, taste, see, smell, more of Heaven on earth. Even still I am unsure exactly if I truly know all of the plans and purposes he has for us. What we are walking through now, is not what we had ever planned, wanted or desired. It is far from what I imagined 'more' meant! I am still in 'AWE' at his majesty, and his deepest love for mankind. We keep our hands in receiving position and use the tools I am sharing in this chapter to continue to move. We still ask for 'more'… but have learned not to 'figure out' what that means.

Today, our business platform takes us into ministry all over the world. I am currently hosting a radio show called, 'Breaking Chains with Kathleen Mailer". We have salvations, healing miracles, deliverances, signs and wonders at almost every business meeting. People are hungry for something more in their life, and when they encounter Jesus through our business ministry – they step up and step out in Faith.

We watch the lights turn on inside of people when they find hope, purpose, and a plan. It is exciting at our 'A Book Is Never A Book' Boot Camp. When our graduates 'experience' the Holy Spirit, they understand how easy it is to walk in his grace. They get to 'see' how the hell they have been through is really the platform to their purpose. They often find their brand, their vehicle in which they express the giftedness they had inside. They learn their gift; match their desires with God's will for them. They find the truth that success can happen right now in the moment. It is SO much fun to witness our Daddy doing what he does best!

We have witnessed the Lord heal a person on his death bed, in a coma from a brain tumour. He was moments away from entering the gates of Heaven. After we prayed and went to war on his behalf – he got up and walked directly to the nurse's station. I laughed so hard when I heard that he said to the nurse, "Can you get my Dr. for me? I am tired of laying around. I want to go home!" He was totally healed from the top of his head to the bottom of his feet in the name of Jesus!

We have seen both young and old- be instantly delivered from demons – suicide, addictions, murder, death, poverty, witchcraft, free mason, and so much more.

We have seen whole families come to Christ; learn to forgive one another; walk in peace and harmony. Couples that are on the brink of divorce are not only set free of the bondage they were in, but find the truest, deepest love – as Jesus loves his bride. Mothers and daughters come to see 'eye to eye'. Sisters and brothers connecting on a level they have never been. Fathers and sons, restored as one.

We have even seen the Lord grow limbs out to balance people, a tooth grow out, a heart healed, brain injury cleaned up, diabetes cured, eye-site and hearing restored, and of course financial miracles, favour and so much more.

This is our daily life in our business. I can't put into words what a delight it is to walk every day knowing that I am, by His design, his hands and feet in a hurting world.

The Lord has just lovingly reminded me of a story from my childhood that made a monumental impact on who I am today. I am sure if my Dad was here, he would love that I have recounted this story to you.

I was 11 years old and my Daddy asked me to go to the city with him and help him with his work. My father laboured tirelessly to put food on the table for us through his water well drilling business. As a result of his push to create a life for us, he was gone much of my early childhood. We moved to the farm when I was 8 years old for what I believe was supposed to be a simpler life. I thought Dad would be home more, but it seemed to me he was gone more. So at age 11- spending any quality time with my Dad, who happened to be in an excellent mood, was like a dream come true.

Earlier in the week, my Dad was moving some cattle around and a calf had kicked him. His leg was pretty sore and he had a hard time getting around. That day, he had to go to the city to see some of his suppliers. The excitement mounted in me as I ran upstairs to get changed into suitable 'business clothes'. Ahh yes… my entrepreneurial spirit was growing in that very moment. SMILES.

While having special time with my Dad (I was the baby of 7 children) was thrilling. This exhilaration was more than just that. Although I didn't know or understand it at the time, his request spoke directly into my spirit. It murmured of how much he trusted me; he loved me; he was confident I had what it took to handle it; and that I was very special treasure.

In the hour it took to drive to the city, I chatted non-stop. My Dad just listened, nodded his head, and seemed… well? …for a lack of better word, pleased. Getting that kind of undivided attention was almost intoxicating. I think I was the happiest I had ever been in my life.

Our first stop was Ernie's shop. Dad had a lot of business to take care of. We went inside and Dad sent me out to the truck to bring back important things. There were papers, his HEAAAVVVYYY briefcase. I could hardly lift it, but I gave it everything I had. He even directed me to bring in different gizmos and parts for the rig. I had NO idea what they were for but that didn't matter! I was determined to do the best job I could. I pushed forward with my heart, soul and strength.

Every time he delegated a job for me. I met him with enthusiasm. Even when I got things wrong he was supportive. He would say, "Dolly, this is the wrong part. The one I was looking for is almost like this – but it actually has grooves in the shank. Does that make sense? You were really close! Good job! You can put this back and bring the other please?"

After Daddy and I had finished all of his business meetings we started on our journey back home. Any bit of fatigue I had from the day's activities disappeared when Dad drove up to Confederation Mall. A mini- exhibition complete with Ferris wheels, games, and other rides! What?? Dad said, 'you did such a great job today Dolly, I think we could stop here and have a little fun. What do you say? Want a Dairy Queen ice cream cone for a treat?"

My head spun with the wonder of it all! Really? DQ was something we RARELY had simply because we lived in the country where none of the fast food places existed and we rarely had extra money for such luxuries in life!

Sitting in the car beside my Dad on the drive back home I rested in warmth of my Father as he put his arm around me. I remember saying to Dad as I feel into a contented, deep sleep, 'Thanks Daddy for letting me be your 'legs' today!'

To me, this story illustrates my thoughts about who I am in Christ. My Heavenly Father owns this business I am in. I get to go to work with my Daddy every day. I get to watch how brilliant he is. I get to watch how deeply he loves people. I get to be his hands, his feet, and... his legs! I get to experience the satisfaction of knowing I made a difference. I get to bask in his praise and his blessing. I get to go to sleep every night, content and satisfied. I fall asleep with his arm around me –

knowing that right now I am the most important, most loved, and most treasured little girl on the planet.

That is the beauty of walking in the power of the Holy Spirit that is ours. Blessed be the one that finds his/her purpose in Christ!

3. **It's time to take a stand:** One of the biggest obstacles I have seen my students wrestle with is taking comfort in the 'fence sitting position' when it comes to God. They are so worried about offending others as they walk into their business dealings. They come across with an air of 'timid", 'shy', or 'with-holding'. Consumers are smart! They can sense there is something not quite 'right' about this entrepreneur. If they feel that you are with-holding They wonder what exactly you are covering up!

What is the proper attitude? Simply BE who you are created to be. You ARE a child of the most-high God! Most people are very loving and supportive of your views if you handle yourself with respect and honour.

A few years ago, when I spoke on various stages around the world, I did have some event coordinators say, 'you can't really use the word 'GOD' in this setting. It isn't really appropriate to 'preach' Jesus here.

While respectful of the platform I was on – I would still be able to share my truth with the whole group. I never once had anybody come at me with negative feedback because I said the word "God" or Jesus.

How did I do it? Easy! I opened my stories with, "Is it ok if I tell this story from my truth? I am not here to tell you what you should or should not believe in – but I have to stay in my truth. Is that ok?" I always got permission to share from my own personal truth. I would then lace it with things like, 'I had a comin' to Jesus moment!' Or, "I felt God nudge me…" It opened the doors to so many discussions with the guests as well as the event coordinators.

You have got to decide what stand you are going to take. Is it what the Word of God says? OR is it what people say?

Don't get me wrong, always be respectful. However, we are dealing with people's eternity, and coming to their aid to give them relief of the pain and struggles they are living in right now. If you know something that can benefit them, and you hoard it, what kind of person would you be?

It's time to take a stand! What will it be?

I would like to share with you, a song I wrote – may it bless you with revelation.

It's Time To Take A Stand

© 2013 - Kathleen D. Mailer

It's time to stand a stand.
What will it be?
C'mon now child it's your eternity.
Heaven is a real a place but then so is Hell.
How do you know? Let me ask you…..
How are you livin' right now?

All my days are running together.
I don't know which end is up.
My life is a roller coaster,
And I don't know just how to stop.

I feel like I am being stalked
By fear, frustration and defeat.
I can't put my finger on it,
I just know I need to be freed.

I've been searching, begging for an answer.
Their ain't nothin' I haven't tried.
All it's done is confuse and daze me,
And left me standing on the out-side.

Late one night I decided to try it.
I cried out to God above.
I was met with an open door, now
Jesus stood in unconditional love.

But, THAT was not the surprisin' part.
As I knew that God was true.
It was these words that he told me,
I knew if I didn't listen I would lose.

It's time to stand a stand.
What will it be?
C'mon now child it's your destiny.
Heaven is a real a place but then so is Hell.
How do you know? Let me ask you.....
How are you livin' it now?

4. **Discernment:** Discernment comes in handy in many different facets of a K.B.O. business. It can help you with clarity. It can aid you with a nudge that things are not as they seem. It will assist you when you need to make a decision to move (or not move) forward with a partner/client/situation. It causes you to 'pause' and really seek the Lord.

The best thing about discernment is the ability to use this devise will keep you walking in Kingdom purposes. When you come across people in your daily routine who seem to be re-active to curses in their own lives (like the spirit of offence); you can turn what seems to be a difficult situation around almost immediately.

When you can establish what is really going on their lives, you can bend the situation into a God moment. You can immediately detect the difference between the **person** and the demon. That way you don't take offence to anything that they say or do.

I was having a meeting with a partner who was, as far as I know, happy with the situation and the arrangement we had in regards to a business project we were working on. One day he phoned me and said he decided that this project was something he could no longer support due to time constraints, financial issues, and other conflicts.

The good news was that I was able to discern that this had nothing to do with the business project, me or any other 'excuse' he was bringing forward. I pressed into the Lord and asked, 'What is really going on? How can I help him Lord?"

I saw the 'unloving spirit' over his life. The one that caused him to over commit, then in the middle of the process caused him to feel used and abused. This was a cycle in his life and it was time to break it.

Lovingly I listened to his situation and asked if we could pray for God's guidance about how to proceed. After he nodded, I prayed the Holy Spirit would reveal a plan and purpose to this situation – and He did! My question to this K.B.O was, 'Who took advantage of your kindness in the past?" That led to a vibrant discussion about forgiveness and healing. From there he was delivered from a cycle that he had learned from his Mother, she from hers and so on. Generational curses are very real. When discernment comes in, we can tackle the issue head on, with love and support.

To this day it was one the most satisfying projects we have taken on. He got far more than just a successful conclusion to a business project – his whole business changed that day. His joy meter grew. His ability to relate to his partners/friends and family had also changed.

That is one of the benefits of carrying around the tool of discernment.

5. **Resist:** *Resist the devil and he will flee.* We have the ability to resist the devil. We have this as a weapon of destruction against the covert operations of satan.

Resisting begins in the mind. It starts with a thought that doesn't line up with the will of God. It starts with a negative place or untruth. It starts with the voice of the father of all lies himself, Lucifer!

How do you know if it is the voice of our Heavenly Father? OR if it is the 'other guy'?

Ask yourself these questions:

- "Does this thought/idea/situation end up stealing, killing and destroying me or someone else?
- Does it line up with the word of God? If so, where do the scriptures tell me this is true?"

When you know it is the enemy – quickly get things right with God. I covered the process earlier in the book – but this point needed to be brought to your attention again.

RESIST the enemy and turn from him. Jesus will see you through the process. Call on His name to help you. Quote the scriptures of truth.

6. **Truth:** A great tool in our tool belt. We have the Bible that tells us what the truth is.

You will know right from wrong, black from white, truth from lies when you study the word. Having Truth on your side, even when there are false accusations, will help you to stay strong in amongst the CHAOS.

7. **Righteousness:** The righteousness of Christ is evident in the way he is consistent in his character. The bible says that *he is the same yesterday as he is today and will be tomorrow.* Because He stays consistent we have a True North plumb-line in our life.

You will never get lost if you know where True North is. It helps us stay grounded in our faith. It keeps us on track and moving forward.

8. Peace that surpasses all understanding: This is a wonderful gift from God as we move forward in our business. Too many times we get snowed under with stress and frustration. One of the favorite tactics of the enemy is to throw us into the pit of worry and angst. When you walk in the Peace of God, you find it easier to - keep on keepin' on.

It had never been as evident for me as it was when the Lord unveiled this gift. We were taking our 3rd 13-hour road trip in 4 days. My husband's Uncle had taken ill and he was dying of cancer. It takes 13 hours to drive from where we live in Calgary, Alberta to his home. We were Uncle Colin's only family and we wanted to be there for him.

Our daughter was being home-schooled at the time but was in final exam day so she couldn't come with us. We drove to Brandon, MB one day, assessed the situation and talked quietly about Uncle's wishes. We came to the conclusion that we were going to stay and take care of him in his final days, we turned around and went home to prepare.

We discussed our findings with our daughter, Dannielle; gathered more clothes; cleared our schedule and back on the 4th day.

Praying for guidance, I looked up from the Bible that lay open on my lap. I began to meditate on the words I had just read. I watched out the window as the miles whist by. The Canadian Prairies can be breathtaking especially in the summer months when the warmth of the sun illuminates the world below. The crops are a heavy lavish green and the cattle are lazily grazing in the pasture.

All at once, I had this warmth envelope me. Instead of feeling worried about Uncle Colin, Dannielle, Dan, Dan's Mom, finances, my house, and physical tiredness, I felt a sense of peace.

[7] *Then you will experience God's peace, which exceeds anything we can understand. His peace will guard your hearts and minds as you live in Christ Jesus.* **Philippians 4:7**

Since that day, the peace of Christ has been with me most all of the time. For the record, this was the start of our desolate wasteland experience. Over the next few years we had trials, tribulations, and tests. There were many deaths of family and friends, sickness and disease, financial hardship, relationship issues, false accusations and court battles – we had it all. Believe it or not, through most of that, I had peace.

It doesn't make sense, but I will tell you- without His tranquility, I don't think I would have been able to make it. Just one of these life altering situations would have been enough to push a person to their limits – but with Christ strengthening me? I COULD do all things!

9. **Faith:** 11 *Faith is the confidence that what we hope for will actually happen; it gives us assurance about things we cannot see.* **Hebrews 11:1**

It truly is our stick-ability to move through the obstacles, the wicked ways of the enemy, and the fiery darts of Hell. Without our faith we have nothing. If we can't believe that we have salvation in Christ Jesus – it means we are all living for not. Or worse, it means that we are all going to Hell. I say that clearly because any other scenario that is given by mankind, other than Heaven, would be Hell in my books!

Faith gives us hope. It gives us warmth when we need a hug. It gives us the peace we require it. It gives us vision when we cannot see beyond our circumstance. It gives us the fight deep within our belly.

Faith is what separates us from unbelievers. It is substance and the fruit of our existence. Whenever people talk about others who have worked hard to realize their dreams you often hear people say, 'Yep, he had faith he was going to make it. Even when everyone told him he wouldn't!'

It is something that K.B.O's around the world need. There will be too many people trying to get you to doubt that your dream, your vision; your goal will come to pass. There will be too many people all too happy to tell you how crazy you are. But keeping your Faith alive will by-pass the neigh-sayers and gets you to where you want to go!

10. **Declare the Word of God:** There is infinite, manifesting power in your words. This is a subject that I would like to write a whole book on. I know we delve into great detail about this in the K.B.O. Mentorship program because it is critical we comprehend the vastness of this machine we call 'the mouth.'

In the Bible there is scripture after scripture that talks about declaring and decreeing. I urge you to do a study, even if you feel you 'got this'. You can learn that there is layer after layer on this subject that makes it feel like a new revelation every time.

There are many books written on this subject but my favorite at this point just might be Joel Osteen's book called, "*I Declare*". Please get it and read it.

We all speak our current life into existence. Please be careful what you declare. God's word will keep you from defiling your lips and using your mouth as a tool for the devil to put strongholds in your life and in the life of others.

Watch out for the negative things you say. Find the right things by looking through the Bible. If you alter the confessions of your mouth, you will transform your life!

Here are some words that I have observed K.B.O's proclaim. Every time I urge them to mind their mouths, God lovingly has me repent for mine too. It is always evolving, but we can get into the habit of saying what is right and true if we work on it.

- I can't or I won't.... you fill in the blank!
- My diabetes (or cancer or depression) … Whatever you do, don't claim sickness!
- I can't afford that! … This makes me cringe.
- We aren't getting ahead ... Another declaration to destroy your faith.
- I know that God can, but will he for me? … What does the Bible say about this?

You get the picture. Write down the 'destroying declarations' you say now, and then find the truth in the bible. Start to declare, proclaim and affirm the truth of God's word. Watch what happens!

11. **Praying:** Prayer changes everything! As a K.B.O. you are moved to pray. We are intercessors at heart. We are problem solvers and the best problem solver is (you guessed it), The Holy Spirit! You have to commune with him if you want to become more in your field, in your family and in your life.

You have to go to battle and to war. You need to ask for discernment, wisdom, favour, open doors, divine appointments, healing, signs, steps, financial provision, giving positions, opportunity, salvations, healings, deliverances, enlarge your territory, find the land, find a solution… the list goes on and on.

Prayer is simply communicating with our Father, with our business partner, with our best friend!

7 "Keep on asking, and you will receive what you ask for. Keep on seeking, and you will find. Keep on knocking, and the door will be opened to you. 8 For everyone who asks, receives. Everyone who seeks, finds. And to everyone who knocks, the door will be opened. 9 "You parents—if your children ask for a loaf of bread, do you give them a stone instead? 10 Or if they ask for a fish, do you give them a snake? Of course not! 11 So if you sinful people know how to give good gifts to your children, how much more will your heavenly Father give good gifts to those who ask him. **Matthew 7:7-11**

I love the story of Nehemiah in the Bible. I think my favourite scripture out of all of it is this book is this one,

10 "The people you rescued by your great power and strong hand are your servants. [11] O Lord, please hear my prayer! Listen to the prayers of those of us who delight in honouring you. Please grant me success today by making the king favourable to me. Put it into his heart to be kind to me." **Nehemiah 1:10**

Let this scripture be one you use daily to help you get to where you need to go. Please God, grant me success today…

12. **Praying in the Spirit:** Is Praying in Tongues Business Tool? The answer is an absolute "YES!"

Praying in tongues is one of the many wonderful gifts of the Holy Spirit. It is given to us in faith. With this faith to believe it works, we can see great benefits in our lives. This isn't a gift that sometimes comes to us and then disappears; we can use it anytime we want, and I believe you should use it often.

My intent here is not to become involved in a theological debate on whether this gift is available to us here and now, but I do encourage you to study the Bible carefully if you have any questions or concerns about it. I would be happy to share more with you about the gift and how we receive it through baptism in the Holy Spirit. (Just a note: not everyone has the gift of tongues, but it is available to everyone who believes.)

To start on this journey to find out more, read Acts 2:1–4!

I can tell you that I have seen a huge shift in my business since I started to incorporate the use of praying in tongues.

• I found that divine appointments (the right people in the right place) started to line up effortlessly. (I still had to follow up with them, so don't think it is a "magic formula," that POOF, you don't have to do anything but sit back and eat bonbons!)

• I also found that it gave me clarity and focus when I needed it. I use it when I feel overwhelmed because I have to speak or write.

• I use it when I need divine wisdom in making tough business decisions. You aren't always popular being the person at the top, but it's important to make the right decisions, according to God's purpose for your business. After all, isn't it HIS business, in the first place?

• If you need strategy, miracles, understanding, they are all there in the power of your tongue. When I pray in tongues, I seem to get an impression in my spirit of where to go next, or perhaps WHAT to pray for, or the next step just shows up in my email, in a phone call, or in person.

• When I find it hard to believe God's promises, I pray in tongues to build up my faith. The more faith I have, the more I can step out and do big things.

• When someone needs intervention quickly (sickness, accident, or help), I don't know what to pray for exactly... but the Holy Spirit does!

Why it works according to the Word:

- Praying in tongues is a PRIVATE prayer language between your spirit and God. The Holy Spirit prays on your behalf when you don't know what to pray (1 Corinthians 14:2; Romans 8:26).
- Praying in tongues is a POWERFUL weapon against the enemy. We all know satan wants to come against us in our business!
- It edifies us; it instructs and improves us morally or intellectually.
- The Apostle Paul himself encouraged us to speak in tongues (1 Corinthians 14:5).
- It builds our faith (Jude 1:20).

There are other scriptures to help you decide whether it is a powerful business tool and how to use it (Acts 2:4; Acts 1:8). Incorporate all of God's gifts of grace and find your business growing to a *higher level.*

13. **Fast(ing) Forward**: When I started to incorporate a lifestyle of fasting, I noticed big changes. There were changes in my business, my mindset, my health shifted. I began to understand that there were many things that I was unknowingly putting ahead of God.

I decided to take a year where I would have a 'fasting' mentality to really seek God and his purpose for my life.

I asked him what to fast; when to fast; how to fast; how long to fast. He showed me scripture and rewarded me with daily revelations. Many of those downloads are shared in this very book!

I went on 7-day fasts, 30 day fasts and some 40 day fasts depending on the significance and the magnitude of the situation I was pursuing.

A couple of thoughts on fasting:

1. **Only fast when the Lord gives you his blessing on it.** Depending on the things you fast, you will need his help! That is the whole point of fasting. If it is super easy on you to do it on your own, maybe you don't need to do it. You are getting rid of something that is taking up the space between you and God. I was amazed at how God helped me through the process. There was a sense of ease, whereas before when I tried to 'stop' doing something in the past, forget it. I couldn't break a habit if my life depended on it.
2. **Fasting isn't just about food**, although it is good to go through the 'food' addictions because it is something that many people struggle with. Sugar, over eating, bread, ice caps at Timmy's ... need I say more?
3. **Some of the things I fasted in the past?** TV, social media, sleep, sugar, bread, emails, shopping, meals.
4. **Some of the things I fasted for?** Answers to our financial situation. For healing for our family. Healing

for myself. Business projects. Our church. Direction. Breakthrough. Deliverance.

5. **Always fill the thing you fast with God, his word, a pen and paper.** Mediate on the things he gives you. You will be surprised at the revelations you receive!

14. **Grace:** *"Pressure of performance vs flowing with grace is what separates the work-a-holics from the true success builders."* – **Kathleen D. Mailer**

Grace is God's empowerment that he has freely given to us if we ask for it! It is how we receive salvation. It is how we walk in the power of the Holy Spirit. It is how we keep our peace.

I know immediately when I am not walking in grace. What is my tell-tale sign that I am walking in my own strength? Wait for it. Can you hear the scary music building the suspense? It is overwhelm!

Drop to your knees and repent when you feel overwhelm. Ask God to restore the grace he has for you and then get up and try again. I can't believe how much I can get done in a day when I am covered by grace. I find that time seems to expand. I am effective even when I am not confident. I am at peace even when my deadlines are looming. I get answers to the problems I need to solve. I have everything I need at my fingertips.

From the end of the earth I will cry to You, when my heart is overwhelmed; lead me to the rock that is higher than I. **Psalms 61:2**

The grace of God is something every K.B.O. not only needs in their tool kit but MUST study in depth. When you are enlightened by uncovering the full meaning of this, you will wonder how you ever made it through life without having full disclosure on the subject.

15. **Supernatural Provision:** *"Portion deliverer does not mean rations.'* – **Kathleen D. Mailer**

The Lord wants to help you prosper! It's a fact! As a K.B.O. if we don't make money, then we don't have a business! Seriously! If we are not making sales, then we have a very expensive hobby. Can I get an Amen?

One of the things my K.B.O students found very helpful was understanding that when the bible talks about the fact that God is our portion deliver – it doesn't mean rations.

Many of us who have grown up in poverty think those portions are small allotments because there is only 'so much' to go around. I think back to the table when I was a child. At supper time, my Mom would dish up certain things for us to make sure we all got our share. There were 7 children, the adults and many times we had other friends and family join us.

Although I will admit that I would have gladly given up my 'share' of liver and boiled veggies; the very act of this portion delivery was impressed upon my young heart. It wasn't until I was working on my mind-set, struggling to pay bills and have enough money when God spoke softly to my heart about the situation.

He said he has more than enough. He told me all of the gold and silver in this world is His. He told me he owns everything and that I can have whatever amount I want and need, anytime I want it – but first I had to get rid of some of the B.S. I had rumbling around in my head and my heart. Of course we already talked about what B.S. stands for! Remember?

Believing that God's portion means rations is really a big deep vast part of B.S. I implore you to let it go today!

God has supernatural provision waiting for you. I could tell you story after story of how He provided for us. I think through the desolate wasteland days, God was delighted to hear me ask him for our daily bread. (Some days I mean that literally!). He was also delighted to show me all of the ways He could provide.

It wasn't just about sales (although that is one way). It was through many other avenues! This includes gifts. I had to really work on my broken receiver! What I mean by that is that it was easy for me to give but very difficult for me to receive. If that is you I implore you to get on your knees and ask for healing. Giving and receiving is the cycle of life.

God's word says so. Ask K.B.O's we have to be able to do both!

19 And this same God who takes care of me will supply all your needs from his glorious riches, which have been given to us in Christ Jesus. **Philippians 4:19**

16. **Lovingly Observe and Correct:** *"Your journey toward the fulfillment of your dreams should be about progress and not perfection."*- **Kathleen D. Mailer**

This is hands down, one of my favourite tools and I use it every day! This is the ability to look at your yesterday and ask yourself, 'If I could do it all over again, what would I do differently?"

I don't hold any judgement, nor do I use it to feel condemned. If I am condemning myself or feeling bad about it, then I am walking in my own strength once again. Condemnation is the devil's tool, not God's. Stop and pray and ask for God's grace to cover you – then continue on.

If you are consistently saying, day by day, that there was one activity you would do if you had that day to do all over, then you can make the proper observations and corrections to your daily choice lists, aka: choose to do list.

Let me give you an example:

There was a time when I looked over my list and for a week I consistently wrote, 'What would I do differently if I had it to do all over again is to make a sale."

Day after day, I found myself writing that down. It caused me to pause and ask the following questions:

1. Does making a sale get me closer to my goals or further away?
2. What is stopping me from making a sale every day?
3. Are the things I am doing every day getting me closer to my goals or further away?
4. Are the things on my list contributing to making a sale or moving it away?
5. What things can I take off my list all together? What will I cease and desist doing? What will I delegate? What will I postpone?
6. What is the most important thing I can do in a day to make a sale and how can I do that FIRST before I do anything else?

Then I just needed to lovingly start doing the things I heard the Holy Spirit whisper to me. Before you know it my days consistently had sales and now? We are working on automatic systems to be bringing sales in without more work from me. THAT is true financial freedom! But I digress…

The "Choose to do List" is a great tool to keep you on track for your goals, find out what you are avoiding; decide what is important and what is not.

Then you can lovingly correct it the next day. You will find that you are getting better and better and within a year you will look back and say, 'Oh my gosh! My life is so different!"

17. **Obedience:** Sometimes this is so hard for people because they look at obedience as something like rules and regulations. That spirit of rebellion be gone in Jesus name!

Actually obedience to God needs to be a part of your regime or a lifestyle habit. I have learned over the years, especially with my prophetic gift, to listen to the Lord and take action when He tells me to. Every time it turns out that God was right! I know! Can you imagine that! (Laughing).

How many times I was blessed by the blessing that God put on another person I couldn't tell you. What I can tell you is that I have never once regretted listening to God and taking steps to implement the requests he gave me.

Even if I was full of fear; panic; doubt; worry, I still pressed on. K.B.O.'s question me, "Kathleen what if I was wrong and I didn't hear God?"

That is a great question! Here are some guideposts. They are a bit redundant because I have mentioned them several times throughout the book and my teachings. However, you can never be reminded enough.

1. Ask yourself if it lines up with the Word of God? Or does it cause you to 'sin'?
2. Ask God for confirmation if it is a BIG thing.
3. Is it something that will destroy another? (God mostly gives encouragement, rarely warnings).
4. Is it getting you closer to your goals in a Godly way?
5. Have you gotten Godly counsel to talk to about the situation?
6. Is it the right time to deliver this message?

What if you make a mistake? Let me say this, God knows your heart in it! He will cover you in grace. If you are moving forward and you have taken time to pray and seek His will-God knows you are trying.

Think of it this way: If you try to teach your daughter how to tie her shoes and she makes a mistake do you get mad and bring about destruction or 'take away' something that you have given her? NO! Of course you wouldn't.

What would you do instead? Well, if you are like me you look at her and say, 'Aww, you are just too cute! Come let me show you again how to do it the right way." That is our God! That is our Heavenly Father. He wants us to learn and grow. If our heart is right, He will make things right when we mess up. Obedience is the right thing to do, always and in all ways!

18. **Worship:** This is one of the most powerful power-tools in our tool chest!

Worship will:

- Build you up and get your 'head on straight' as you start your day.
- Help you declare the word of God in and over your life.
- Connect you with the All Mighty, bringing you closer to Him.
- Bring down the enemy, shut him up, stop his evil tricks, and slap him upside the head.
- It will help you focus, get answers you seek, increase your love, put joy in your heart, and position you for prayer.

Worship Works! Use it!

Let's put the word into action:

1. Go through this chapter and then book in your day timer certain 'fast periods' where you will take each section and do a powerful study on it. This isn't something you read once and put away. This is why this book is a reference guide… you refer back to it time and time again!

2. Ask the Holy Spirit to reveal to you, which power tool you need to work on first. Then when you are done

with that, repeat this step to see what is next. He will guide you through the process. Only He knows which one is imperative today.

3. Remember, lifestyle changes and implementations take time. Stay patient, calm and loving with yourself. It is a journey and not a destination. Step by step you will find yourself in a different place at the end of the year. Praise Be To God.

Let me pray with you,

Simply say this prayer with me, 'Lord please show me what I need to implement in my life right away. What is the most important tool I can incorporate in my day to day business? Show me what it is I need to do to become more like You. How can I use it to its maximum strength in my business with my partners and my friends? Help me to share your truth. In Jesus name, Amen."

CHAPTER TWELVE

Develop a Foundation of Success Principles

The Bible is bursting with success principles that we can apply in order to accomplish our God given purpose as a K.B.O.

Here are but a few success principles you can apply to your life. My hope is that you will study each one and develop it into a lifestyle change. We are developing this as part of our curriculum for the K.B.O. Monthly Mentorship Resources.

In the meantime, my prayer is that you can use this to get started NOW!

Each section in this chapter is a chapter in of itself.

1. BECOME A MASTER RELATIONSHIP BUILDER (MRB)

MRB is the K.B.O's reason for being. I won't spend a long time here on what this means. I have dedicated a full chapter to this. What I want to say is: this is the foundation of our purpose for business (and life). Our business is our vehicle in which we continue to follow in Jesus' footsteps.

He truly was a MRB – He saw deep into our souls, He challenged others to *be more, do more, have more* life (in abundance). He knows our hearts, hurts, and hurdles. He has a solution to every problem. He is the gateway between Heaven and earth. He is our salvation, which is the essence to everything we are created to be.

As a K.B.O – you too can do and be all of these things and more, just as Jesus commanded from us,

18 Jesus came and told his disciples, "I have been given all authority in heaven and on earth. 19 Therefore, go and make disciples of all the nations,[a] *baptizing them in the name of the Father and the Son and the Holy Spirit. 20 Teach these new disciples to obey all the commands I have given you. And be sure of this: I am with you always, even to the end of the age."* **Matthew 28:18-20**

2. PLAN/GOAL SETTING:

I believe that the next 12 months is going to be one of the MOST amazing years of your entire life. You don't have to start at the fiscal year (January); you can make your year begin today!

For K.B.O's, God is putting HIS plans and HIS promises into action. The thrilling news is we GET to experience it WITH Him.

While this section is a lot to absorb, setting and keeping goals is essential to every K.B.O.

This overview is something I get into great detail over in the K.B.O. Monthly Mentorship Program – however this will give you an excellent start, right now.

This new season of our lives is where, I believe, we will see the tangible, physical release of HIS power through HIS people.

Electrifying! Even as I write this today, I feel a stirring in my spirit and an ache on the heart of God for His business ministers to take CONTROL of the market place. Can you feel it too?

What WE need to do is awaken the FAITH deep inside us. We need to believe that His WORD is true today, just as it was yesterday and will be tomorrow.

We need to set some concrete steps down on paper so that we can accelerate our effectiveness, our impact, our message in the world. God has placed BIG dreams on our heart. Don't we owe it to Him to get focused and methodically forge ahead with confidence and clarity – seeing to it that we bring a Jesus' solution to a hurting world?

K.B.O.'s Belt of Truth: Our mandate is to bring a Jesus solution to a hurting world.

While I want you to set goals in every area of life, for the purpose of this chapter we are going to work through **ONE complete BUSINESS goal**.

Please allow me the privilege of taking you through this process, step by step.

This IS going to take some time, so after reading this chapter – go back and put these words into action.

In our K.B.O Mentorship Program we first:

a) **Set the Vision:** (Lessons we learned from the book of Daniel.)
    1. What would my life be like if this next year was 10 x greater?
    2. What if I had 10 x more time? What would I do with it?
    3. What if I had 10 times more money?
    4. What if my business were 10 x larger?
    5. What if my relationships were 10 x greater?
    6. Don't forget, ask the Holy Spirit to guide you through this process

b) **Who do I, personally, have to become – to be 10 x greater this next year?**
    - Characteristics?
    - Habits?
    - Learning/Growth?
    - Mindset?
    - Patterns?

c) **Who will help me on my journey?**
    - This should always include God – but write down people you know that could help. Mentors, Church, Pastors, Trainers, Friends, Family.
    - People you don't know yet, but should get to know.

- How will you implement this?

Then we work through this MONTHLY PLANNING SYSTEM:

The K.B.O's at our monthly mentorship night love this easy formula. It helps us to keep GOD at the focus, while we take action. In other words, we do what we can do best, and GOD will do the rest.

I learned to set goals in a *"tough, hard business, no nonsense, unspiritual, sheer determination to do things on my own*" model. It was a model where by sheer will and determination, I **made** things happen and I had a 'GET 'ER DONE' mentality.

Did I achieve my goals? OH YES! I sure did. From the outside looking in, month after month, year after year, I would accomplish what I set out to in business. I even received awards and accolades from my 'higher ups'.

I had a new car, a nice house, a great hubby, etc. All of these things only built a house on sand. Since I did it on my own accord, with my own strength – I learned how tough I really was. NOT!

I found myself getting sick. I found myself working seven days a week, 12-14 hour days. I found myself looking good to the world… but in my house?? It was all a house of debt, no time to build relationships, an unhealthy body, severely lacking in my walk with Christ.

As a K.B.O – we don't TRY to achieve balance. We GET to have balance as a by-product of keeping God at the center point of our life. We GET to have TRUE success because we are working HIS plans for our life… Not OUR plans. We get to enjoy these wonderful gifts (house, car, children etc.), but they don't define us.

Success is a measurable word. As a K.B.O what is your definition of success?

It certainly is a lot let stress, because of God's promise to us…

Zechariah 4:6 *So he said to me, "This is the word of the Lord to Zerubbabel: 'Not by might nor by power, but by my Spirit,' says the Lord Almighty.*

Proverbs 19:21 *Many are the plans in a person's heart, but it is the Lord's purpose that prevails.*

This takes a TON of pressure off of us, and shifts us to see clearly… 'What's God's job? What is ours?"

Step One: Building The Foundation

1. **It is GODLY to set plans into action**: God is a planner! We are created in his image.

Jeremiah 29:11 *For I know the plans I have for you," declares the Lord, "plans to prosper you and not to harm you, plans to give you hope and a future.*

If we are NOT setting our aspirations, we are not living in the fullness of our blessing. Is it any wonder many K.B.O.'s don't have the success that they are promised?

On a K.B.O's Belt of Truth: God is a planner, and so am I!

Isaiah 32:8 *But the noble make noble plans, and by noble deeds they stand.*

2. **Your plan must be measurable:** You need to KNOW that you KNOW you achieved what you set out to do. It also MUST have an end date attached to it.

3. **It must be written down:** Proverbs 16:3 *Commit to the Lord whatever you do, and he will establish your plans.*

4. **It must have a certain number of distinct steps you can take to achieve it.** Proverbs 21:5 *The plans of the diligent lead to profit as surely as haste leads to poverty.*

5. **You must include helpers:** God is a social being. When the world began, He started it with the Father, The Son and The Holy Spirit. The three did it 'as one'. Why would you set a target with no one to be in your corner? Maybe you haven't 'met' the person to help you yet then put down the 'type' of person you need to help with each plan.

6. **You must include what you need to acquire:** In other words, are there certain skills, habits or a mindset you need to use that you don't have yet? OR is there a person you can invite into your vision that has these things?

7. **It must be set into your day timer:** Yes, put your plans into action and you have to actually set aside time to achieve them. Get a day timer if you don't have one! Do it now!

8. **Set a goal every month (see below) for EVERY area of life.**

Let me give you a list of examples of monthly goals I might set for myself.

I have also given you some SUBSET projects I may work on, in certain months.

a) **Spiritual:** My walk with God, bible study, personal soaking time, courses and programs to strengthen me.
b) **Health:** exercise, eating right, sleep, habits.
c) **Business: Today's Businesswoman Magazine,** Today's Businesswoman Conference, subscriptions, sponsorships, outreach, website, writing.
d) **Business: Aurora Publishing Authorship**, marketing, author helps, outreach, website.

e) **Business: A Book Is Never A Book Boot Camp**, registration, product creation, outreach, website.
f) **Business: CCKBO (Christian Collation of Kingdom Business Owners)** building home study programs, international membership, building 'helps' for churches world-wide to equip business ministers world-wide.
g) **Business: International Business Evangelist.** Writing my books, creating programs, speaking schedule world-wide, encouraging and equipping.
h) **Friends and Family:** My husband and children, my sisters and brothers, my relatives, my friends.
i) **Cleaning up Messes**: There are always a ton of messes available for one to clean up. This could mean physical messes in your home that you have been putting off. This could mean a relationship issue that needs to be cleaned up. This could mean messes, (physical, emotional and mental) in your community or your business. It feels GREAT to clean up a mess, and it makes it easier to have 'room' in your life for the wonderful miracles God is putting on your path!

Step Two: Backwards Effect

Now take your BIG VISION and break it down in steps. What 'chunks' of things would have to happen in order for this to come to fruition over the next 12 months?

Yearly Plan:	
Date:	On Dec. 21st, 2014
Set God's Vision	Praise God for 10 X More Clients this year, over last year.
Measurable	• 100 people purchased my mentorship program at $2000.00 each • $200,000.00 for one year. • Now I can give 10 x more to the ministry that rescues women from the sex trade! • Now I can spend time with my family on the vacation to Disney Land. • Now my church will grow, because my tithe is even higher than last year.

1. **List the steps you need in order to set your goal.** Easy chunks that you will need in order to achieve that wonderful end result. How did you do that? Remember, to do what you CAN… what YOU know to do and God will fill in the rest.

Let's start to use an example now:

Yearly Plan:	
Date:	On Dec. 21st, 2014
Set God's Vision	Praise God for 10 X More Clients this year, over last year.
Measurable	• 100 people purchased my mentorship program at $2000.00 each • $200,000.00 for one year. • Now I can give 10 x more to the ministry that rescues women from the sex trade! • Now I can spend time with my family on the vacation to Disney Land. • Now my church will grow, because my tithe is even higher than last year.
Steps: HOW DID WE DO THAT?	
1	Word of Mouth: Video tape my current clients and put them on the website, ask them for referrals, create a referral program and create a marketing copy for the website and flyers.
2	Create a FREE EDUCATIONAL NIGHT- sign people up at the end of the night. I need to have 100 people in the room to sign up 10 people. Do this once per month Feb through November.

You get the picture, keep listing as many as you can think of. It doesn't matter how many you have listed, just write them all down until there is nothing left to write.

Many of my students find that new and better ideas come to them now which they hadn't thought of before. THIS is the HOLY SPIRIT helping you. Don't forget to invite him to work WITH YOU on this list.

2. **Set a SUBSET PROJECT:** Organize your steps into the most effective use of your time with the greatest results. This is going to be one of your **Monthly SUBSET PLANS.**

Let's take our example from above: My word of mouth marketing example can actually be a great part of creating a FREE EDUCATIONAL NIGHT.

If I can use the word of mouth technique, with videos and marketing copy, I can fill up my room.

SO, in my goals I would put this subset project in as 'FREE EDUCATIONAL NIGHT'.

Notice I am also dating it carefully and thanking God for His help to achieve it. This is a 'project' we will be working on throughout the year.

Let's start to use an example now:

Yearly Plan:	
Date:	On Dec. 21st, 2014
Set God's Vision	Praise God for 10 X More Clients this year, over last year.
Measurable	• 100 people purchased my mentorship program at $2000.00 each • $200,000.00 for one year. • Now I can give 10 x more to the ministry that rescues women from the sex trade! • Now I can spend time with my family on the vacation to Disney Land. • Now my church will grow, because my tithe is even higher than last year.
Steps: HOW DID WE DO THAT?	
1	**Word of Mouth:** Video tape my current clients and put them on the website, ask them for referrals, create a referral program and create a marketing copy for the website and flyers.
2	**Create a FREE EDUCATIONAL NIGHT**- sign people up at the end of the night. I need to have 100 people in the room to sign up 10 people. Do this once per month Feb through November.

Step Three: Monthly Plans

Now that you have broken your yearly plan down to smart, effective, and highly do-able projects (with God everything is possible!), you need to further chunk it down into monthly plans.

1. Let's walk through my work sheet, carry over all of the information we have acquired so far and put into our worksheet **this month's plan.**

2. **Creating Goal Levels: M - is for "ME" , T - is for "TRUST GOD", M - is for "Miracle"**

   I have taken a lot of 'goal setting' advice from many different gurus over the years. Each time, I had never found a sustainable, wholesome plan that would help me work WITH GOD. I admit, this plan has come from a mish-mash of earthly influences, but my Heavenly Father taught me how to pull it all together and take it to a HIGHER LEVEL. I am so grateful for the honour of being able to teach you this, here today. I am thankful that He showed me an easier way to be all He called me to be, without trying to separate myself from His heart.

These next steps are where the real miracle of fulfillment begins. We will start to see do-able, bite sized pieces appear before us. God will make the path straight, with our eyes focused on Him.

We need to set miniature goals in order to achieve great success.

This not only stops overwhelm from happening, it also takes planning for success into a whole other level.

When you look at your monthly plan:

Here is mine: Set the foundation and fill the room for the first Educational night on Feb. 28/14

Ask yourself the question: What can I count on myself to do, no matter what, to reach this plan in the next 30 days?

What does that mean?

This is what you can do, not what someone else can do.

This is what you can COUNT on yourself to do, no matter what.

This is where you need to be extremely honest with yourself.

Let me give you another example to help illustrate this point.

Devin has been trying to set monthly goals by number of sales for years.

His company begins a ritual every month by arranging a sales meeting where they have a motivation moment and a time to share in each other successes.

Their goal was to inspire their sales team to take action. For Devin, in the past, all it had done was bring shame, guilt, frustration and pain. No matter how hard he tried, he could only average 2 sales. He felt less than the others, discouraged, like a loser EACH and EVERY month. This certainly didn't end up motivating him. It did the opposite. So much so, it was hard to get out there to do what had to be done, day after day. Sound familiar?

It does to me! Sends shivers of YUCK down my back as I remember my own journey.... But I digress.

He used to HATE these meetings. And now? As a K.B.O, he has a NEW and FRESH ANNOINTING that he is taking into his sales office. Now he can stand on the platform and share success that makes sense.

He spends more time with his family than ever before.

He is more clearly focused.

He is much more excited about his future.

Let's continue to use Devin's story to illustrate this remarkable technique.

His SUBSET GOAL?

I have 10 New Sales by Feb. 28th.

His reality:

Every month, I average only 2 sales in a 30 day time frame.

M - Is about REALITY as you currently know it.

So, M is what you can count on doing this month, no matter what… Devin can count on himself – for sure- to do 2 sales in 30 days.

He has been doing that every month anyway.

He knows he can do that again.

Does that make sense?

His **ME Goal:** *I close 2 sales by Feb. 28th*

T - Is about TRUSTING in GOD.

This is setting the next level of the monthly plan that helps you stretch every month. Getting a little out of your current comfort zone can bring you a long way to reaching what may be potentially the best year ever.

This is about setting something WITH God's help, and having you TRUST in Him. This is about activating some FAITH, mixing it with your ACTIONS, and SEEING GOD coming through!

In this case, Devin's T Goal-

TRUST Goal: *I close 4 sales by Feb. 28th*

You can see this is a stretch, but by golly if everything came into place… you can believe that you can possibly to do it. You just need a bit more planning, a bit more focus, and a bit more help. It is a goal worthy of going for, that's for sure. It builds excitement.

M - Miracle Goal

A miracle is simply that. A miracle. Something that you would have no idea what you need to do in order to achieve it. A miracle is something that only God can help you accomplish. You know that IF you get it, according to your current reality, it would HAVE to be God!

You will GIVE GOD THE GLORY! That is for DARN sure, because YOU KNOW it didn't come from you.

Does this make sense?

In this case, Devin's M Goal would be.

MIRACLE GOAL: *I close 10 sales by Feb. 28th*

Now let's see how this plays out in our plan of action that we have been working on together. I have used this exact process to break it down to the Goal Levels that I just explained.

Let's have a look at what that might look like shall we?

Yearly Plan of Action:	
Date:	On Dec. 21st, 2014
Set God's Vision	Praise God for 10 X More Clients this year, over last year.
Measurable	• 100 people purchased my mentorship program at $2000.00 each • $200,000.00 for one year. • Now I can give 10 x more to the ministry that rescues women from the sex trade! • Now I can spend time with my family on the vacation to Disney Land. • Now my church will grow, because my tithe is even higher than last year.
SUBSET MONTHLY PROJECT: FREE MONTHLY EDUCATIONAL NIGHT- 100 people in the seats	
Monthly Plan: Due – Jan. 30th, 2014 Set the foundation and fill the room for the first Educational night on Feb. 28/14	
M- ME	Call all of my current clients and ask them if we could do a video testimonial. Create the website with marketing copy and videos so that people can sign up. Book the location and get it ready to set up. Ask my current clients to bring new friends.
T- TRUST	Register 10 NEW people into the education nights. Get my presentation finished and ready to go Plus my M done
M- MIRACLE	Get my M and my T done REGISTER A TOAL OF 25 NEW people into the education night

Do you see how this works?
Ok, don't wear out on me yet, we are almost done. I promise, once you learn these tools and techniques it will be easier to implement as you gain momentum.

Persistence is a KEY ingredient to seeing your dreams come true. Keep pushing through this process and it will prove invaluable.

3. **The HELP line:**

   Now is the time we need to think about who will help us with this project. Remember, we are not alone. This is YOUR vision, but God in His wonderful wisdom has also given us help mates.

   Look at your WHOLE picture you have written down. Ponder on each level goal (M, T, M) and ask yourself, **'Who can help me?"**

   Who do you know that could help you with some of the details?

   OR, maybe you haven't met anyone yet who could get you to where you need to go – but you DO know you need to have them help.

   Also ask yourself, **"Who do I need to become to achieve this?"**

   Are there certain habits, mindsets, learning materials you will need to have in order to accomplish this task?

Let's check in and see what we have happening in our example.

Yearly Plan of Action:	
Date:	On Dec. 21st, 2014
Set God's Vision	Praise God for 10 X More Clients this year, over last year.
Measurable	• 100 people purchased my mentorship program at $2000.00 each • $200,000.00 for one year. • Now I can give 10 x more to the ministry that rescues women from the sex trade! • Now I can spend time with my family on the vacation to Disney Land • Now my church will grow, because my tithe is even higher than last year.
SUBSET MONTHLY PROJECT: FREE MONTHLY EDUCATIONAL NIGHT- 100 people in the seats	
Monthly Plan: Due – Jan. 30th, 2014 Set the foundation and fill the room for the first Educational night on Feb. 28/14	
M- ME	Call all of my current clients and ask them if we could do a video testimonial. Create the website with marketing copy and videos so that people can sign up. Book the location and get it ready to set up. Ask my current clients to bring new friends.
T- TRUST	Register 10 NEW people into the education nights. Get my presentation finished and ready to go Plus my M done
M- MIRACLE	Get my M and my T done REGISTER A TOAL OF 25 NEW people into the education night
Help Center:	
Who do I need?	God, a good V.A., Cheryl (to book at the hotel she has her events in), My family- to give me quiet time to write, someone to video tape our interviews for us.
Who do I need to become? Or to learn?	An early morning riser, making it easier for me to get my writing down. A great planner and delegator. How others fill a room for FREE educational nights.

Are you starting to see things take shape a bit better?

4. **Putting it into your day timer:**
   This is where MOST people fail. They get tired of all of the planning they had to do (remember you have done a yearly goal plan with us… that is a lot of homework).

   Then, they don't follow through with the final last stages.

   Look at your plan and place these tasks directly into your day timer.

   Knowing what you 'get' to do every day makes it easier to achieve the plans you have set before you.

5. **Making it a game:**
   I did love it when I learned to make this process a game. By assigning a point system to the different levels, you can see each have a market – something measurable, on how close you are to your end goal.

   Here is how it works: The score is out of a total of 10. Give yourself the following points at the end of the month if you,

   1- Wrote down your goal
   2- Reached your "ME" goal
   3- Reached your "TRUST" goal
   4- Reached your " MIRACLE" goal

If you achieved your ME goal, then you are 30% closer to achieving your yearly goal than you were last month. (1 for your written goal and 2 for reaching your M. The total is 3 out of a possible 10 points)

If you reached your TRUST goal? You are 60% closer. It helps you want to be better without pressure.

6. **Final Step:**
   Fill in the final last questions:
   - What did I notice about myself this month?
   - And, "What can I do to improve next month?"

Don't forget to incorporate these things into your next planning phase.

Also, please remember to PUT YOUR PLAN INTO ACTION FOR NEXT MONTH.

You have all of the tools. It will be easier to implement next time. By setting a consistent plan into action WITH GOD, you will become extraordinary and you will distinguish yourself above the rest of the businesses in your genre.

Don't forget to have fun with it and celebrate your successes along the way.

- I pray that the Lord establishes His Kingdom in you!
- I pray that you become the greatest success story for God this year. It is time for us to lift our Shields of Faith and ARISE!
- I pray that this not only inspires you, but also motivates you to take the action steps you need..
- I pray that it will sustain you through the month to keep your momentum from one day to the next.

Putting 'The Word' Into Action Worksheet

Yearly Plan of Action:		
Date:		On Dec. 21st, 2014
Set God's Vision		Praise God for 10 X More Clients this year, over last year.
Measurable		• 100 people purchased my mentorship program at $2000.00 each • $200,000.00 for one year. • Now I can give 10 x more to the ministry that rescues women from the sex trade! • Now I can spend time with my family on the vacation to Disney Land. • Now my church will grow, because my tithe is even higher than last year.
SUBSET MONTHLY PROJECT: FREE MONTHLY EDUCATIONAL NIGHT- 100 people in the seats		
Monthly Plan: Due – Jan. 30th, 2014 Set the foundation and fill the room for the first Educational night on Feb. 28/14		
SCORE	**1**	**I wrote my goal down**
M- ME Score 2	2	Call all of my current clients and ask them if we could do a video testimonial. Create the website with marketing copy and videos so that people can sign up. Book the location and get it ready to set up. Ask my current clients to bring new friends.
T- TRUST Score 3	3	Register 10 NEW people into the education nights. Get my presentation finished and ready to go Plus my M done
M- MIRACLE Score 4	1	Get my M and my T done REGISTER A TOAL OF 25 NEW people into the education night
TOTAL: 6		**Out of 10 - 60% closer to my ultimate plan**
Help Center:		
Who do I need?		God, a good V.A., Cheryl (to book at the hotel she has her events in), My family- to give me quiet times to write, someone to video tape our interviews for us.
Who do I need to become? Or to learn?		An early morning riser, making it easier for me to get my writing down. A great planner and delegator. How others fill a room for FREE educational nights.
What did I notice this month?		I had a hard time getting up early
What can I do to improve next month?		I am going to start going to bed at 10PM

Putting 'The Word' Into Action
BLANK WORKSHEET

Yearly Plan of Action:		
Date:		
Set God's Vision		
Measurable		
SUBSET MONTHLY PROJECT:		
Monthly Plan: Due –		
SCORE	**1**	**I wrote my goal down**
M- ME Score 2		
T- TRUST Score 3		
M- MIRACLE Score 4		
TOTAL:		**Out of 10 - ___% closer to my ultimate plan**
Help Center:		
Who do I need?		
Who do I need to become? Or to learn?		
What did I notice this month?		
What can I do to improve next month?		

3. BEFORE YOU DELEGATE, PRIORITIZE:

It's as simple as the steps we took when we worked through our goal above. What needs to come first, what can you delegate, what can you do yourself? Is it your giftedness that you are doing it yourself or is it something someone else can do?

Remember, if someone else can do it and they require less finance, time, and frustration to do it – chances are THEY should be doing it, not you!

4. LEARN TO DELEGATE:

Wow, I have to confess it took me far too long to learn the art of delegation. A poverty spirit over your life may have a lot to do with a lack of execution of this success principle.

It will help you become more efficient and save you time and money. It will also be a great platform for a MRB. An effective delegator will help others accomplish their God given duties. It will help them want to be more, do more and become more. Sound familiar?

Jethro, Moses' father-in-law was a very successful businessman. I can imagine him sitting on the sidelines and watching Moses' rise to his calling in leadership. The problem arose when Moses found he had to put so much of his time into hearing the people's disputes against one another.

Putting out fires was NOT the best, highest use of Moses' time! He was called to lead the people, not mediate!

Jethro asked Moses a very important question, that I think every leader should ask themselves time to time. He asked, 'What are you accomplishing here?" Whoah! Seriously?

How many times do we get distracted by putting out fires instead of doing the very tasks that get the results we want to achieve?

Open your Bible with me, let's get the whole story.

Jethro's Wise Advice

13 The next day, Moses took his seat to hear the people's disputes against each other. They waited before him from morning till evening.

14 When Moses' father-in-law saw all that Moses was doing for the people, he asked, "What are you really accomplishing here? Why are you trying to do all this alone while everyone stands around you from morning till evening?"

15 Moses replied, "Because the people come to me to get a ruling from God.

16 When a dispute arises, they come to me, and I am the one who settles the case between the quarreling parties. I inform the people of God's decrees and give them his instructions."

17 "This is not good!" Moses' father-in-law exclaimed.

18 "You're going to wear yourself out—and the people, too. This job is too heavy a burden for you to handle all by yourself.
19 Now listen to me, and let me give you a word of advice, and may God be with you. You should continue to be

the people's representative before God, bringing their disputes to him. [20] *Teach them God's decrees, and give them his instructions. Show them how to conduct their lives.* [21] *But select from all the people some capable, honest men who fear God and hate bribes. Appoint them as leaders over groups of one thousand, one hundred, fifty, and ten.* [22] *They should always be available to solve the people's common disputes, but have them bring the major cases to you. Let the leaders decide the smaller matters themselves. They will help you carry the load, making the task easier for you.* [23] *If you follow this advice, and if God commands you to do so, then you will be able to endure the pressures, and all these people will go home in peace."*

24 Moses listened to his father-in-law's advice and followed his suggestions. **Exodus 18:13-24**

Incorporate these steps to help you to be a Delegation Master in your life!

a) **Share the vision:** Take time to prepare an overall picture of where you want to go. Often times, K.B.O's are lost in confusion and they are not sure where they are going, let alone being able to lead anyone else. If you take the time to sit with the Lord on this, and truly get clear about where you want to go, you will find that He will bring you people, the provision, and the grace you need to see it through.

b) **Purposefully position:** Decide what qualities, characteristics, and gifts that the person you need to complete this task will have to bring to the table. It is important to fill a position with someone who has a willing heart; they have to be able to act the part.

Let me give you an example: I had a Pastor come to me with a broken heart and spirit. The problem was, her church had averaged their numbers at 150 and couldn't seem to break that point for years. Sure, there would be times that it would grow to 200 and other times it would dip to 120. Frustrated, she asked me to pray for her and see if God could give me an answer.

What God showed me was incredible! It has changed the way I do business, and the way so many leaders, pastors and trainers are doing their business.

The curse of an 'unloving spirit' is unfolded in so many areas of life. In this instance, the Pastor had no idea that this could seep into the hearts of leadership, including herself. I want to say, this is in NO way a 'blame game' – it is taking ownership and becoming better at what God has entrusted us to steward.

What I was able to see was that the blinders were on to delegation (unloving spirit) - she couldn't see that she put someone in the leadership role of administrator. This person is a gifted Pastor/Trainer, but not so gifted in administration. Although both the Lead Pastor and the Administrative Pastors' hearts were for God – (whatever it takes right?) - that didn't mean that they were qualified to do the job.

Here is what happens… The Administrative Pastor (AP) would, try as he might, keep dropping the ball on follow through. This caused frustration for the AP and the LP. It also caused huge tension between the volunteers and leadership. The unloving spirit began to take hold (in the hearts of people because they could not let it go)… This, in turn, made the AP feel awful and start to have thoughts of condemnation toward themselves. (That is the devil's tool, right?). The devil sits back and laughs, because the cycle continues to grow. The unloving spirit takes root and runs rampant in the hearts of the people.

Once the LP got this concept, she changed his thought process and renewed the delegation goals. With proper alignment, all things came together. The church started to hum with a burning heart for God – and it continues to grow today.

Ask yourself how this works in your business? How many times have you put someone in a position that they shouldn't be in because you really wanted them to be there? Hey, they were great people! OR, perhaps you kept them there for FAR too long. They didn't grow with the position (or in my case, refused to grow). This cost me more than you can know: money, time, pain, and relationships…because I didn't get this small step about learning to delegate.

c) **Write out your request clearly, complete with time frame, and the why:**

Try to keep your request as crisp and short as possible. It is a good idea (if it is a multi-task job) to put it down in bullet points. Adding a short, descriptive 'why' helps to rally and join people together for a common goal.

d) **Confirm that they understand:** Have them repeat back to you, in their own words, what it is you want from them so they are clear. Clean up any misconceptions or misrepresentation of what it is you have requested. If there was a misunderstanding, make it more clear in the job description that you gave them so that the next time you request this same job description, you won't run into the same problem.

Just a note, most job or tasks we delegate to others are the same tasks over and over. This is part of the 'systems' we want to put into place. Let me give you an example of what I mean:

I have several businesses and each business has a blog posting that I want handled in a certain way. I have this sheet on hand, and send it to whomever I need. It can be sent to Darren who uploads for my blogpost on our Aurora Publishing website. I can send it to Kerry who uploads to our Today's Businesswoman website and I can send it over to Alicia who updates my Kathleen Mailer website.

I have used this delegation sheet time and time again and just tweaked the details that need tweaking on the page. Now, it is a system I have in place so that I will always be clear in my message AND if someone gets sick, or leaves the company, or becomes another subcontractor - I will always have an easy way to delegate that task.

It saves me money, time and frustration. Does that make sense?

Today's Businesswoman magazine

Job Description: ______________________

____

____

Due date: ____________ **Assigned to:** ____________

Job details: ______________________

____

____

____

____

____

e) **Avoid taking the job back or giving it to someone else:** This is a warning.

Oftentimes, an 'unloving spirit' will show up when we give someone a job and then we take it back or put someone else into that position.

I can think of one K.B.O. who put a qualified candidate in the position of starting a branch of their business in another city. That always grows with great leadership and delegation. There will be problems to overcome and new situations that must be dealt with.

Instead of dealing with the situation when the new Lead Manager was discouraged, (that is a sign of success NOT failure by the way), the K.B.O took back the position. He went in and took over the company and demoted the Lead Manager to a lesser position with less pay. How do you think that Lead Manager felt? He felt unloved, not cherished or respected.

Here are the dangers of doing that: a) you run the risk of killing the person's spirit. They end up not wanting to stand up and do more, be more – but become less and less. b) If you have prayed about this, and that person was the one that GOD ordained to take over – pushing him out is the wrong thing to do! You end up 'stealing' that person's anointed position. You will find yourself under a curse for sure if you do that. That is what happened to this K.B.O. He kept loosing great quality people on his team. He kept losing his flock.

The proper way to handle this would be to find out what was causing the greatest amount of grief. To find out the strengths and the weaknesses. Teach them to lead in the strengths, and delegate their weakness. Ask what are the 3 CORE values or attributes this person brings to this position? WHY was he there in the first place? Have him do what he is called to do – help him to farm out the rest?

f) **Ensure accountability**: Put in check points to ensure That they are on task. Date those checkpoints. Ask the questions: “How are we doing on that situation? Do you have any questions? What can I do to help you make this successful?” This will elevate the last minute problems and procrastination when people run into a snag.

5. TAKE ACTION TO RID YOURSELF OF PROCRASTINATION:

Believe you me, I am preaching to myself. Procrastination is one way the devil likes to keep us stuck. How do you get yourself unstuck from the tumultuous cycle? Simply take action.

I know how simple this sounds. The good news is, if you have taken time to set your goals, prepared your 'choose to do' list; there will always be a next step. One foot in front of the other makes great things happen, when you don’t feel like it.

If you are finding that you have these same steps on your plate, day in and day out take the time to ask yourself:

a) Is this really important to the overall picture of my success? In other words, is it getting you closer or further from your goals? If the answer is no… don't do it. Take it off the list!
b) If the answer is yes, ask yourself, am I the most qualified person to complete this task? If the answer is no - delegate it! If the answer is yes…
c) How can I make this task easier? Do I break it down into mini-steps?
d) Finally, if you have done all this and you still can't seem to have breakthrough, after prayer and making sure you have been delivered from spiritual issues… DO IT ANYWAY! Do it first thing in the morning, before you check your email, before you get into other situations, do it first and foremost.
e) Practice that over and over until you get it right.

6. SELF DISCIPLINE:

"Self-Discipline is not about inflicting pain, it is an act of love'. – **Kathleen D. Mailer**

I used to think discipline meant pain and suffering. I thought it had more to do with 'bringing out the belt, condemnation and guilt, than lovingly correcting oneself to become as one with Jesus.

Perhaps you too have a problem with rebellion against discipline. Please take time to really study the scripture and work toward becoming more of who Christ is, and less of the old you – you want to change.

What helped me to make this transition is reading what the bible says about self-control. In essence it is one in the same. The exciting thing is that it is one of the fruits of the Spirit!

Because we have these promises, dear friends, let us cleanse ourselves from everything that can defile our body or spirit. And let us work toward complete holiness because we fear God. **2 Corinthians 7:1**

When I realized what it really meant, it became a great way to connect with Jesus. The Holy Spirit began to unveil certain choices I was making that took me away from Him. Then, together, with the strength of Christ and the tools I explained in the last Chapter… I began to see magnificent results in my life!

I am a work in progress. I am reminded of Paul's struggles and I don't feel so bad. Even he had issues, just as I – but he knew what to do to get things right. Let this scripture be of comfort to you to work toward lifestyle changes and be the K.B.O that takes nations!

15 I don't really understand myself, for I want to do what is right, but I don't do it. Instead, I do what I hate. 16 But if I know that what I am doing is wrong, this shows that I agree that the law is good. 17 So I am not the one doing wrong; it is sin living in me that does it.

18 And I know that nothing good lives in me, that is, in my sinful nature. I want to do what is right, but I can't. 19 I want to do what is good, but I don't. I don't want to do what is wrong, but I do it anyway. 20 But if I do what I don't want to do, I am not really the one doing wrong; it is sin living in me that does it. **Romans 7:15–20**

7. SET DAILY REMINDERS:

Finding the right software to use is imperative to helping you keep your goals and commitments. The program I used is so wonderful I want everyone to find out about it! SMILES. I will share this with you later in the book.
This particular principle really separates the super successful K.B.O from the mediocre one. Invest in the right tools to see this work well in your life. I am learning to be better and better at this.

This includes following up with emails and promises you make. Remember too, this is a work in progress so don't get overwhelmed. Just START now. Get better every day and soon you will find yourself a pro!

8. MENTORSHIP IS KEY:

The greatest mentor ever known to mankind was Jesus Christ. Many religious doctrines acknowledge that Jesus walked on this earth and that He was a powerful teacher.

We know that He perfectly exemplifies the "attitude of mentorship". A mentor educates and leads others; yes true, but before he or she can do that, a mentor must first be a devoted and avid student.

John 5:19

So Jesus explained, "I tell you the truth, the Son can do nothing by himself. He does only what he sees the Father doing. Whatever the Father does, the Son also does.

John 5:20

For the Father loves the Son and shows him everything he is doing. In fact, the Father will show him how to do even greater works than healing this man. Then you will truly be astonished.

The uncomplicated truth is as Christians we have the GREATEST Counsellor who EVER was or ever will be. Our God knows all. He sees all. He IS All.

The Bible is full of truth, and if you seek the truth in its pages, you will find it.

God has also put people on our paths to teach us ways to continue to grow and mature. His primary objective is for us to build a relationship with Him and with each other. To this end, He has created the gifted instructor to help us bring our dreams and plans to fruition: dreams we, with the Lord, have created for our lives.

Sometimes it is our parents and siblings, teachers at school, pastors, friends, or our spouses who are used to keep us on the right path to our destiny.

Sometimes they are what I lovingly refer to as "reverse mentors", people who do something SO wrong that you change everything to NOT be like them!

Both mentors and "reverse mentors" have an impact on us.

We must remember that our business isn't simply a J.O.B. It is a mission. Therefore we must act accordingly and treat our daily business activity as a highly treasured honour, serving the Lord and doing His work.

We must live our lives "on display", just as Jesus did. Simply stated, this means that whether you are in the supermarket or in church on Sunday, you should be the same person. You must be kind, have compassion, integrity, love, joy, and peace. You must be looking good, and feeling good. This should be the fruit that you are continuing to generate day in and day out.

The truth about mentorship is that it is again founded on being a Master Relationship Builder (MRB). Too many people don't know how to build solid relationships. In all honesty, some people lack friendship skills (as crazy as it sounds). With advances in technology, our ways of communicating have become less and less face-to-face encounters, and we often avoid and give up on close relationships.

We stay hidden in our comfort zone and never step out into the beautiful, joyous world of close friends and teams.

As a leader in your field, business relationships can sometimes be tricky. Often tough questions arise like: “Who do you ‘go the mile’ with in friendships, if you are trying to lead them?”

This uncertainty causes you to step back or step out of relationships, so that you do not end up on the receiving end of the crash that happens when your client has put you on a pedestal and you fall off!

A great way to eliminate this pain is to no longer have clients, but partners in business. Keep the word alive in your relationship and you will find that ‘grace’ will take you a long way.

Together you confess and share the difficulties you are having with some, and pray about the outcome you want to have. If it is time constraints, ask your partner for prayer that God’s grace will come into the situation. Be up front with one another and ask for mercy and forgiveness quickly. In this true heart to heart connection you don’t have to be on a pedestal like the world would like you to believe you can lead – side by side - following Jesus all of the way.

You grow in mutual respect, admiration, strength and love – all things satan hates! Too bad so sad satan, because we don’t really care what you want. We live as MRB – and that is that!

9. BE AN AVID STUDENT:

Be hungry for the Word. God often speaks to us through the written word. It is not only in the Bible where He highlights some great aha's for us, but He also does so in books, seminars, radio shows, and audio books.

Every successful person on the planet is an avid reader/learner. There is a direct correlation between how much you read and what your income will eventually be. I once heard Jim Rohn (a world famous motivational speaker/mentor) say that if you read one book a week, you will have consumed 52 books in a year.

If you read a book a week, you can rise to the top of your field and find out from masters, past and present, how to change the things you can, and allow God to do the rest.

I always say,

"If you do your best, God WILL do the rest."
– Kathleen D. Mailer

If you read as if you are consuming life through the written word, your wisdom will increase your capacity to learn and earn.

10. LIVE A LIFESTYLE OF FORGIVENESS:

While I dove into this in great detail in a previous chapter, I knew it was important for you to understand that this is actually a success principle.

Without forgiveness we crowd our cup of life with 'junk' making it impossible for God to send us the blessings He has for us.

It goes without saying this is one of my favourite passages to meditate on. I pray it helps you too.

5 *"When you pray, don't be like the hypocrites who love to*
pray publicly on street corners and in the synagogues where
everyone can see them. I tell you the truth, that is all the
reward they will ever get.
6 *But when you pray, go away by*
yourself, shut the door behind you, and pray to your Father in
private. Then your Father, who sees everything, will reward
you.

7 *"When you pray, don't babble on and on as people of other*
religions do. They think their prayers are answered merely by
repeating their words again and again.
8 *Don't be like them,*
for your Father knows exactly what you need even before you
ask him!
9 *Pray like this:*

Our Father in heaven,
may your name be kept holy.
10 *May your Kingdom come soon.*
May your will be done on earth,
as it is in heaven.
11 *Give us today the food we need,*[a]
12 *and forgive us our sins,*
as we have forgiven those who sin against us.
13 *And don't let us yield to temptation,*[b]
but rescue us from the evil one.[c]

[14] *"If you forgive those who sin against you, your heavenly Father will forgive you.* [15] *But if you refuse to forgive others, your Father will not forgive your sins.* ***Matthew 6:5-14***

11. ACCOUNTABLITLITY:

Accountability is so important for so many reasons. One reason in particular is to keep your goals, reasons, and focus at the forefront as you move quickly toward your goals.

I have a few accountability partners in different projects and areas of my life. It helps me to stay on track and go that extra mile if I have promised to get something done. I don't want to come to the table without finishing what I started. It is extra incentive to keep motivated and moving.

The other reason that I think accountability is so important is that it helps 'flush' out ideas to help you plan and prepare better. I often find if I have a dilemma just talking to my accountability partner helps me answer my own questions.

This extraordinary person can serve as a great brainstorming buddy because they bring their knowledge and point of view to the surface – helping you get where you are going while making the journey faster, easier and more fun!

WARNING: Be careful to whom you are accountable.

Not everyone is created equal. Make sure you love, admire and respect this person. Also be sure that they have your best interests (and you have theirs) at the base of the co-operation.

We are all showing accountability to someone even if we don't realize it. People can be crutches that can totally crush our business and our life. What happens if you find yourself in a situation where you don't have anyone that fits the job description above? Here is something to think about.

Change your life? Change your friends! Seriously, we all need to take this into account when we are doing a makeover of our business.

I once heard that if you take the income of five of your closest friends and divide that by five, you will find the cap on your own income. I've found this to be so very true in my own life.

I once worked at a financial services company, and we were all just starting out. The sad, but nonetheless true, issue was that we were all broke and broken. No matter how hard I tried to pull myself out, there were always situations and circumstances that pulled me down so that I could never get ahead financially. We hung out together. We worked together. We lived and breathed inside our own bubble. It was time for new friends, wasn't it?

I suggest that if you are in a similar situation, you should look around and find networking functions, social situations, and your local church with a membership that encompasses a high calibre of learning and growing. They should be people who are working for God and His Kingdom: People with His TRUE values who have learned that God wants more for us than we could ever imagine. Only then would you be able to reach for the stars.

This is one of the primary reasons I want to bring together the Christian Collation of Kingdom Business Owners (CCKBO). We need to grow one another to be all who God has called us to be. We need people in our lives that don't feed us fluff (God's truth above all else). We don't want to have people who bring you down or carry demonic spirits to the table (like the Spirit of Jealousy). We want to build a movement of an army to take control of the Kingdom that Jesus gave us – and win their souls to Christ! Amen?

12. CELEBRATION TIME, C'MON:`

Ecclesiastes 3:4 ESV *A time to weep, and a time to laugh; a time to mourn, and a time to dance*;

It came as quite a shock for some of my friends who haven't found Jesus yet. Often times they get the "deer in the headlights" look when they see how much fun I have in life. I laugh, I joke, I dance, I sing – I can't help it! I am filled with the Joy of the Lord. In church we play rock and roll music – we praise – we get filled and we have fun!

I think on one level, I too thought that all of the 'fun stuff' in my life would be over if I accepted Christ. Nothing can be further than the truth! God loves to celebrate. As a matter of fact, HE invented it!

Scriptures all throughout the Bible talk about festivals, celebrations, dancing and singing to the Glory of Christ. The best part is, when you are His… nothing fills you more than doing it God's way as opposed to the world view.

I know so many of whom I have led to the Lord say the same thing. I love parties, rock and roll, having a good time. The drugs I took, the alcohol I drank – nothing – NOTHING - gave me what I was searching for like serving Jesus does.

While all of that is true, I want to say that with every milestone, give God the glory and you will find that your life will transform into something you can't describe. As you celebrate each and every achievement, you will find out that you are more productive, more pro-active, more excited, more filled with joy, have more time, more money and more purpose than ever before.

Celebration with the Lord – is truly the best celebration you can have. Unbelievers will have a hard time understanding this until they experience it themselves. But the truth be told, we need to remember to celebrate your success.

What's the alternative? satan steals the joy right out from under you. I want to give you a very good example that just came up for me. I am still unpacking everything I found out about myself while I went through the cleansing process. I pray that this example will truly help you to examine your life and help you be able get to the next level God is bringing you to.

I used to own a company called 'The Exclusive Lady'. I designed and manufactured my own line of lingerie from sizes 2-52. I knew nothing of fashion designing. As a matter of fact, I couldn`t (and still can`t) sow a stitch!

I was going through my old files, doing a cleansing clean up. I found tucked away my paperwork on this company. With it, I found something out about myself. I did remember I had a $1.2 million dollar contract with a large department store. I did remember that certain things happened, like my investors drug their feet, and I lost it all. I did remember that I struggled with being a Mom and a businesswoman at the same time. I do remember how hard it was to leave my daughter and how many times I worked in my business as I was worrying about my husband and daughter. I also remember when I was with my husband and daughter, I was thinking about the business.

This nasty cycle is what I remember. I remember when I folded the company how painful it was and how I felt like such a failure. I remember feeling like I was such a loser and there is no way I could be a good C.E.O of any company because I am not the `corporate type`. As a matter of fact, when Shark Tank aired I really loved the show. Who wouldn`t who is in business? One can learn a lot from the Sharks just listening to their comments. I did think to myself, 'Oh my goodness I would NEVER want to be the one to pitch something to them'. I could never do that. I will stick to what I am doing now and making my millions, thank you very much!

Here is where the devil stole so much joy from me.

1. He stole my joy because the success was so hard. I pushed and willed my way through the process instead of letting go and letting God take care of situations and circumstances.

2. He stole my joy while I was with my family – I really don't remember a lot about those times - although, praise God, memories are coming back!
3. He stole my joy while I had success with my business. Do you know I didn't even really tell my husband a lot of the success I had? I noticed I had an approval for a $5.125 million dollar loan for a manufacturing plant. I NEVER told Dan! Can you believe that? That is SO unlike us now that it seems impossible. I never put my signature on that (thank God!). I assume it was because my investors didn't move forward in the end and I didn't get my contract. The truth is, I can't remember! I also looked at the pitch I gave the investors. It was worthy of Shark Tank! Seriously. I put a LOT of work into that. There wasn't any doubt, yet I can't remember even doing it. It was my work to be sure. I didn't have anyone to help me at the time, nor the money to invest in it. It was in my words, with my flavour – but I don't remember it at all. I found the letter from the investors. They said, 'We are in, what a GREAT presentation! One of us needs to check the availability of funds and when that comes back, we will be set to go." You will see shortly how I took this note. How the devil stole this out from under me. What I also want to say here is, thank God – it didn't go through! In hindsight, I am so relieved. I can't imagine running this kind of a business now. It doesn't serve God's people, like I do now.

4. I didn't really remember the fashion shows, the catalogues, the new designs… how did I do that?

I will tell you how. I had the favour of God over my life! What I didn't have was God in my business!

Yes, the day that I lost this contract was the worst and the best thing that ever happened to me.

Part of Kathleen's testimony, learning to do business God's way:

All business owners wake up wishing that today would be a life-changing day for me in business. Today was no exception for me. I was full of fear, excitement, focus, and stress… oh so much stress. Stress? That was NOT new!

I started that morning with a ritual worthy of Tony Robbins. He would be so very proud of me as he watched me in the mirror that morning. I looked into my eyes and said, 'You can do this! You are a business mogul. You are worthy. You are the best! You are ready."

Dannielle (my daughter) was around 3 at the time. Like all beautiful children her age, she was getting ready to go to the babysitters. First she needed help to get a glass of water. Then she needed help to find her blankey. Then, while I am getting dressed in my most perfect power suit, she needed help to pack her bag with the essentials. When it was time to put my makeup on, she had decided she didn't want to go to the sitters. Today she was ready to stay at home. She started pushing me and my buttons. (I hate to admit it but it was true for me then.) Finally she said, "I want to go to the sitter by myself because I'm a big girl Mommy!"

At my wits-end, I agreed she could go to the babysitter's by herself. The walk was 2 houses away for goodness sake, what could go wrong?

I loaded the truck with my presentation gear – I was to pitch to the investor today for my big break! I had a $1.2 million dollar contract on the table. I was set for my manufacturing plant. All I needed was some capital to move to the next level of living in my business.

I watch her walk to Barb and Len's house, open the door and wave good-bye to me! She made me smile. She is really getting big! Lifting my voice I said, 'Bye honey have a good day today!" and I hopped into the truck in a big hurry to get going. I didn't want to be late and now? I am on the brink.

Walking into the office of my potential partners in business, I was as prepared as I could be. I had been up night and day in the last 3 weeks preparing for this meeting. After saying what I needed to say – I was well received. They asked me to step outside and wait for a bit before I left and they would be able to give me a 'yes or no' answer before I go.

I was excited, scared, and really thinking about how I had 'blown it'. Thoughts of failure and defeat were going through my head. The sinking feeling came when I received a note that I took as a 'no way' was put at my fingertips. The secretary had a pathetic look on her face – like 'yeah it was never gonna happen'.

I went home, feeling a bit numb. It was now noon. I had been pitching since 8:30AM, answering questions, walking through my plans for the future. I had decided to stop by the store to pick up some lunch. Danni was at the sitter, and today? I think I might leave her for the day. I am so bummed out. I had to figure out what to do now.

When I got home it was close to 1:00pm. I walked into the front door and saw the messages on my answer machine. 28? What the heck? I hope they are orders! Bills are coming due and I don't have enough money to pay everything.

The first message, I didn't even compute it. My heart dropped. My ears rang. "Mrs. Mailer, we have your daughter. I live across the street from you. She was on your front doorstep crying. Her babysitter wasn't home."

The second message, one of the same, "Please Mrs. Mailer, call me as soon as you are in. Your daughter is crying for you. I don't know how else to connect with you."

All 28 messages were from this kind stranger. We lived on a VERY busy street – anything could have happened to her! My world whizzed by in fear with the 'what if's'… The honest truth is, to this day I have no recollection of the person that took her in. I have no idea how they found out my last name! I have no idea if I even thanked them! Truly… I still don't remember… what I DO remember is feeling like my world died that day… and it did.

Bringing Dannielle home I clung to her like my life line. I was done with business. I was done with trying. I was done with everything. I just wanted to be a Mom and a wife – nothing else matters.

It turned out that Barb forgot she was taking Danni in that day so she and her husband went shopping. None the less, it was MY fault for not taking the time to wait.

After I tucked Dannielle in for a much needed nap, I went to God. I threw myself at his feet and asked him to help me.

That day was the third time in my life that I heard Him speak to me clearly. After all, I only consulted Him when I needed something. His mercy and grace are so beyond words. He still was there for me, when I obviously didn't deserve it.

His words, 'How is your way working for you?' Stab me in the heart why don't You? That is when He talked to me about doing what I loved. Doing what was right. It was about serving others. It was time to start doing business His way – stop trying to do it on my own strength.

I begged His forgiveness, and said – I will only do business if You tell me to. I want nothing more than to focus on my daughter now. He shook me to my core when he told me I could have both.

God fixed this situation for me, even though I still can scarcely believe it. He made it so Dannielle didn't even remember that situation. She was not scared or haunted by it. Praise God. (As a matter of fact she found it fascinating to hear this story!) God gave me a new business, imagine that? One that served people and my first book was born! He helped me clean up The Exclusive Lady. He helped me find the balance I so much needed. He helped me make sure it never happened again.

How? I still do not know… I just know that I serve the BEST Master in the world!

The point I am making is that we need to celebrate our successes on the way. Enjoy life! Don't get so caught up in the work hard mentality that you forget why we live. We are Master Relationship Builders remember? The best way to build relationship is to sing and dance unto the Lord. Do it with our community, then we all enjoy life to its fullest. We all will enjoy and experience God's greatness. Then? Our focus is on the abundance of Jesus. We then live a happy and fun life, solving people's problems and making a way to the best life ever!

13. RE-EVALUATE WHAT YOU HAVE AT YOUR FINGERTIPS:

It is time for us to start fresh and take stock/inventory of what we have. This is time for us to sort through the gifts, talents and abilities. What products or services do you have to offer?

Let me help you with a few steps to get us ready for the next 12 months of your life. Let's build our business bigger, better. Let us get ready to position ourselves to prosper.

1. Make a list of all of the products or services you offer right now.
2. Ask yourself, "What products or services do I make the most amount of money on right now? What is it that is my top seller?"
3. What hasn't been selling?
4. What do I want to try to sell? If there are several possibilities pick the one you think will generate the most. Then start to 'add' to your portfolio, one thing at a time.
5. Focus for the next 30-60 days on your top sellers FIRST. Get a strategy in place that will help you sell MORE of what is working.
6. Take a look at the situation. What do I need in order to sell more?
    - Do I need more clients?
    - Do I need more quality clients?
    - Do I need to put a package together to sell more of this to one client (i.e.: Buy one get one at 50% off).
    - Is this a perishable product/service where my client needs it over and over again?

If yes, do I have a plan in place to get them to come back for more? Do I have a system to touch base with clients I already have? Can I do that now? What do I need to make this happen?

This goes hand in hand with the next success principle.

14. ELIMINATE WASTE, CLEAN UP YOUR RESOURCES:

I think elimination is the easiest principle to put into practice and often brings great results in little time. It is time to eliminate and clean up our business and your life to make it easier, faster, more productive, more enjoyable, and more prosperous!

Let's walk through the elimination process. I have given a few examples to get you started. If you live a lifestyle of cleaning up resources, and elimination of waste you find your business doubling and your give-ability increasing!

1. **Eliminate clients that don't work for you anymore.** Seriously, the greatest gift I gave myself in business is to 'fire' my clients. Let's face it, as your business grows (and as you grow); your quality of client grows as well. That is the way it should be. Some of us can find 'clients for life'... which is wonderful. However, that means they need to grow alongside you.

   I am very grateful for my new language: partners vs clients. The very word 'partner' brings the perfect client to me. Later in the book, we talk about our perfect target market. Be sure you know exactly WHO you want to partner with. When you do know that, you can actually eliminate the clients who don't fit your criteria.

   Elimination questions:

   a) Has this client bought from me in the past year?
   b) Do they fit my criteria of my new business partner?

c) If not, can I share the vision with them of where my business is growing – will they be open to that?
d) How was the experience I had with them when I worked with them? Is it something I would do again? If not, eliminate.
e) Who are the clients I currently have that bring in most of my income? What can I do to 'romance' them and build a better relationship?

2. **Eliminate products and services that don't serve you and your message.**
   The same strategy we put into place with clients is the one you need when it comes to your products and services. What products are your top selling products? How can you make them even better? What products are busts? Eliminate them immediately. Go through and take stock, have a clearance sale to get rid of them or give them away. God always blesses a giver. If you can give them away to make room for something BIG BIG BIG – do it. You will be glad you did.

3. **Eliminate waste in your food budget.**
   Most people have no idea how much they actually eat out! I have heard so many of my K.B.O. students tell me how they don't have any money whatsoever! They can't afford a $39 book to invest in themselves in order to change their lives.

   If that is you, I challenge you to go over your bank statements. Highlight every transaction that you made that you purchased food or beverages. Add it up every month.

One K.B.O. student took this challenge. She and her very busy family were always on the go. She tried to make good meals and eat healthy, but time isn't always on her side. She found out the small trips through the McDonald's drive through, and the quick stop at Timmy's added up to nearly $400/month! She and her husband went out for the odd meal out. It really didn't seem like a lot.

I am not saying you should not treat yourself to these things – but we must all be careful not to make 'treating myself' a lifestyle habit! Does that make sense?

I showed her how she could budget only $100.00 to still do these things and put $300 into investing into a business or elimination of debt. By the end of the year she would have nearly $3600.00. Can you imagine that? She could have a published a book to set her up as an expert in her business. She could have paid off her Canadian Tire MasterCard. She could have invested into many books/programs to help her get better at marketing.

Just sayin'… eliminate waste and you will FIND what you are looking for!

4. **Eliminate waste in your time:**

Time wasters are the worst! They makes us feel like we have gotten nothing done. Many of us go day by day feeling frustrated because we had so many time wasters in our midst.

Here are a few time wasters to watch out for: television, emails, social media, social visits during your work day (physical or through technology), open door policy in your office, answering phones when you are focused, pets, not letting family know the proper rules around you working, broken tools, lack of knowledge, cluttered work stations and so much more.

Ask yourself the questions, 'What can I do to eliminate distractions and pressures on my time?" Put the answers into action right now! More time is more money and more give-ability.

5. **The hemorrhaging in your finances:**

Go through all of your expenses. Seriously take stock of where you are at.

After you have listed all of your expenses, ask yourself the following questions and take action accordingly:

For each expense, ask yourself:

a) **Do I need what this expense is providing?** An example would be a monthly trailer payment on your RV. Do you even use it? How much do you use it? Can you go back to the tent for a few years until you get caught up – assuming you want to camp? How much does it sit there? If you use it for only 2 weeks out of the year and you are making payments of $250/month – can you put that money aside and 'rent' an RV for those two weeks? If you realize that this is true – get rid of it immediately. Does it make sense to sell it? Rent it out to someone else? Make it into something that can bring you money every month to pay for the privilege of having it. Think about what you can do to keep it, get rid of it and with it the expense.

b) **Can I make this payment less expensive per month?** For example, cell phone expense. Are you paying for a family plan? Look through what you have. Do you use the data plan to its full extent? Can I get a cheaper plan? Will a 'pay as you go' plan work for me and be cheaper? Is there someone on my plan that can start to pay for their share of the plan?

c) **How can I eliminate this payment all together?** If you have a credit card and it is killing you with interest every month, this is a good way to eliminate it. Find things around your house to 'sell', a by-product of the next success principle. Put everything you make from that sale onto your credit card until you have eliminated it. My suggestion is that you pick 1 Visa and/or 1 MasterCard that best serves you and get rid of the rest! This is only my opinion: get the help of an expert for advice. Credit cards and debt are a huge way that the devil keeps us in bondage. Ask me how I know! I have been there and done that, thank you GOD that you delivered me from this evil.

You will be surprised at how elimination can be a lifestyle change when you start to see the physical results of a few minor changes.

Here is some scripture to ponder on 'waste'.

Don't waste your breath on fools, for they will despise the wisest advice. **Proverbs 23:9**

[7] *Do not waste time arguing over godless ideas and old wives' tales. Instead, train yourself to be godly.* [8] *"Physical training is good, but training for godliness is much better, promising benefits in this life and in the life to come."* [9] *This is a trustworthy saying, and everyone should accept it.* **1 Timothy 4:7-9**

Making the best use of the time, because the days are evil. Therefore do not be foolish, but understand what the will of the Lord is. **Ephesians 5:16-17 ESV**

15. **CLEAN UP YOUR MESSES:**

I truly learned this lesson years and years ago. I am so excited to bring this to the forefront of your success principles.

You wouldn't think that there was a direct correlation between messes and income, but there is. If you find yourself looking at a messy desk every day you will find that you struggle with powerful income opportunities.

When you live in a 'mess mentality' your cup of life is so full God can't fill it with blessings. Don't take my word for it, start cleaning up messes and asking God to fill the void you created with something you want. Be sure to journal everything, including the all of the blessings that follow. Soon you will have a lifestyle that says, "I must clean up messes!"

It is VERY important, though, as you clean up the messes in life, to ask God to fill it with what you want. Nature abhors a vacuum and the devil would love to fill that space with whatever he can to open doors. A simply prayer and thoughts of God will help you to move forward in your success. Soon you will be living a life of freedom and abundance.

Some messes we must consider cleaning up.

a) **Relationships:** If you need forgiveness, ask. If you need to forgive, do. If you need to release toxic relationships, do it now. Make sure that God is at your core when you do so. Listen to the whispers of the Holy Spirit. He loves the heart of a MRB.
b) **Physical messes**: messy desk, filing cabinet, stacks of paper, unfinished projects, (you should always finish what you start!), broken tools or technology, client lists, house, bedroom, cupboards, closets and more.
c) **Finances:** We talked about this already. Get focused and clear. You are a K.B.O. this is an area that is very important.
d) **Use the RRR (Release, Recycle, Re-use) approach to the cleaning**:

Release the things you don't need or want. Is it a recycle bin project? Is it something someone else can use? Then be a K.B.O and 'give' it away. See, your give-ability starts at your core! Who else can use it? Or, you can re-use it. You may find things you haven't used yet and that you can now use in a clean environment.

Even if you need help with this, hire someone. It is worth it. OR, incorporate family help. They can be more objective when it comes to the RRR method. Study up on the best approach to take when you get serious.

Remember, you don't have to do everything all at once. DO schedule some time in to do it though. I remember when I decided it was time to go through my office (I try and do it once per year). I set my monthly goal: My office is cleaned up, cleaned out and ready for action on /before 30 days. Then, every day, I started with a shelf, a cabinet drawer or something. Sometimes I would do more than one thing, but I discipline myself that at least that thing I wrote down would get done. The work was about 15 minutes to 1 hour every day, and before the end of the 30 days I got everything accomplished.

Something else you might want to note is the fact that the more you live the 'clean my messes' lifestyle, the easier and less time it takes to get it done!

WARNING: remember to ask God to fill the void you create as you go through and clean up. You don't want to give the devil any leeway in your life. Focus on what is good and true and right – the Bible tells us our life will be lived to the fullness.

16. **BE EARLY, NOT ON TIME:**

It seems like this should be something I wouldn't have to even mention. However, this is one place the devil seems to really play havoc in a K.B.O's life. Always being early (five minutes before) will be something you will be known for. It builds up your credibility. It makes people feel cherished, valued and respected.

If you are always late, your lack of respect will soon show up in your relationships. People won't believe a word you say because you can't even be on time for a meeting. Your integrity gets shot. Once that happens, your business launches into a downward spiral.

17. **SIMPLIFY AND MULTIPLY:**

Wherever you can, take time to simplify your steps. We do talk more about this at greater lengths throughout this book. When you simplify, you save time and effort and you make your life much more enjoyable.

This is another reason I help my K.B.O students to write a book. If you get asked the same questions over and over again, writing a book can be so rewarding. Your client/partner will get the answer they need. You will save time and effort explaining it. You will also benefit by putting money in your bank.

Take time to simplify your marketing methods, your delegation, your sales strategy, your website, your scheduling, your meetings, and your health routine.

Then watch how God will multiply you in more ways that you can count! Praise His Name!

18. **BE A DECISION MAKER:**

Wow, this is one place that I find K.B.O's really struggle. Getting good at making decisions will separate you from the mediocre business owners.

While I agree we do need to take time to pray to make good business decisions, I often find Christian business owners use this excuse to procrastinate, or put off making tough decisions. It becomes a 'cop out' for them and leaves them in a place of perpetual poverty.

How do you learn to make good decisions? How do you know it is 'God's will' for my life?

Easy! Does it line up with his word? Does this take you closer to your goals or further away from your goals?

If you are K.B.O. and you KNOW that God has called you to this business, then ACT like it. You don't have to take every little decision to Him to see if you should move forward or not.

Let me give you a very good example of a K.B.O student that has been transformed by making her lifestyle a decisive one.

It was time for, "A Book Is Never A Book Boot Camp"; God had been calling her to write a book for years. Years before she even met me, she knew it was time to write and publish her book.

She had been praying, the week before, 'God please help me as I don't know what to do to write this book! I know you have put it on my heart again. I want to make sure it is for you!" That week, a friend sent her an email saying that I was doing 3 Free Videos on how to write, publish and market your own book. Make money even before your book is done!

She saw it as a sign from God. She went to the website and signed up. With each video, she felt the stir of the Holy Spirit. She knew this was from God. She even called the office and I took time to chat with her on the phone. She knew, without a doubt, it was a call from God.

When it came time to sign up for the boot camp, she said, "I need to pray about it." Of course! Why not? However, the truth was she didn't want to spend the money. She understood the value in being there. She listened to the countless testimonials of change that our graduates freely gave. She knew it was from God, yet she could NOT make the decision to come or not.

Time went by and the early bird price was coming to an end. She had to keep praying (not because she couldn't come up with the money) but she was unsure if this is what God wanted for her.

The price mark changed and still she agonized over the decision. Now she had to pay $500 more to come to the boot camp! The next one wasn't for another year! Her answer to me was, "I just don't know if I should go!"

I am not interested in 'making' people decide if they want to go or not. That is the Holy Spirit's job. My job was to pray for her and break off the spirit of indecision. Just decide one way or another. She asked herself, "Does this get me closer to my goals or further away?" Of course, it was closer – but still she was unsure.

Next, we were sold out and couldn't take any more people into the boot camp. She was so upset, but the truth is, when we do it only once per year – that is the price you pay to wait! She missed out this year.

The next year came and she signed up right away. Unfortunately for her, the early bird price (and the course price) went up as we changed from 2 days to 3 days. It cost her to wait. It cost her to not move. She knew it was God's will yet, she was so unsure.

For the record, she did come to the boot camp. She had a life altering experience. She was delivered from the spirit of indecision. She wrote not one but two books. She created income within 30 days – which covered her ticket price AND the cost of publishing/marketing.

She told me that this indecisiveness had affected her marriage – aka: divorce, her relationship with her children, her business. People looked at her as a 'flake'. People took advantage of her – people who forced her to make a decision to buy because they grew impatient with her. Thus, the cycle began… bad decisions came from being pushed.

If this is you, I pray that you find a way to become a better decision maker. The little decisions you should make quickly and effortlessly come when you trust God and trust yourself. The more you make, the better you become. The more you know the heart of God, the easier it is for you to make decisions. Focus on making decisions, right or wrong – and following through.

Take 100% responsibility for your life and you will find that you live a blessed life indeed.

19. **DON'T GET AHEAD OF GOD:**

Major lifestyle change in the making! I hope through this chapter as I shared examples with you that you can see the value in NOT getting ahead of God. Doing things on your own steam truly is not fun and it can be devastating, not just for you, but those around you.

Overwhelm, worry, stress and frustration are often the fruit you receive when you are getting ahead of God. Peace, joy, prosperity, good health are a result of letting God guide you through processes.

I will never forget the ease that we had when our daughter got married. Leon and Dannielle had such favour over their union it was incredible. I was focused on the things I was to do, which was building God's ministry - and God took care of the details for this wedding.

Seriously, we needed a photographer – we prayed that day and we got a great one. We needed a cake? That came effortlessly too. I could write a whole book on the blessings of this wedding!

What I am getting at is the fact that God led, and we walked in his wake.

The wedding went along with minimal stress and frustration. As a matter of fact, I wondered if I was doing it right because it was so easy and stress free! God was good! The day was outstanding, the couple ecstatic, the guests happy and Mom and Dad? OVER JOYED with the goodness of our God!

Let's put the word into action:

1. Go through this list and check off which one you have a pretty good handle on.
2. Ask the Holy Spirit to reveal to you which one, of the number that is left, that He wants you to incorporate into a lifestyle change first.
3. Study the subject, get a deeper knowledge and work on just one principle at a time.
4. It is a journey, not a destination. It takes years to develop lifestyle habits, a bit at a time. The more your practice, the more it will integrate deep within and you will begin to walk it habitually.

Let me help you pray,

Dearest Father in Heaven, I pray today for your help to show me what lifestyle change I must make first. Help me to prioritize my changes and then help me to follow your guidance in making these changes. Let these next 12 months be the best learning curves and strides I have ever made.

I also pray for the results to be clear and easy for me to read, as signs that I am on the right track. Help me to see the miracles in my life as a direct result of the changes I am making. Let my life be a living sacrifice for you. Let others see the 'fruit' in my life as a result so I can give you the glory. In Jesus name, Amen

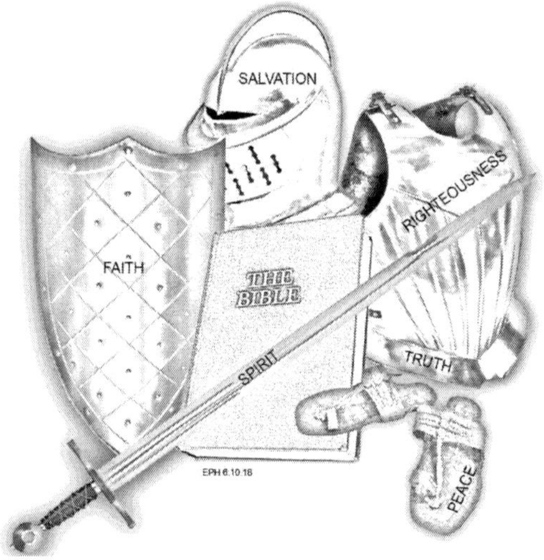

(c) 2014 Kathleen Mailer - KBO

CHAPTER THIRTEEN

Becoming a Master Relationship Builder

The primary difference between doing business God's way and the way of the world is the fact that K.B.O's are business evangelists. Like our Father, they care more about the people than the monetary show of cash flow.

This puts the K.B.O in a terrible conundrum. Do they focus on making money? Or, do they do as they have been commanded and make disciples of men?

The good news is that you can do both. You don't have to opt for love or money.

When you have a Holy Spirit filled business, money is simply a great and tangible fruit that is produced out of your capacity to love and live.

When Jesus enters the picture, you will see that you don't lack a thing. Let's review a story of a simple businessman named Simon. He was a hard worker. Often, you could find him working all night just to put food on his table for his family.

On this particular day, he had found himself even more exhausted than usual. He had just come off of a brutal shift that seemed like it would never end. He worked and worked and had nothing to show for it at the end of the day. These days were tough for everyone since the economy was in a bad way. As a matter of fact, everyone in his industry had the same problems. He had to face the cold hard reality, no fish were biting right now and that is bad news for a fisherman who makes his money selling fish!

I can imagine the inner turmoil that plagued him. I am sure he had bills to pay. His family needed to eat. I can believe that he was bone deep tired of fighting this battle physically, mentally and emotionally. What was he going to do? When was he going to 'catch' his big break?

Does this remind you of anyone you know? My heart aches right now, in remembrance of my own life as the Holy Spirit urges me on to continue my story for you today.

Ready to pack it in and pack up – he docked his boat and started putting away his tools. At this deep moment of business despair, Jesus walks up to the empty boat.

Jesus had a way about him, that was for absolute sure. With just a sentence, he asked Simon to help him reach the ears of the mob of people who were hungry for something more. They needed to hear some good news. All Jesus asked of him was to push the boat into the water so that he could teach from the boat. (Which just so happens to be a business platform – hear what I am saying?)

After he was done, the Lord then did what he always does and decides to bless Simon. You see, Simon offered Jesus his time, his resources and vehicle (his business) to reach out to the people who were in desperate need of what Jesus freely offered them.

They needed to be set free, loved, healed and released from captivity and oppression where the devil's lies had blossomed.

What happens next really nails it to the cross for me. Jesus tells Simon to go back out where it is deeper, then cast his nets out.

C'mon! Simon had tried all of this before! It was like he was saying, "Hello Jesus! We ALL know sales are down. Nothing is happening. I have tried that avenue and it was an epic fail!" Somewhat skeptical and tired, he reluctantly agrees.

I don't know about you, but what I do know is that many people at this point tell Jesus to *'forget about it!'* (Say that with a heavy Italian accent). Their excuse meter comes to the surface… I have already been there and done that.

They continue to say, "This doesn't work. Seriously, I have tried and tried. Do you know that no one is biting, Lord? Not one customer, let me tell you! It is the same all over in my industry. There simply are not any fish in the sea." (Sound familiar?) Well, Simon basically pulled out the same excuse we all have used for thousands of years.

Here is what happens when you use an **excuse**:

"You **EX**it your **C**alling and you need to **U**nderstand that this is when **S**atan **E**xcels"

I want you to notice two very important things here:

1) **God wants to revive our dreams and our business ideas of the past.** The old ways aren't working for us anymore. The reason it no longer works the old way is because God is calling us to go 'deeper' with him. He wants to take our business to a whole other level. For many of you reading this right now, I want you to hear this word – *he wants to resurrect the dreams you once had, dust it off, tweak it ever so slightly - making it God's way.* Then, you will have great success. This success is greater than ever before. This success is boat loads more. Forget about the cup that runneth over, we are talking about boatloads. Boats are spilling over with blessing. So much blessing you can't contain it. So much bounty you will need to call in your team to help you harvest it all. So much abundance that those (that the world would like to classify as competition) in your industry will have to help you with it because you can't possible do it by yourself.

2) **You have to be obedient and believe in your Jesus, not in your circumstances.** Simon thought the Lord was crazy. He didn't put it in those terms, but he did explain that there were not any fish there to be had. I actually laughed as the Holy Spirit showed this to me. Imagine, Simon Peter is telling JESUS how business is done! He actually explained to Jesus why his way wouldn't work.

It's like a new business owner telling a Mentor that owns all of the gold, silver and money in a Kingdom how business is done.

Confession time, I kind of did that a time or two – just like Simon Peter. "Lord? I have tried it, that doesn't work!"... Yep, I am moving on....

The key words that Simon used that showed his brilliant mindset was 'never-the-less, I will do it anyway.'

I learned a valuable lesson from this years ago when we started the Today's Businesswoman Magazine. I had run very successful businesses in the past. God had given us incredible blessings and help to succeed. Then, our life hit a major season of 'paring down' – and God was teaching both my husband and me new thoughts, new avenues and new ways of doing life (a.k.a. business). We had many struggles emotionally, relationally, physically and financially. Through it all God, gave us a life line of grace. Most would crack under the pressure of 1 of these situations (let alone 22) life changing circumstances in less than 3 years. I continue to stand amazed at how great our God is. We should be basket cases by now, but we aren't and we know it is by God's grace. We saw him protect us, love us, provide for us, heal us and care for us in tangible ways.

One day, I was sitting in worship and thanking him from every fibre of my being for his faithfulness, grace and mercy. I asked, "What can I do for you?"

Let me tell you, unless you mean it, don't ask God this question! He said, 'Actually I would like you to put together an international magazine called Today's Businesswoman. I want it to provide quality, affordable mentorship for Christian Businesswomen around the world. I want it to be quarterly. I want you to charge this much. I don't want you to sell 'advertising' in it – I want to do that differently."

There is much more, obviously. The point I want to make here is this: He wanted me to do business in a totally different way than I was used to.

For example, I was sure you should have 'sales' before you work on content. After all you have to make money first don't you? The way He wanted me to do it, it was clear that that wasn't his agenda. It is a long story, maybe I will tell you later.

I was ready, though, to follow Jesus. In my life, I was totally done with MY way of doing business. These ways were taught to me by mentors of the world. What I wanted was a deeper, intimate relationship with God. I wanted to do business God's way – and since I didn't fully know what that looked like – I followed the gentle voice of the Holy Spirit.

Like Simon, I found out what a blessing it is to be in the boat with Jesus as we take His message out to the world. I also found out that the blessings and provision come by the boat load when you focus on Kingdom ways.

Ok, let's get back to our story. **Let's read it directly from the Bible now, shall we?**

Luke 5

The First Disciples

5 One day as Jesus was preaching on the shore of the Sea of
Galilee, great crowds pressed in on him to listen to the word
of God. 2 He noticed two empty boats at the water's edge, for
the fishermen had left them and were washing their nets. 3
Stepping into one of the boats, Jesus asked Simon, its owner,
to push it out into the water. So he sat in the boat and taught
the crowds from there.

4 When he had finished speaking, he said to Simon, "Now go
out where it is deeper, and let down your nets to catch some
fish."

5 "Master," Simon replied, "we worked hard all last night
and didn't catch a thing. But if you say so, I'll let the nets
down again." 6 And this time their nets were so full of fish
they began to tear! 7 A shout for help brought their partners
in the other boat, and soon both boats were filled with fish
and on the verge of sinking.

8 When Simon Peter realized what had happened, he fell to
his knees before Jesus and said, "Oh, Lord, please leave me—
I'm too much of a sinner to be around you." 9 For he was
awestruck by the number of fish they had caught, as were the
others with him. 10 His partners, James and John, the sons of
Zebedee, were also amazed.

Jesus replied to Simon, "Don't be afraid! From now on you'll
be fishing for people!" 11 And as soon as they landed, they
left everything and followed Jesus.

I also want you to catch another few nuggets as you go through and read the actual account.

1) Notice it says that **Simon had to bring in 'partners'** from the other boats. This is significant to us as K.B.O's because our language is changing. Later in this chapter I will expound on this.
2) **Simon Peter had the right attitude**. After the work was done he fell to his knees before Jesus and confessed his sins. He humbled himself before the Lord. He was 'awestruck'. AWESTRUCK! When was the last time you really felt AWESTRUCK by what the Lord has done for you? Did you position yourself on your knees in front of him to thank him from these depths of your soul? OR, did you look at it and say, "What about all of the other areas in my life where I could use some breakthrough? What about that?" I just want you to think about this.
3) **Notice the fruit of what happened** as a result of this one business transaction with JESUS in the boat when Simon Peter was just minding his own business? His company *caught the attention of others*. Even *his 'partners' were amazed*! *They followed Jesus too!* Sounds like business ministry to me! Just like my husband and myself, Peter went on to walk in the power of the Holy Spirit - miracles, salvations, healings, signs and wonders followed him where ever he went. POWERFUL.
4) **Notice Jesus' response?** He put peace on Simon's heart and told him not to be afraid. From now on you will be fishing for people. Doing the work that God himself ordained for each one of us.

I don't know about you, but I am excited! We just need to remember, it really is NEVER about the enterprise itself, it is about the people. It is about you becoming a Master Relationship Builder with everyone you meet (just as Jesus was). It is about who you become in the process.

Again, my words come back to you not to be redundant, but to impress upon your heart the importance of this phrase as we prepare to implement the physical transactions of our everyday dealings.

"God gives us a business so that we can go out and DO God's business!"
- Kathleen D. Mailer

There is no business like the 'family' business. Instead of complaining to the Lord in our heavy Italian accent (yes we are talking *'family business'*), *"forgetta bout it";* let's realize we have a great inheritance.

This really is the FAMILY business that has been passed down to us from generation to generation. The King himself started it all! This isn't something we 'earned', we 'inherited' it. It is in our blood to be entrepreneurs! The characteristics we need are right there, in our D.N.A. We need to start to act like we 'got this!'

Wow, OK - another word from the Holy Spirit right now to really drive this section home:

"The true difference between a worldly business and a kingdom business is that real power and influence show up in your NET-work and not your NET-worth!

If you focus on your NET-work your NET-worth grows too. It comes naturally, easily and readily." – **Kathleen D. Mailer**

But how can we become a fisher of men? Easy, just like Simon-Peter, Mathew, Luke, and all business men and women of the day – they followed Jesus.

27 Irrefutable Attributes Of A Master Relationship Builder (MRB)

Another way to look at this is that you are getting your MASTERS in relationship building. We will call our new position a "MRB" as we move through the rest of this chapter.

The first thing I would like to address is the fact there is SO much more I could add to this list. Maybe it will be another book. This certainly isn't an exhaustive list but it is one that is a great start to 'add' to your life. My prayer is that it will help you find the results you need to set you apart from anyone else in your industry.

My intention is for us to create a movement, not just momentum. In order to do that we need new language, new thought processes, new avenues of doing business from a God's eye point of view.

I pray that these attributes become a lifestyle rather than just great 'habits' we have.

In no particular order:

1. **MRB, thinks partnership *vs* clients:** the best thing I ever did when God asked me to work directly with Christian writers was change my language and my ideal client.

   My company, Aurora Publishing, helps K.B.O's take their message to the masses. I help Christians write, publish AND market their own books.

   God calls us to share our testimony and K.B.O's need to understand the value in doing so. You will get the fullness of what I am talking about in the next section of the book.

   I bring this to your attention because I want you to actually 'feel' the difference in your heart when I talk about my potential customers or clients in terms of 'partnering' with them.

   In the past, I had 'clients'. They wanted me to help them self-publish their books. They needed help to write the outline, understand the publishing process (and get it published) and also some marketing venues to get the book out there. It worked for a while and we were very successful. However, God had asked me to put down the business the way we were doing it – and wait on him.

This is when my education took place! These customers of mine had a **'client' mentality.** Simply put, deep within their heart they have a belief that it is up to the company they bought the service from to do ALL of the work and ensure they are successful.

Their mindset is, 'I paid the money and now you have to make sure I get what I paid for.'

The problem with that is they, too, have to do some of the work involved in order for this process to be successful. In my case, the customer/client had to actually write the book in a given time frame – to send to us the finished manuscript and then our services can kick in. It was expected that they would do that and then we could help them finish the process.

When they realized that they dropped the ball, it becomes commonplace for them to put the blame on other people aka: the company they are working with.

To make a long story short, I only give this example because now God has breathed new life into this. I now PARTNER with Christians to help them achieve their goal. They understand that they have to do certain work, as do I – and together we can give God the glory! We have a beautiful thing together.

We combine our resources, talents and gifts – working toward the work of the Kingdom and POW! You have something so powerful that the devil himself can't sway.

The difference is incredible and I have been incredibly blessed with partners, just like you reading this book right now. My readers are my partners. My team, I partner with them too. My authors, yes they are partners. My suppliers? Oh, definitely partners. K.B.O students? Yep, they are partners too.

Let's face it, I NEED them to fulfill my purpose (Oh God I thank you for my flock!). I love what I do! And, the truth is, they NEED me, too. When we know that God is the one in our midst we have a boat overfilling situation! Halleluiah!

Consider working with partners. Explain why you changed the name. Your clients and customers will love it. It doesn't matter what business you are in – if you frame yourself with the **'partnership' mentality,** your life just got better.

2. **MRB has a multiplication mentality. They duplicate and make simple systems.**
   It is a great idea to actually think in terms of systemizing everything you do. I have started my business from what seems like the ground up again – adding what I have learned from the Holy Spirit to the success tools I had before.

   I won't get into specifics in this chapter, but I do want you to think carefully about the following questions:

   What can you do (that you currently do over and over every day) to make things run automatically?

This would cover things like creating a F.A.Q page on your website to answer questions for your guests. If you are getting asked the same questions all of the time, why not take the time now to put it all together and not WASTE time every day doing the same old thing over and over. Just as a side note, this is also a great way to write a book! Just sayin....

What can you do to write down the steps you take so that someone else (other than you) can take over? This includes delegation of certain tasks. A great example for you would be the process you take to create your newsletter every month. Is there a step by step technique to getting it done? Can a Virtual Assistant do it? If they can, then this is becomes a procedures manual for them. You will never again be stuck in a situation where one person has all of the control in an area – and no way to duplicate it. If that person gets sick, or moves on... you won't have to re-invent the wheel.

When you have these types of things written down, then you can hire almost anyone to come in and handle the job. It takes a little time now, but later? Oh baby, life is simple and good!

3. **MRB gains fresh perspective from a God's Eye View:**
   We already talked about perspective in previous chapters. Whenever an MRB is faced with a challenge, they look at it from God's point of view.

Ask the Holy Spirit to reveal to you what is really going on in the situation you are facing. Is it about something you need to change? Perhaps it is habits or behaviours? Is it about the other person? Is it even about the situation at hand?

A great way to gain perspective is to continually learn and grow in the word, from great books and mentors. Have an accountability team (ideally all working under the same mentor) that have no problem telling the truth. Stay in prayer. Find someone who is gifted in perspective and ask them to be a part of your team.

This gift is a life-saver (literally and figuratively) for K.B.O's everywhere.

4. **MRB's know that integrity is everything:**

This should go without saying. However, this is one area the devil loves to play in. If he can get you to break your word, he has a good chance of taking over in your life.

It is open season on your business for his little minions.

If you say you are going to be somewhere then be there.

If you say you are doing to do something, do it.

If you are to be somewhere, be ahead of time.

If you, being human, make a mistake – own it, ask for forgiveness, and lovingly correct it – formally un-commit – whatever. Seriously, integrity is everything.

5. **MRB's have an attitude of mentorship:**
   I have already discussed this at great length, but I feel that it is important enough to share more thoughts on this again, right here.

   We must always be learning about our industry, taking courses, reading books and receiving mentoring. We must be learning from the Holy Spirit every day. We must be having great conversations that inspire us to be more, do more and have more under God's grace.

   An attitude of mentorship will change your life. Always know you can learn from your next door neighbour, your clients/partners, your pastors, your friends, your children, your spouse and from nature. God speaks – as K.B.O's we NEED to listen.

6. **MRB's have intimate knowledge that we are all Mentors whether we choose the profession or not:**
   I have said this to my students for years. We are always teaching others how to act and be MRB's. We are mentors to our children, partners, and even the men and women at the grocery store. Act like it! This thought naturally brings me to the next attribute.

7. **MRB's understand the concept, "I am always under surveillance".**

   This is no joke! This is something I take very seriously. Do I always succeed at being my best? No! I wish I could say I do. However, once I really got this thought in my head I understood so much more.

   This is important as we move into places of significance for the Kingdom. satan is always watching us, waiting for an opportunity or an open door to burst open our defenses and get in.

   A good illustration of this is a rule my husband and I put into place. We had heard some other Pastors talking about this very same subject and God began a work of 'warning' for us.

   We never get into a car with a member of the opposite sex by ourselves, NOR are we in a room/meeting by ourselves with a member of the opposite sex (unless it is a family member of course).

   It isn't because we don't trust each other OR the other person. It has nothing to do with that. It is because I know how the enemy's mind works and how he uses situations to try to kill, steal and destroy all that is good.

   This is a protection piece. Being under surveillance seems a bit creepy - but creepy is satan's middle name! In what areas is the enemy watching you under a microscope? Are you giving him any power in that area of life to bring up smoke and mirrors?

8. **MRB's know that they have everything they need at their fingertips:**
   God gives us everything we need at our fingertips to move forward. Sometimes we just don't see it. Sometimes, even just 'knowing' this to be true can bring a paradigm shift in your thinking that results in life changing actions.

   Take stock and inventory of what you do have, then ask God to fill in the rest. Sometimes it is a physical tool, or a characteristic. It may also be a person God has placed in your life.

9. **MRB's have a rule they live by, "Don't Eat Your Seed":**
   Just like a farmer, we should always put away 'seed' to grow our business. I have had many K.B.O clients that struggle with this aspect. For example, if someone buys a product from you, make sure you replace the hard cost from the product into an account where you can manufacture another one. That way you have a never-ending supply to fill the orders that come your way.

10. **MRB's know that they have to give a hand-up NOT a hand out:**
    If I have said it once, I will say it again, "Free has no value!" I am NOT saying the things we get for free are not valuable, look at our salvation! I am saying that

we don't always accomplish what we set out to do when we give away for free things we should be paying for.

Look at what Paul said about this very subject.

[13] *The only thing I failed to do, which I do in the other churches, was to become a financial burden to you. Please forgive me for this wrong!* **2 Corinthians 12:13**

People have to have 'skin' in the game. Often times if they do not put out something of value to them, they will not prosper or use what they were given. If they purchase your product or service, they will find value in what you have to offer.

This goes the other way, too. MRB's know the value of paying for the things they need and want. It boils down to value and respect.

One K.B.O student said to me, "I always try to get what I need by trade or by always asking someone to give me a discount. When you told me that THAT was the reason my business was not succeeding I took a good look at it. I decided to change my 'mind' on this subject. When I started to pay out, people started to pay me! I couldn't believe how quickly my business turned around. AS the bible says, 'You reap what you sow!' Whew! How true!"

I could go on and on about this subject, but I will leave that for our K.B.O. Monthly Mentorship program. For today, don't take my word for this. Check it out for yourself!

11. **MRB's have a call to live a life of generous giving:** I don't think I need to say more… the Word says it all!

A Call to Generous Giving

8 Now I want you to know, dear brothers and sisters, what God in his kindness has done through the churches in Macedonia. [2] They are being tested by many troubles, and they are very poor. But they are also filled with abundant joy, which has overflowed in rich generosity.

[3] For I can testify that they gave not only what they could afford, but far more. And they did it of their own free will. [4] They begged us again and again for the privilege of sharing in the gift for the believers in Jerusalem.[[5] They even did more than we had hoped, for their first action was to give themselves to the Lord and to us, just as God wanted them to do.

[6] So we have urged Titus, who encouraged your giving in the first place, to return to you and encourage you to finish this ministry of giving. [7] Since you excel in so many ways - in your faith, your gifted speakers, your knowledge, your enthusiasm, and your love from us - I want you to excel also in this gracious act of giving.

[8] I am not commanding you to do this. But I am testing how genuine your love is by comparing it with the eagerness of the other churches.

[9] You know the generous grace of our Lord Jesus Christ. Though he was rich, yet for your sakes he became poor, so that by his poverty he could make you rich.

[10] Here is my advice: It would be good for you to finish what you started a year ago. Last year you were the first who wanted to give, and you were the first to begin doing it.
[11] Now you should finish what you started. Let the eagerness you showed in the beginning be matched now by your giving. Give in proportion to what you have.
[12] Whatever you give is acceptable if you give it eagerly. And give according to what you have, not what you don't have.
[13] Of course, I don't mean your giving should make life easy for others and hard for yourselves. I only mean that there should be some equality.
[14] Right now you have plenty and can help those who are in need. Later, they will have plenty and can share with you when you need it. In this way, things will be equal.
[15] As the Scriptures say,

"Those who gathered a lot had nothing left over, and those who gathered only a little had enough." **2 Corinthians 8**

12. **MRB's know, "It's NOT About Me":**
    I had to create a magnet for this to remind me that this business ministry is NOT about me, but about the one who lives and breathes through me. The Father has given me this business for a reason. That reason is to be a MRB.

    Sometimes I get caught up in my own 'schedule' I forget that when certain people call, or certain tasks need to be done, or circumstances occur that feel overwhelming – I need to step aside and let God work through me.

A great example is one I will never forget. I had a particularly flourishing week. I had deadlines on the magazine, Today's Businesswoman; my daughter needed help with her grade 12 final exams; my husband asked me for some time to go through our real estate projects; I had 5 authors ready to go to layout and design; I had just started a new exercise routine (therefore several new habits).

One author in particular, who had put off writing her manuscript forever, sent her manuscript to me and expected the layout and design done within 24 hours! She called, emailed, texted. I explained as best as I could that we had to put it in the docket now because she passed her deadlines 3 times (which I had an open docket for her).

The next day, the process happened again, call, email and text. Call again 2 hours later. Call again and leave another message to call her back.

Feeling frustrated, I knew I was not walking in peace. I put everything down and went to my room to pray. (Ok, maybe I vented a little to the Lord first!). Then I got quiet and listened to him.

Lovingly, he reminded me that this was not about me. He asked me to call her back and ask her why all of the sudden the 'push' was on. I was to ask her what I could do for her. At this time we were not working exclusively with Christians as we are now.

I phoned her and listened to her vent about the fact this process takes too long, what is wrong with me and my company, and things should move along faster. I heard her tell me why it wasn't her fault she didn't get her manuscript in on the deadline dates, that I extended 3 times. I heard her complain that she should not have to be penalized for missing those deadlines even though she agreed to them. When she was done, I simply said,

"I hear you saying that you are feeling frustrated with how long this process has taken. I was just wondering what else is going on in your life right now. How can I help you, not only with this process, but with other things?" I then softly spoke her name and said, "Are you ok my friend?"

She burst out crying to tell me that her father was dying in the hospital. Her husband was also pressuring her because she spent money on several things for her business and never finished the projects. His hours were cut down and there were many people in his company who have been laid off. She was scared that he was going to be next.

I asked if it was ok for me to pray, and she was so very grateful. When I was done praying I said, 'why don't we make a plan of action together?"

I basically gave her the same steps I had given earlier, however this time she could hear them. I am happy to say her book came out and it was a doozy! Awesome! She and her husband both gave their life to Christ – and now she is making an impact around the world.

Yeah, it's not about me! Always seem to need a reminder! How about you?

13. **MRB's have strength in perseverance**:
    In my life, was there any time when I felt like giving up? OH YES! While we were going through our desolate wasteland experience there were 3 times I can say I truly wanted to give up. I had had it with everything we were doing. It was so hard to keep working toward a goal that seemed unproductive.

    I pushed into God more and more through each of these times. What kept me going were the words the Lord spoke to me one day when I was complaining about things.

    'O.K let's say you decide to quit helping people write and publish their books. Let's say you close down the magazine and you don't write anymore for it. How about you quit writing your books, mentoring people, and praying for people? Then what? WHAT IS THE ALTERNATIVE?"

    Oh my Gosh! Scary! If I throw away my dream, what would the alternative be? What would I do if I had nothing on my plate anymore?

The funny thing is, I would most likely end up gravitating back to what I am doing now. I learned to give up my 'complainer attitude' and decided to put on my 'sustainer attitude'.

"Success happens when you give up the ' complainer' and decide instead to be a 'sustainer'." – **Kathleen D. Mailer**

I was never ever going to give up! I decided I would persevere if it meant that we had to lose everything. That was it! Now that we are through the process, God has made it better than we could have imagined. Being on this side of the learning curve is nothing if not awesome.

[7] *But as for you, be strong and courageous, for your work will be rewarded.* **2 Chronicles 15:7**

14. **MRB's know the difference between, Perfection vs Pure-Affection.**

This is, simply put: perfectionism kills. It causes you to live under a constant strain of people pleasing. When we are trying to please people only, we offend God. Truly, it is time to hang up the 'good ol' perfectionist' attitude and decide it is more about the people we are leading.

"God doesn't want perfection, he wants pure-affection" **– Kathleen D. Mailer**

15. **MRB's keep everything relevant:**

You need to be in constant update mentality. Lovingly correct your behaviours, your products, your services, your team. You have to make things relevant to the people you lead. If you are too 'preachy' or 'pushy', you end up pushing people away.

Help others to see what is in it for them, and you will find your relationships in business will grow, sustain, find grace and mercy. It will be a wonderful life to live.

16. **MRB's live a prayer filled life:**
The power of prayer is so important. You need to pray for direction. You need to pray for wisdom. You need to pray for your flock, family, and your business. You need to pray for doors to open or to close. You need to live a life in constant communication with the Lord.

When you do, all things will be added unto you! God will fill your heart, your life, your health, your finances, your home, your entire being with His presence. Best present ever!

17. **MRB's live authentic lives:**
In the same way let your light shine before men that they may see your good deeds and praise your Father in Heaven. **Matthew 5:6**

MRB's are real! When I speak I hear that statement all of the time. "Kathleen you are so real! I love that about you! I feel I know you. I feel I can relate to what you are saying."

You want to be authentic and real. There is nothing to hide! You are who you are. Let people know that you, too are a work in progress. After all, no one is perfect! The only perfect one did a lot of work to help us to walk toward being the best we can be.

18. **MRB's walk in compassionate leadership:**
Always chose compassion even when you are in the 'right'. When you do you will find that you can accomplish so much more. Your understanding and wisdom will grow each and every day. You will become more like our Master, Jesus. You will reach out. You will touch someone's heart, and life. You make an impact in the world around you.

Compassion will lead to you pouring into projects that the Lord will be proud of. On that day of Judgement, you will hopefully find him saying, "Well done, good and faithful servant!"

Remember, people have issues, just as you do. Look past them and 'see' the person that God sees. Help to lead them through their obstacles - so they too can see who they are in Christ.

19. **MRB's are always lifting others up:**
One of my favourite scriptures of the bible is:

"So encourage each other and build each other up, just as you are already doing." **1 Thessalonians 5:11**

MRB's are natural encouragers. Our attitude is one of always lifting up others to help them see who they truly are in Christ. Because this is a natural gift for me, I had never stopped to realize how important this one attribute is to the body of Christ.

I often speak about how when one is gifted in an area, they don't always see it as a gift. They think, 'doesn't everybody act like this?" Do you know what I am saying? It was the same for me in this area. I remember vividly when I realized that, 'no, Kathleen, not everyone acts like this – AND - so many people desperately need that encouragement."

I was speaking to a K.B.O. who was in her 60's - obviously gifted in so many areas of life. She had finished a great project that had made an impact on the lives of so many people. It was a tremendous accomplishment. I was so thrilled for her! I felt the nudge in prayer, as I was praising God for what He was doing in her life, to send her flowers. The response to that floored me! I could barely hear her speak through tears and sobs.

She told me that no one. NOT ONE person ever gave her flowers! NOT ONE! Not for her graduation (high school, university, other…), not when she had her children. Not even for her wedding shower or her wedding (she bought her own). Her secret desire was to be acknowledged one day for the good she had done…. and have flowers show up at her door with a note that would speak to her heart!

After that, I had several K.B.O's speak to me about how alone they felt; how no one ever encouraged them - the way I do; how they always feel uplifted after talking to me.

It was then I began to see a new perspective through God's eyes… it is hard for people to be encouragers if they have never been encouraged.

Take heart dear one, if this is you. Simply sit down and ask the Holy Spirit how it is done! Read how Jesus made people feel. Watch what he has done. Think about how you would want to be encouraged. What are things that you would want to hear? Start to use the SAME things you write down to encourage others around you. What you give out, you get back!

Hmm… I must have read that somewhere. Have you heard that before? (SMILES).

20. **MRB's master the art of discipline:**

We have talked about this already earlier in this book. I won't go into great detail, but discipline is very important to an MRB. It takes discipline to put God first. It takes discipline to put others first. As a matter of fact, if you take a look at the root of discipline you will find 'disciple' - being one of Jesus' disciples is being the BEST you can be.

Study their lives. Study their habits. Study what they did - in the name of Jesus… teach, write books, heal, share the good news, release the captives, set free the oppressed, help the blind to see, have a relationship with Christ. I could continue.

If you get the picture, then get the picture of YOU as one of his dear ones. Why? YOU ARE! Help others to be disciples by becoming more and more disciplined.

21. **MRB's have learned how to be great decision makers:**

We all know that we have to understand what it takes to make not just good, but GREAT decisions. I know that the more success you have, the more decisions you will have to make. The more decisions you have to make, the quicker the process MUST become.

If we lack in this area, we find ourselves getting into trouble. I liken it to being 'double minded'.

Here is what the bible says about that!

7 For that man ought not to expect that he will receive anything from the Lord, 8being a double-minded man, unstable in all his ways. **James 1: 7-8**

We are called to solve problems as K.B.O's – that means quick decisions filled with wisdom.

22. **MRB's have the heart of a server:**

As an MRB - we have to remember the 'WHY' we serve the Lord. We must never lose or 'wonder' at the situation. We must always be in awe of who he is.

An MRB has a servant heart when he/she easily remembers this scripture,

But thanks be to God that, though you used to be slaves to sin, you have come to obey from your heart the pattern of teaching that has now claimed your allegiance. **Romans 6:17 NIV**

23. **MRB's keep the vision first and foremost:**
As a MRB, we are called to keep the vision as we lead others through their desolate wasteland We will need to remind our team where and why we are going on a continual basis. AND, there are times we will need to remind ourselves where and why we are going!

I love the way the KJV captures this scripture:

18 *Where there is no vision, the people perish: but he that keepeth the law, happy is he.* **Proverbs 29:18 KJV**

24. **MRB's have learned to walk humbly:**
James says it best so I won't try and re-create it here. Of course, we go into greater detail in the K.B.O. Monthly Mentorship program. It is SO vital to who we are, and what we are called to do.

This is one attribute that is hard to maintain for those who are called to greatness. I pray this scripture becomes a prayer for you daily. Why? Because you, my friend, are one that is called to greatness!

7 So humble yourselves before God. Resist the Devil, and he will flee from you. 8 Draw close to God, and God will draw close to you. Wash your hands, you sinners; purify your hearts, you hypocrites. 9 Let there be tears for the wrong things you have done. Let there be sorrow and deep grief. Let there be sadness instead of laughter, and gloom instead of joy.

10 When you bow down before the Lord and admit your dependence on him, he will lift you up and give you honour. 11 Don't speak evil against each other, my dear brothers and sisters. If you criticize each other and condemn each other, then you are criticizing and condemning God's law. But you are not a judge who can decide whether the law is right or wrong. Your job is to obey it. 12 God alone, who made the law, can rightly judge among us. He alone has the power to save or to destroy. So what right do you have to condemn your neighbour? 13 Look here, you people who say, "Today or tomorrow we are going to a certain town and will stay there a year. We will do business there and make a profit." 14 How do you know what will happen tomorrow? For your life is like the morning fog -- it's here a little while, then it's gone. 15 What you ought to say is, "If the Lord wants us to, we will live and do this or that." **James 4:7-15**

25. **MRB's are team players:** Jesus led a team! He played on team! He lived and breathed team.

As an MRB, you have to have a team mentality. With a team, you have the ability to create a movement. This is something bigger than just a marketing platform. These are radical, life changing, culture changing, world changing, and paradigm shifting concepts I am talking about. And you can't do it alone.

"If you want to create a movement you must first join a movement." – **Kathleen D. Mailer**

26. **MRB's love the local church:**
It is obvious we would love the local church, especially if our mandate is to reach nations. Jesus loves her, we love her too.

Our church takes care of those we evangelize as we go through our business ministry. It is a place we can honour God and we can take our tithes and offerings. They help us to multiply our talents, gifts, and our time! They do the day to day things, in our community and beyond, that need to get done.

The relationships we build within these walls of the church, become a foundation to how we do business and life. Everything you experience in your business ministry with regard to relationships will play out right there, within the body. When you are dedicated and committed to your church – you work at becoming a vital part of this living and breathing organism.

This is a place where you have someone to cover you, protect you, love on you, mentor you, take care of you and have your back. As an MRB, you NEED this.

You can't be a loner in ministry anymore. You must have the power and the authority that Christ gave the church walking with you as you venture out.

Oh yes, your local church is what you live for – sending new babies in Christ to find a home; sending others to be part of your community.

It is also the place in which we do corporate worship – when we need to recharge, refuel, revitalize, grow and learn.

We are called to 'fund' the Kingdom purposes – and the church executes these purposes well.

You need a faith-filled, Holy Spirit led, Bible believing, born again church to plant your roots in so that you will not be blown over by the strong winds of the enemy. That is why I am firmly planted in our church. I pray you are too!

I am for the **Christ's local church of nations**… I am called to equip, empower, and encourage Pastors, Trainers and Business Leaders so that their church can be a vital, leading-edged, faith finding, relevant, community reaching church – wherever it may be.

Wherever I speak in the world, I am there for any and every church that has Jesus' vision. It is time for us to RISE UP! LINK ARMS! BUILD RELATIONSHIPS regardless of denomination and theology. We need to get the good news of Christ to the world. It is an urgent, powerful time in the history of world. Let's join in peace – we need each other!

27. **MRB's wake up with God every morning:**

A 'God first' lifestyle is truly the cornerstone every MRB works from. Put Him first with our tithes and offerings. Put Him first – the first day of the week. Put Him first - with your first morning wake up. AND, as the Bible assures, we will be blessed!

The more blessed we are, the more we can be a blessing! The more we can be a blessing, the more blessed we are… this is one cycle I do NOT want to break! It comes from putting God first every morning.

I wake up with a worshipful heart first thing. I pray before I get out of bed. I take my quiet time with a pen and paper in my hand – and my bible – and I talk to God. I write down what He says to me - for me – for others - for his business.

I have come to LOVE my time. The habit wasn't always there, and I still realize that I need to set a time first thing in the morning (mine is 6AM). Make it an everyday occurence of each week. Make it a solid, vast part of your make up. You will see success like you have never seen before.

Jesus is inspiring, motivating, awe-creating, wonderful, counselling, forgiving, peacemaking, and a whole lot more.

This is one lifestyle habit you will most definitely NOT regret! I will pray for you, as I did for myself, that Jesus will help you put this into practice.

The Holy Spirit is nudging me on right now to share this with you: I need to answer the question, "Kathleen, is it ok if I do it later in the day as I am not a morning person?"

It is always ok to do it later in the day! AND – waking up in the morning and giving God your FIRST of the day is the whole point of this.

Jesus did it, we should do it. I hated getting out of bed in the morning at first, too. But the truth is, I started to love the time more. The more I did, the less I fought it. The less I fought it, the easier it became.

Very early in the morning, while it was still dark, Jesus got up, left the house and went off to a solitary place, where he prayed. **Mark 1:3-5 NIV**

Let's put the word into action,

1. Go through the checklist above. Check off as many as apply to you.
2. Write down the things you want to change in your life, or add to your life.
3. Create steps and space to incorporate new belief systems into play.
4. Do a check every month, and see how many of these things change as you grow and learn this next 12 months.
5. There are, obviously, many more attributes I could mention. When you think of them, write them down for yourself. Are you walking in those great leadership steps?
6. Study the life of Jesus and continue to grow and expand your skills to become the BEST MRB ever!

Let me pray for you,

Father I pray that this K.B.O. reading this now understands the power of being a MRB. I pray that this chapter will grow for them, in their mind, in their soul and in their business. Give them what they need to succeed, dear Holy Spirit. Let my heart stand with them as they become the ministers they are called to be. In Jesus name, Amen

CHAPTER FOURTEEN

Building Your Success Team

God has stepped in and you have stepped out. He is calling you to bigger and greater things. The only problem is, you have no idea how to plan for this let alone execute it. You have to know that you are in the right place!

When we realize that we have absolutely no clue how to bring something of this magnitude about. We know we are walking in God's purpose for our life. When we can't do it on our own, he rejoices. The only way we are going to get there is through relationship and grace with the Father, Son and the Holy Spirit!

I know it can feel uncomfortable right now. You might even feel a little lost, or overwhelmed. God knows I have felt this MANY times on my journey to where I am today. I want to encourage you by sharing with you my definition of overwhelm.

"Overwhelm is God's set up for breakthrough!"
– Kathleen D. Mailer

If you are feeling like this is too big for your britches, that is a correct feeling. As K.B.O's we often feel that we are meant to do things on our own. We are leaders after all, right? The truth is, the Master Relationship Builder himself, Jesus - had a team around him too. Why would we think we should be any different.

God wants us to be in relationship with our brothers and sisters. He wants us to work together to grow and learn. He wants us to put Him in our midst and take care of the 'family business'. In order to do that, we need to build a success team.

Simply put, you do need to fine-tune what you are good at and farm out the rest! You need to find other people who are aligned with your goals and ambitions to change the world. They ARE out there! I promise you that. The problem that you may be having is finding the right people.

When you have gone as far as you can go, that is the right time to bring in new, fresh faces. God has called many others to their destiny under the same mandate as you've been called. He wants us to help one another.

In the secular world, we have learned the fear of competition. In Kingdom alliances, we realize there is no such thing. If we pool our resources, tools, and gifts, we can help others reach their goals and accomplish our own objectives.

A great example is my friend Christie Love with *LeadHer*, a wonderful networking group, has the same mandate as Today's Businesswoman magazine - to encourage, equip, and educate. If I believed in competition, I would never have contacted her. When I did, much to my delight, I found a warm and generous person who cares about those whom God has asked her to look after. Just as we do! We will work together to accomplish God's true desire, and He will get all of the glory as we watch people change and receive healings and miracles every day. That's our God.

If you do not reach out and align with others whose destinies fit within the sphere of your assignment, you are not only holding yourself back, but them too. Isn't it time you went beyond your own limitations? Let's find out whom, exactly, you should have on your team so things will start to happen faster and more easily. Once you build a team of powerful beautiful people, you will find our life much more joy-filled, less stressful, and exciting.

Let me give you a reminder of whom you should have on your team. This isn't to leave out your wonderful flock whom God has called you to Sheppard. Remember, there is power in your NET-work and your NET-worth will grow!

Here is an idea generator of those you may want to have on your team.

1. **Prayer team:** These are the people who want to pray with you and for you. It is important that you schedule a perfect time when you are all praying. My team, the department editors of this magazine, pray almost every morning - Monday through Friday. We pray for the magazine, for ourselves, for our readers, for our team, for our distributors. We pray for the content, for our cover person. We pray for breakthrough, healings, and that which allows us to link arms and eradicate poverty in the nations, one businesswoman at a time. As I mentioned to you before, it is imperative that you keep prayer central in your life.

2. **Intercessory prayer team:** These are the people around the world who pray for you, a continual support - offering wisdom, discernment, and assurance that your plan works like a well-oiled machine. They take care of so many people. They are a covering so you can move boldly into the plans and purposes God has for your life.

3. **Church:** You need a good church! Why? It IS a very good way to continue to learn and grow, but you NEED the spiritual support and family-bonding aspect of a great church. My church is amazing. They really believe in me and my business ministry. If your church doesn't believe that business is a good thing, OR perhaps believes that you are only good for paying the tithe, then I respectfully say that you need a new church. This could get me into hot water, but I DO know the difference between a church that believes in you (increases your faith) and one that doesn't. It is miraculous what you can do with the right church family. Be sure to gain access to a faith based, bible believing church. You need all of the help you can get!

4. **Spiritual Leadership:** You need a good spiritual leader helping and guiding you on life's journey. He or she can encourage you, pray for you, and sometimes give you the prophecy you need to hear.

5. **Mentor:** You need practical leadership - someone who has done what you want to do or knows something you need to learn. You need to find a mentor who will help you become a MASTER with your God-given gifts. Our magazine is a good example of practical mentorship. Every quarter you examine

your goals and move forward. Having a mentor will keep you on track and focused.

6. **Health Coach:** You need advice on eating right, exercising right, and learning how to manage your body. You need energy to do what you need to do in this lifetime. If you can't cope physically, you will find so many more obstacles that you need to overcome.

7. **Family:** Get your family on board as best you can. I know I can hear the screaming and the temper tantrums already: "Kathleen, MY spouse never supports me in anything I do, so I can't reach my goals because he is always pushing me down or sabotaging me!" I respectfully say this to you: Truly, I DO know that some of you are going through a very hard time in this respect. Find another family member you can count on. Family is someone you choose; a relative is bonded to you by blood.

8. **Virtual or personal assistant:** The need speaks for itself!

9. **Mortgage Broker:** Sooner or later, you will be called to "take the land". Real estate adds value to your portfolio, whether it is investing, for living, or to house your dreams. Remember that as you grow.

10. **Realtor:** Need I say more?

11. **Public Relations person:** Get your face out there so people can see it. Seriously, if you want your light to shine, you've got to get up to the top of the tower. That is why we

don't believe in advertising - we believe in marketing. We want your voice to be heard!

12. **Dentist:** Yep, it is important, just like the next two team members are.

13. **Doctor:** Check

14. **Salespeople:** Can you imagine if there were more people out there sharing your message? Would it help them? You? Your client/partners? I am thinking, yeah!

15. **Printer:** you need to make sure your marketing materials and products go to the next level

16. **Money Lender:** This could be investors, bankers, or other provision opportunities.

17. **Investment advisor:** You will be making money, and you need to be a good steward of it! Be prepared to prosper!

18. **Insurance agent:** personal, business, health, dental

19. **Financial advisor:** Sometimes you need funds! Or someone on your team to help counsel you on which way to go!

20. **Networking/Event coordinators:** good source of information from likeminded people

21. **Breakthrough Coach:** someone who can see what stops you and helps you break free!

22. **Website professionals:** People who really know about marketing and S.E.O. (if you don't know what that means, YOU NEED THIS PERSON!)

23. **Personal Stylist:** You MUST dress for success.

24. **Optometrist:** Yep, them too.

25. **Nanny/daycare provider**

There most likely are many others, but this gives you a good list to start the creative juices flowing.

Let's put this plan into action,

1. **Decide who you need on your team** - pray about it.

2. **Ask others you trust**, in your church, online, or in your community. We have a great community on Facebook (Today's Businesswoman Magazine) where you can connect with the people you need to. The C.C.K.B.O's are building a network behind the scenes for this very reason.

3. Start by **contacting prospective team member** via email. Be sure to thank them for their time. Tell them clearly what/whom you are looking for and what your goals and dreams are (be concise!!!). Ask them what their personal ambitions are, and whether your goals are compatible with what they want to achieve. If everything seems to match at this point, ask them if you could set up an appointment. This is the next step. OR, if they have a website, check it out to learn more about them.

4. Ask the question: **How can I help you reach your goals?** Remember it isn't about you? Help them succeed and you will find, by God's grace, they are exactly who you need too.

5. **Make an agreement** that is mutually beneficial. Do not underestimate the value of excellent expertise! Pay someone what they are worth! Joint Venture with them. Bless someone with a bonus if you feel they went above and beyond. You reap what you sow!

Position yourself to prosper! Watch the time and money you'll save and the things you'll get accomplished!

If it is not a fit, no problem, simply say… "NEXT!"

Let me pray for you,

Lord I am asking for divine appointments to begin happening even as we read this chapter. We know you have everyone that we are to partner with already sitting there. This is your business Lord, and I know you are ready, willing and able to take care of this business. I pray an anointing of divine appointments come into play as we give you our list of people we know we need.

I also ask now Lord for revelation. If we are missing something/someone important on our list, I pray that you show us right away who that maybe. I also pray that if these appointments are not aligned with your plans, you reveal that to us too. Lord, it is your business and we are ready, willing and able to boldly move forward to connect as you would have us do. In Jesus name, Amen

May you find the right people, at the right place, at the right time! May your business now move above and beyond your wildest dreams.

SECTION TWO

CREATE A PLATFORM THAT PAYS

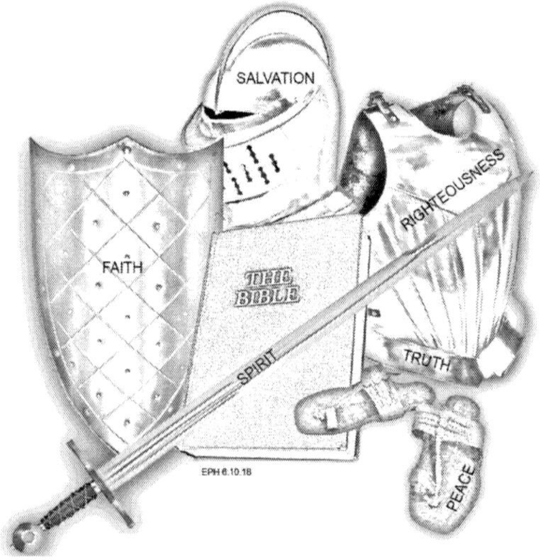
SALVATION
FAITH
THE BIBLE
RIGHTEOUSNESS
SPIRIT
TRUTH
EPH 6.10.18
PEACE

CHAPTER FIFTEEN

Mailer Business Model, You Need 3 Pillars Of Income to Weather Any Storm

***"God is the same yesterday as He is today and He will be tomorrow."* (Hebrews 13:8)**

What I love about this scripture is that God shows us how reliable and dependable he truly is. Since we are made in His image, we need to realize that we need to replicate this security and safe place within the walls of our business.

Let's review where we are right now:

1. **Do we have the foundation securely in place?** Are we solid on the "rock"? Do we understand that our business is our ministry? Do we really get that we are Master Relationship Builders? Do we do the Lord's work every day? Do we seek HIM first? If we can say yes to these questions we can check the "foundation set" as "DONE".
2. Now – **look for the cornerstone**. It is with this anchor that we can make sure the rest of this structure is firmly in place. Jesus is the cornerstone - my Bible tells me that is true. Jesus is Lord - Money is a tool - my heart is for Him. All set? CHECK!
3. NOW… we need to **put the pillars into place** in order to build a Godly stronghold for our business to grow.

Just a reminder that as K.B.O.'s we are to "fund Kingdom Purposes through our Business Ministry"... which means we need to get down to the business of making money.

Why don't we start by setting up the 3 Pillars of Income so that we can weather ANY storm that life may bring?

This is what I call the,
"Mailer Business Model" **- The Three Pillars of Income**

It is a "system" that really works!

Imagine with me 3 different pillars in front of you. Each pillar has a mantel with the words, Immediate, Intermediate and Legacy etched in its foundation making it steadfast and true in your house of business.

Pillar 1 Immediate Income - This is where money is coming in as a simple exchange, a product for cash - right now in the immediate moment.

Pillar 2 Intermediate Income - This is where you know how much money is coming in each and every month for a pre-determined length of time. This will help you to budget, count on your bills being paid and create financial freedom. This is set up so that there is little or no effort on your part - you KNOW for the next 6, 12 or 18 months how much is coming into your storehouse. No matter what – you have security.

Pillar 3 Legacy Income - This is money that comes in from now until eternity. This is often where you have residual income set up so that not only are you financially free, but your family will be free too. It comes in whether you work or not. You can be called to do what you need to do, yet you and your family are taken care of. This is an excellent resource to have – to fund those special projects that tug your heart - for the lifetime of the project! That's got your interest right? I will give you more about this later.

Now, obviously there is much more to cover on this topic than I can share in a few pages – but I hope that these pages will give you some grounding and education to get you set up and ready to prosper in a way that you have never done before.

Let's take a closer look at these three pillars and start to implement them into our lives.

IMMEDIATE INCOME:

As I mentioned, this is where we can go out and create money to come in at a moment's notice. This is where you have a PRODUCT (not a service) that you can sell and someone gives you cash for it. It is an exchange, product for cash.

Since I work so closely with K.B.O.'s who have a book, all my examples in this next section will be given from that point of view. **I believe that EVERY business owner SHOULD**

have a book (and later I will give you all of the reasons why). I just want to plant that seed right now for you – as you work through the set-up and process of creating immediate income in your business.

Please remember, there is POWER in your testimony – and it is time that Christian entrepreneurs begin to see this incredible opportunity at their fingertips.

Here is the example of immediate income: Simply put, I give you a copy of my book, and you give me $40.00. That is immediate income. It is a simple exchange for product and cash.

Every business must have an immediate income system and stream in order to make it in business. The beauty of this is that YOU are always in control of how much money you make and how much work you put into something. As you go about your business, you have something right with you which you are passionate about - that you can share with a prospect. It helps you to start a relationship with a "taste" of who you are and what you do. Those bigger ticket items can be immediate income earners, too – but often, new people love a "sample" of who you are and what you do. In my opinion, nothing says it better than a book!

This works for other products too! Not just books. Let me share a few ideas off the top of my head here. If you are in a coffee company – bring your product! If you are catalogue sales, make sure you have some popular "products" on hand to share and sell.

If you are in a service related industry like Real Estate, figure out what you can have for immediate income. A book is an excellent product to create. Many of your clients have questions, concerns, or problems that you can solve via information. Imagine if, for every tire kicker you get – someone gave you $20.00. How much would your income grow in one year? Not to mention, you are an expert - when they ARE ready, they will think of you first!

What about you? What do you have at your fingertips right now that you can sell to get cash flow immediately?

Let's take some time right now to put your thoughts on paper – and see how you can incorporate immediate income into your house of business.

- Make a list of all of the immediate income streams in your business.
- If you don't have one you are passionate about - create one. What would that look like? Think about (if you don't have this already) writing a book or another information product that you can sell immediately. What problem do you have information enough about to sell? (Remember a book doesn't have to be 200 pages to be effective).
- Do you have a systemized approach to bringing the immediate income in?

  Using our example of a book above – here is an easy and effective way of making sure you are ready for God to bring divine appointments and bless you financially.

Your Immediate Income Tool Kit Includes:

1. Your product (a stack of books for sale in your vehicle) or at least one for "show."
2. An invoice/receipt system. I use a printer to create a "sell page" with carbonless copies. One for me, one for the customer. It is a way of writing ALL contact information and taking convenient payment options.
3. Yes, the ability to receive credit card orders is VERY important in business today. There are many options available to you - no matter where you are in business. It is also important to note on these invoices that you have your contact information to make it easier for your new client to come to you if they lose your card.
4. Your business cards: always offer them two. "Take one and give one to a friend."
5. Your word that you will connect with them in a week (or some pre-determined time) to see how they liked it and if they would have any other questions for you at that time.
6. Your day timer. Schedule it RIGHT NOW - to get back to that person. Your constant contact leads to a relationship-building place – where they KNOW they can count on you.

Don't despise these small beginnings and don't be so quick to dismiss this process because it isn't a $2000 sale! I happen to know of one of my K.B.O's who started with my mentorship over 15 years ago at the time of this writing.

He always carried his books in his car to go out at a moment's notice to have for sale, gain speaking engagements, or give as a thank you to someone who had blessed him. He ALWAYS had a constant stream of cash flow even in the most unbelievable situations. Why? His message is imperative in ANY setting, because there is POWER in his testimony.

God is good, he will make a way and if you are ready for it, he will use this platform to help you grow your business.

INTERMEDIATE INCOME:

I want you to think more about implementing intermediate income into your business. This is an income system that brings in a set amount of money in for a set amount of time.

You can think about things like having a membership, a monthly program, a continued education platform, a consumable product every month delivered to your customer's home.

Let me give you some real examples of a few things I was able to help my students put into practice over the years.

Flower shop owner: I helped her to create and introduce the, *"Romance Your Wife"* program. She partnered (remember how we use the word 'partner' now instead of 'customer'?) with top male executives, high earning real estate representatives, company directors that travel a lot.

1. She had them fill out a form on her website (setting up automatic systems are crucial to your success - more later).

2. They told her their wives special dates - including birthday, anniversary, date of the first kiss, special occasions that make her know she is loved.
3. Of course, the obvious, Christmas and other holidays that are important.
4. She asked questions about his wife's favourite things: flowers, chocolates, jewellery etc.

When she had her background in place she recommended a specialized program. Her partner would be billed once per month, once per week, or even bi-weekly to suit his needs.

She then expanded her flower shop line to be sure she had products that would fit into certain categories.

Delivered to this special woman's door were flowers, notes, chocolates and other specialized gift items from the man that cares. He got an email reminder 1 week before the delivery and the day of.

Needless to say she found it fulfilling and was able to create intermediate income on the platform.

Each package she provided (Bronze, Silver, Gold and Platinum) had a per month fee attached to it: $250/month for 18 months - charged to his credit card – gave her security in her business. Her client? Priceless!

Think about this for a moment. What if she had 100 executives doing this each and every month? Would this help her business? That is right, you do the math: $250 x 100= $250,000 in sales each and every month! How many months until this woman becomes a millionaire? How much can she give every month to feed widows and orphans, free women from the sex trade, care for her neighbours at home?

Whoa! I just felt some excitement leap to the forefront as the Holy Spirit just hit someone as they read this.

You can do this too, in your business. Let me give you more examples.

My friend, a **Pastor** who works tirelessly for the gospel in Asia, just informed me that she has found the perfect building for their church and she can use the top floors for lease of office space and a gym etc. This is great intermediate income (and could actually fall into the Legacy category). What she needed was more ways to cash flow this property.

When she asked for my help, she told me that the huge wall of the building faced two main interstate highways, so the building was very visible to tens of thousands of people every week. The Holy Spirit nudged me that she needed intermediate income to put toward her ministry. She had to know she was making money every month for the next 6 -18 months.

What came to mind is a billboard business. On the side of the building she could put a banner ad for the CHURCH FIRST… then under it – build an income from leasing bill board space for a 12 month contract. Even if she charged big name companies only $1000 per month and she could fit only 5 banners (besides the church) - that is $5000/month on contract for the next 12 months. She could break it up into categories and set up $1000 for a large banner, $700 for half sized banner… that means she could make more selling ½ sized banners, am I right?

Do you have 'real estate' that you are not using right now? We have done it on our prosperity and it has evolved to a much bigger place and purpose. This plan will be used so one of our properties can take care of all of the bills and expenses, thus making it fully functioning on its own and giving the over-abundance to our many international/local projects that need monthly income to survive.

God is about leverage and multiplication. The more you give, the more HE gives to you. Solving people's problems is not just a 'one shot deal'… it can stretch to something long term.

Just like my student at the flower shop: solving a one shot problem with the "I'm sorry I missed your special day bouquet"… into a problem solving monthly program.

Let me give you one more example before we close this section. Truthfully, I would love to give you tons of ideas all day long. This avenue of wealth building is something that really excites me. I love the freedom we all can get from it.

If you are a **counsellor/therapist/trainer/chiropractor** - you should pay special attention to details here. One of our Aurora Partners came to me with a wealth of information that was built up inside of him. He is a therapist and had developed a strategy to help people break free from limitations and addictions in their life. He had been in business for nearly 40 years and he felt he had to do something.

Of course, I told him he needed to write a book – and THAT he did! Oh my goodness! I have helped thousands of students write their books. There has not been even one that has taken me completely by surprise like Dr. Tim did! Oh no.

Many times at our boot camps I have writers ask me, "How long should my book be?" My answer is ALWAYS the same! Write it until you are done! If you use the formula I teach in the workshop it is easy to follow and flow.

He took me at my word and the next week he delivered his manuscript. He loved the formula so much because it freed him up to keep focused. He printed his manuscript off and set it on the table in front of me.

At first I thought it was a joke. Then… I realized he was dead serious! He said he was motivated to finish his book. It was literally two feet high! I kid you not! Upon closer inspection I realized the first small portion was his book – and the rest was his coaching program. Not just ANY coaching program but a specialized TRAINING program that he could teach others (in order to teach his material). It was a 'Train the Trainers' type of coaching plan.

A coaching program is an extension of what you write in your book. It is taking your reader by the hand to go deeper with you. A book, as you will find out, is the lead generator and a way to connect…a coaching program or monthly training program which takes you into a deeper relationship and allows you to expand your impact on people and the world.

We packaged his information to automatically send out a monthly workbook, DVD, CD and goal setting for $250/month. The initial training (done once per year at a live event) was $2997.00. It also included a 'wholesale' element to it - meaning the Trainers could buy his books, tapes, and other products for a wholesale price and sell it at retail in their own practices.

This procedure will build great income for you. I have done it before and it changed our lives. My husband was able to retire because of a program similar to this (he was 36 and I was 34). If we stayed at the same standard of living – we could live comfortably. I want you to truly digest what I am saying here. It can be a life changer.

In full disclosure – I am doing it again. Walk with me as I unfold this thought a little more for you. I would like for you to truly experience the reality that you too, can add this strategy to your portfolio. When you do, it will be like a rose, slowly opening its petals and sharing its delightful aroma and unsurpassed beauty as you drink it in with your eyes.

This very book, "Prepare To Prosper, Taking Your Business To A Higher Level" - will become the lead generator I need to start to build my relationship with you, a partner and a K.B.O for God's army. My prayer is that you get a ton of value from my gift of time; that you begin to see with clarity your passion, purpose and platform.

I am also in the process of building the *K.B.O. Monthly Mentorship Program* – that helps K.B.O's expand and grow their business. It helps you set and achieve GODLY goals. It gives you monthly encouragement, prayer partners, and tools (right to the comfort of your computer) to help you grow and expand your business. It covers the ins and outs of platform building and introduces you to the right people you need in order to succeed.

There are several levels – that range from $9/month - $49/month - $97/month - $297/month. This depends on your circumstances and strategy.

This program is set up to build our K.B.O movement and equip churches and Christian business networks with tools and helps – to build business ministry.

All of that will create immediate, intermediate and legacy income for me, my family and, most importantly, the ministry projects God calls us to fund. It is time to evangelize the nations and that takes money. As K.B.O's we have to step up to the plate and pour ourselves into the purposes of God. Time is getting short – ours – and the rest of the world's.

You can do the math - but understanding intermediate income is paramount in your business. Take the time TODAY to sit down with the Holy Spirit and brainstorm. Take stock of what you have, like the woman with the oil in the bible. All she had was a little bit of oil – but God used it for her to start a business. He used it to get her out of debt. He used it to make her a strong, pillar in her community. God will use what you have, too. If we just think differently he can come in and change our lives!

LEGACY INCOME

After you create a solid system where immediate income can come into place, and then add the intermediate pillar into your house of business – you really need to extend that to a Legacy Income portfolio.

Legacy income is simply that: Money that comes in on a regular basis for the rest of your life - investments for the future of your children and the continuation of sharing the good news with the world.

Some examples of Legacy income are as follows: royalties, real estate, licencing agreements, automatic membership, programs, multi-level marketing companies, investments. Not ALL of these things are created equally and not all of them can be legacy income. However, if you work right with the Lord – there can be place where this money can come in no matter what, alive or dead, for generations to come.

For my purposes in this book - I won't delve deep into this practice. I just want you to think about this now and decide to start to add something to your portfolio that would fall into the legacy category.

You need all three pillars to build a safe, secure building as we move forward into creating a Platform That Pays. As we do, more ideas and logistics will be shared.

Putting the Word into action:

Let's recap our time together.

1) Create a system for **immediate income**. Then put together your tool kit and have it with you at all times. Be ready, willing and able for God to use this to bless others AND bless you for your obedience.
2) Add a system in place that will bring about **intermediate income**. Work towards solving a reoccurring problem your flock may have. Solve the problem and get blessed. Be sure to have clear paperwork that people must sign as they go into contract with you. You don't help anyone unless they commit. Commitment is truly key for you, for me, for everybody.
3) Start to write down ideas and do research on what types of things constitute **legacy income.** In your day timer, book in certain days that you will sit down with the Lord and 'think' together. Keep track of all of the downloads he has given you. There may be many 'million dollar' ideas.

Let us pray,

Father I thank you for this Kingdom business that you are expanding right now. I pray for wisdom for the owner. I pray for a peace and a joy of discovery. I pray that she/he is able to glean what they need to from this chapter. I pray, Holy Spirit for more grace to come on to him/her right now in Jesus name. We praise you Lord. Thank you for allowing us to serve our flock and be YOUR hands and feet today. In Jesus mighty name I pray, AMEN

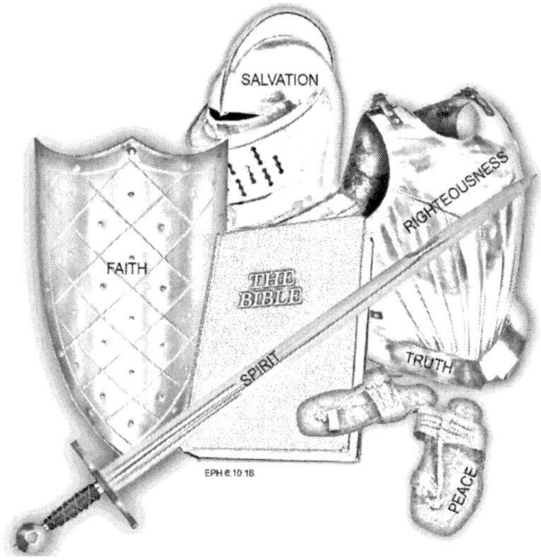

(c) 2014 Kathleen Mailer - KBO

CHAPTER SIXTEEN

It's Not God Enough to be Good Enough. Become An Expert.

I am truly very excited about this next stage of our journey. We have walked through a ton of information and I know that you will reference the last section over and over. It was designed to give you foundational principles to help guide you through the learning process.

I pray that you take each and every section and really work it through. Set time aside in your day timer over the course of the next 12 months and 'plan' your learning curve. I would love to hear about your successes through the process! Feel free to connect with me and share! My contact information is at the end of the book. I hope I have a chance one day to meet you face to face, if not - social media is the next best thing! Don't you agree?

Here is an quick overview of what we have previously covered,

Now that we have done everything to prepare, we must intentionally position ourself so that we can channel all of the blessings of God into a vehicle, a system, or a focal point.

There are key components to positioning yourself as a true expert in your field. Over the next few chapters, we will work together to cover each component and I will give you some guidance as to implementation.

7 Key Components To Position Yourself As An Expert:

1. **A Book:** fastest way to really set you up above the rest. Writing and publishing your core message isn't really as hard as you might think. The end results are well worth the effort. Writing a book changes lives. People tend to look at you with respect, and value your time a whole lot more.
2. **A Store-front:** A well designed website that has transaction capabilities will become your best friend. Like a book, K.B.O's tend to look at this process as overwhelming and huge. It doesn't have to be. It is only an issue if you get some web-designers in the process that charge you thousands of dollars to do a website – and it doesn't even have aspects to it to generate income! That is one of my pet peeves, as you will find out. After you look through this chapter, you will know what you are looking for, and you will know if you can go ahead and create the website yourself or hire someone competent, trustworthy, and kind.
3. **Relationship Marketing:** Every marketing platform you take must bring results from the constant 'pouring into' of your flock. You need to feed them, encourage them, help them, and work beside them. Marketing is NOT selling! - Sales come as a result of your marketing platform. K.B.O's have a 'client/partner' first mentality. When you take care of them, they will take care of you!
4. **Media Moves Mountains:** Using the media will multiply your efforts, time and budget! It is time to get your voice heard and you will need to learn the ins and outs of media marketing. The media can be your best

friend. After all, I have heard it said, 'It was on TV so it must be true!' - Oh my gosh! Don't listen to that! Instead, BRING truth to the TV - and let His voice stand!

5. **Conference Centre:** A way to communicate effectively – it is an easy-access point for you to share with your partners all around the world. With technology today, you can do so much to help others, like you never could before. There are FREE versions of this – so there is NO excuse for you not to be able to make cash flow. This Conference Centre, will give you the ability to plug in all three levels of income we described in an earlier chapter. Immediate, Intermediate, and Legacy Income is close at hand!
6. **Coaching Programs:** by far the best way to create intermediate income which leads to legacy income. There are simple ways of creating the product to sell, distributing the product, and simplifying the process.
7. **Platform: Speak Up! Speak Out!** There is power in your testimony! Even if you don't consider yourself a public speaker, it is time you came out of hiding. This is a tough one for most people, but the sooner you make peace with this – the better you will be. Experts are able to send their message out. They themselves become the brand. They may be the 'brand' behind the 'brand' – but I will tell you - the world knows who the experts are! Let me give you an example of what I mean. Donald Trump is a brand and he is the brand behind several brands including: 'Celebrity Appreciative' (and many others). Bill Gates is a brand; he is the brand behind the brand 'Microsoft'. Does that make sense to you?

Are you ready to roll up our sleeves and get to work.?

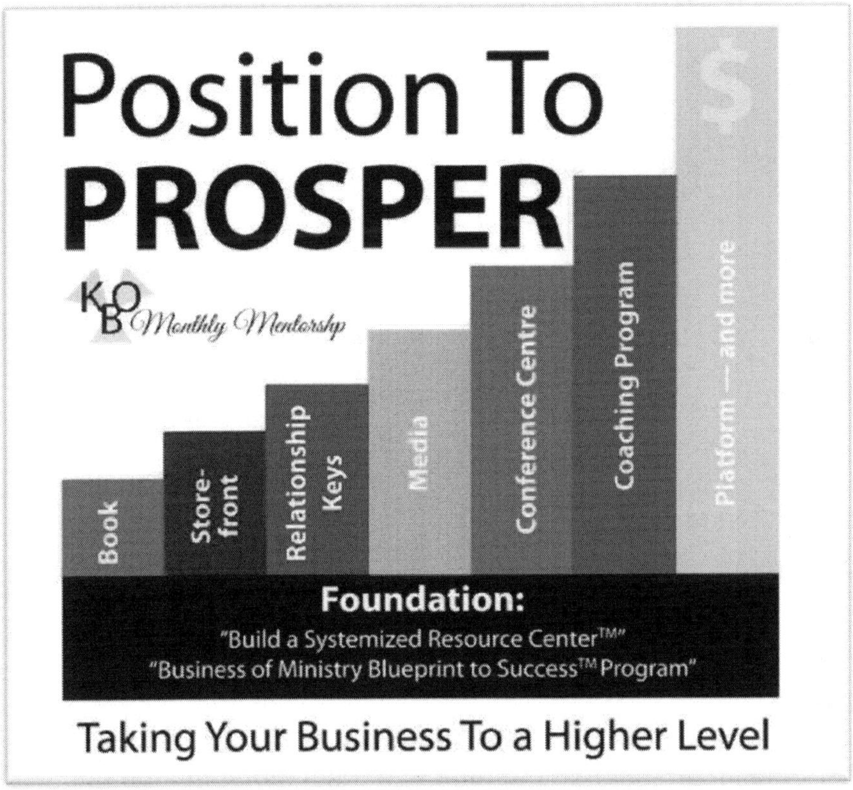

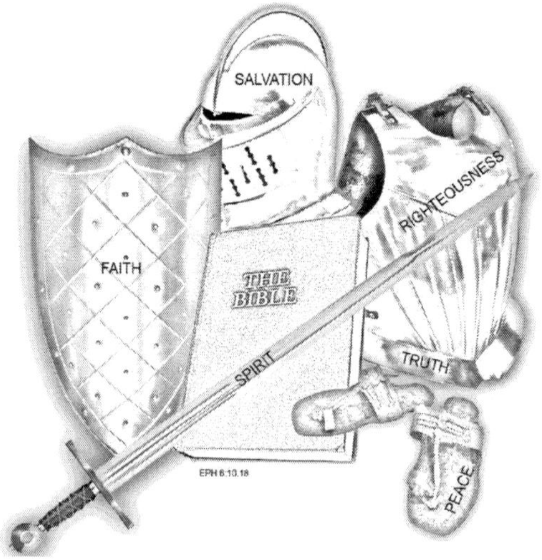

(c) 2014 Kathleen Mailer - KBO

CHAPTER SEVENTEEN

Add A Book To Your Business & Double Your Income.

This just may be my most favorite chapter. Anyone that knows me knows I light up like a Christmas tree when I talk about K.B.O's getting their message to the masses. There are many reasons why I feel that a book will launch you into the next level of your business!

First let's cover the **scriptural reasons WHY you need to write, publish and market your own book!**

(Bold words added by the author for emphasis…)

Isaiah 30:8

Now go and ***write*** *down these words.* ***Write*** *them in a book. They will stand until the end of time as a witness*

Jeremiah 30:2

"This is what the Lord, the God of Israel, says: ***Write*** *down for the record everything I have said to you, Jeremiah.*

Jeremiah 36:2

"Get a scroll, and ***write*** *down all my messages against Israel, Judah, and the other nations. Begin with the first message back in the days of Josiah, and* ***write*** *down every message, right up to the present time.*

Jeremiah 36:6

So you go to the Temple on the next day of fasting, and read the messages from the Lord that I have had you ***write*** *on this scroll. Read them so the people who are there from all over Judah will hear them.*

Daniel 5:24
So God has sent this hand to ***write*** *this message.*

Habakkuk 2:2
*Then the Lord said to me, "****Write*** *my answer plainly on tablets, so that a runner can carry the correct message to others.*

Luke 1:1
Many people have set out to ***write*** *accounts about the events that have been fulfilled among us.*

Luke 1:3
Having carefully investigated everything from the beginning, I also have decided to ***write*** *a careful account for you, most honorable Theophilus,*

Romans 15:15
Even so, I have been bold enough to ***write*** *about some of these points, knowing that all you need is this reminder.*

1 Corinthians 16:3
When I come, I will ***write*** *letters of recommendation for the messengers you choose to deliver your gift to Jerusalem.*

2 Corinthians 7:12

My purpose, then, was not to **write** *about who did the wrong or who was wronged. I wrote to you so that in the sight of God you could see for yourselves how loyal you are to us.*

Revelation 1:11

*It said, "***Write** *in a book everything you see, and send it to the seven churches in the cities of Ephesus, Smyrna, Pergamum, Thyatira, Sardis, Philadelphia, and Laodicea."*

Revelation 1:19

*"***Write** *down what you have seen - both the things that are now happening and the things that will happen.*

Revelation 3:12

All who are victorious will become pillars in the Temple of my God, and they will never have to leave it. And I will **write** *on them the name of my God, and they will be citizens in the city of my God - the new Jerusalem that comes down from heaven from my God. And I will also* **write** *on them my new name.*

Revelation 14:13

*And I heard a voice from heaven saying, "***Write** *this down: Blessed are those who die in the Lord from now on. Yes, says the Spirit, they are blessed indeed, for they will rest from their hard work; for their good deeds follow them!"*

And of course, The foundation of our "A Book is Never a Book Boot Camp":

Purpose of the Book

[30] The disciples saw Jesus do many other miraculous signs in addition to the ones recorded in this book. [31] But these are written so that you may continue to believe[d] *that Jesus is the Messiah, the Son of God, and that by believing in him you will have life by the power of his name.* **John 20:30-31**

My story,

The sun was shining but the air was still chilly. My moist eyes took in the landscape that was once my home. I took a deep breath. A heavy sigh escaped my lips as I urged my feet to move forward – one step in front of the other. "That's right, Kathleen. You can do this."

I remember it as if it were yesterday, not 15 years ago.

My heart was shattered, heavy with the ache of deep personal regrets. My head swam with "would have.... should have... could have...". But I knew I could not change what once was.

I fell on the ground – my knees sinking into the still wet, still soft, sticky dirt beside my father's fresh grave.

"Oh God!" I cried, "What will we do without him?" My father, my mentor, my friend and, in the end, my inspiration to step into my true calling, was no longer a phone call away.

Slowly God began to speak to me. I started to create a hole in Daddy's grave. I didn't know what I was thinking – perhaps that somehow Dad could "see" what I had accomplished? I thought to myself, "I am dedicating this first book to the man who believed in me."

I am this man's flesh and blood. I am an entrepreneur because he installed 'freedom' within me. I am who I am because he urged me to follow my dreams and not give up. My Dad, who inspired me to know that we can all change; who became one of my best friends; who showed me what it was to truly care for and love someone unconditionally.

My Lord now spoke to me about my ***obedience*** - or perhaps my 'lack' of obedience - to Him, my Heavenly Father. He talked to me now about how this word pertained to my life and my business. I felt ashamed – He reminded me of the times I had fought with Him about who I was in His eyes. "Surely, Lord, I am NOT an author, or a true mentor to others!! Don't You know that I am not good enough? Who is going to buy MY book anyway? God, do You know how many business books there are out there?"

Yes, it was true – if I had believed God and taken His Word for fact (that I WAS to be somebody and DO something HUGE with my life), I would have been able to hand my Dad the final and completed copy of my book before he passed away from cancer.

I would NOT have been one week too late.

I begged God, "Forgive me and show me how to forgive myself so that I can begin to heal the searing pain in my heart." I knew immediately – somehow, someway – "YOU will make this right, Lord."

I sat back on my heels, torrents of tears flowing and sobs racking my body. I looked into the heavens. I knew it was time to face up to the choices I had made.

His voice, a whisper in the breeze, actually sounded like thunder above. I fought the howling agony...**"Life is too short to wait to go for your dreams!"**

Stabbing truth – a flashback across my mental screen from 2 weeks before:

"I get what you've been sharing with me, Dolly." Dad sounded urgent as he spoke through his pain. "You don't have to opt for love over money – you CAN have both! You are a teacher and a mentor. Don't let people suffer the way Mom and I did. Show them, it is okay to have money AND to love with all their hearts!"

I took a VOW – I promised my earthly father, AND my Father in heaven, that I would do WHATEVER it took to change thoughts, habits, and mindsets (my own included) so that all would know what it really means when the Bible says, "Jesus came to give us life and give it in abundance."

I settled down on the grass, back to the moment at hand. Leaning back against a tree, I started to sob (deep and cleansing), moving through the fear I felt. "I don't know what

I am doing, Lord! But You picked me... why, I will NEVER know. What I DO know is that You have Your reasons. I AM Yours! If you will take me as I am, I will be your hands and feet. The message you gave me, I will take to the world."

Over the next two hours, I stared at Dad's grave. I was reminded of many truths. I was a baby Christian then, but I sure grew a bunch that day.

Here is what I took away with me:

1. The Lord helped me to create the book that has now launched other products and services worth a million dollars (and soon I will be able to say "millions").

2. I made more money that year than I had made in my entire life up to that point., even though I had spent a lot of time with both my parents (I lost my Mom on December 31st of that same year). I hardly worked, and realized that you don't have to work 24 hours a day, 7 days a week to get ahead!

3. That moment in time was crucial in terms of my destiny. I needed to share my knowledge with others. My attitude became one of "servitude".

"The Hell you have been through
is the platform to your purpose!"
Kathleen D. Mailer

"We are all mentors whether we
choose the profession or not!"
Kathleen D. Mailer

A BOOK CHANGES LIVES!
That is why a Book is NEVER a Book!

1. **A book can change your reader's life.** Some of you reading this chapter know that people are literally "dying" for the information you have for them. You must share your passion with others.

"Are you hoarding your story?"
Kathleen D. Mailer

2. **A book changes your walk with Christ.** It brings you deeper and to a whole new dimension and level of trust. It works like a healing balm, changing the way you interface with others.

"After you write a book, you then can speak from your healing and not your hurt!"
Kathleen D. Mailer

3. **A book changes your relationship with yourself**. When you learn how to write quickly and easily, suddenly you feel as if every goal you have in life IS achievable. You have proof. You are what God says you are. You make a difference!

4. **A book changes you and your family.** They are proud of you and they tell the world. You inspire them. You can suddenly provide much more than you ever dreamed you could – paid vacations, mission trips, you name it - you can do it.

5. **A book changes your relationship with your banker.** A book can provide you with immediate income. It also leaves you with "legacy income" (income that has a continuous R.R.O.R., aka: re-occurring rate of return). You can use a book as a tool to become debt-free. After all, God does tell us "you will lend to many nations but will never need to borrow".

"Books don't just generate income...
they leave a legacy for years to come!"
Kathleen D. Mailer

6. **A book changes your relationship with your clients or partners**. You gain expert status. You never have to explain why you charge what you do. It helps eliminate objections, even before your customer can form them.

7. **A book mentors others**. When you are there connecting with people (being an MRB), you will make an impact on their life. You need to have something for people to take home; mull over who you are and what you are about; digest the depth of change you had talked to them about that day.

A book is an excellent way to continue to mentor even if you are not with your flock. If you are truly helping people move through life, then you NEED to have something to give them in your absence. Otherwise it is like opening them up to bleed, and then leaving them hanging until the next time they can bond with you. Please don't do that! Hold them together with some hope, to remind them that Jesus is there and will never forsake them.

"Writing a book isn't just a product to sell,
it is your moral obligation."
Kathleen D. Mailer

8. **A book is a lead generator.** It reaches out to increase your contacts, opens door to publicity opportunities, sets up a platform for speaking, and so much more.

9. **A book is a disciple, takes your message to the masses**. You are only one person – you need someone/something to go before you.

10. **A Book is a cash-flow machine,** bringing in a never-ending platform for immediate income.

I could go on and on, about why you need to add a book to your business. There is a lot we can do together to changes lives.

Let's put the word into action:

1. Go to **www.ABookIsNeverABook.com**
2. Sign up for the **3 FREE videos** I have for you.
3. **Video 1:** How to write your book in record breaking time. Start writing and send me a note on what you come up with.
4. **Video 2:** Publishing Made Easy. You will find some real helps here. Send me all of your 'aha's' on the subject.
5. **Video 3:** How to make money with your book even before you have it written! This is really fun. I love to hear so much feedback from people who GET what to do. Let me know what your thoughts are.

6. Come to the boot camp: We would love to have you join us for a Holy Spirit Inspired, Life Changing Event - because every graduate knows that **A BOOK IS NEVER A BOOK!**

Let me pray for you,

Lord God, I pray that You give this wonderful K.B.O full revelation on what it means to have a book as their companion guide and business tool. I pray God that through this chapter and the videos they can 'see' themselves not only writing a book, but being successful in the publishing and the marketing.

It's all about You, Lord! I pray they see that it is really YOUR story, and not theirs.

I pray, Lord, that they understand the truth to this quote,

"In order for people to see God's glory,
you have to tell your story."
Kathleen D. Mailer

Lord, above all, I pray that your message for their lives bring purpose, passion, and prosperity, in Jesus name!

Amen

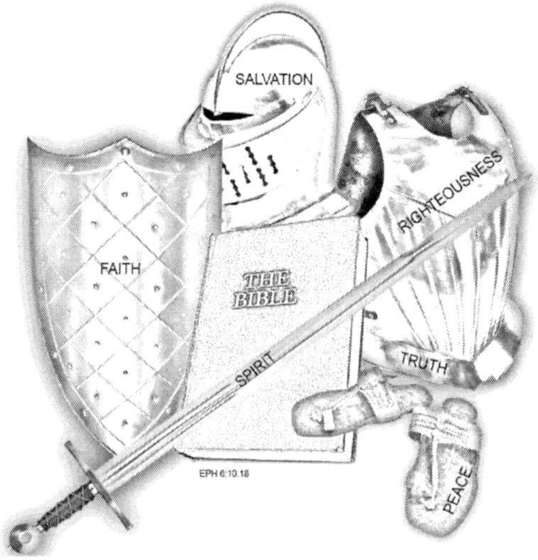

(c) 2014 Kathleen Mailer - KBO

CHAPTER EIGHTEEN

If You Are A Sheppard, Then Who & Where Are Your Sheep?

Understanding exactly who your target market is can be daunting. I find that many K.B.O's who have prosperity issues have clarity issues.

Questions come up regularly like,

- Who exactly is my target market?
- Who am I supposed to lead?
- What does my flock look like?
- Where are they? I can't find them.

Then they emphatically state, "My marketing is obviously not working!" or worse, "Maybe God doesn't want me in a business!"

Well, nothing can be further from the truth! What I have found is most K.B.O's who struggle with finding the right partnerships actually need to deal with a few other issues first.

Let's discuss the B.S. that stop K.B.O's from succeeding. I find that it is this deadly duo that keeps K.B.O's stuck.

1. **Competition:** Sometimes business owners think they are in competition with other experts in their industry. Nothing can be further from the truth!

    a) There are well over 7 billion people on the planet! Lots and lots of people are out there to help and minister to. Don't start thinking there are only a 'few' clients that you could help and your competition is hoarding them all!

    This even feels yucky to me to talk about!

    b) God gave you a special calling!

5 "I knew you before I formed you in your mother's womb.

Before you were born I set you apart and appointed you as my prophet to the nations." **Jeremiah 1:5**

There is no one like you; never has been, never will be. Only you can give your flock the guidance, love, support and protection that they need.

I believe that God has the perfect sheep for your flock. It was all set out for you at the dawn of time, even before He formed you in your mother's womb! You were meant to be together, even if it is for a season or a lifetime.

2. **Comparing:** When we start to compare ourselves to others in our industry we must be careful not to over-analyze the situation. While it is always good to see what others are doing, there is danger in comparing your gifts, talents and abilities to others.

satan revels when we start to compare ourselves. It opens the door to things like the spirit of jealousy, or spirit of condemnation. There is a very real possibility that it will open the door to being a 'copycat' or 'stealing' other's intellectual properties.

This also begets thinking like, "Why would these people come to see me, when they can get it from that guy?"

Why? Again, it is because your flock is your flock. When you start to speak up, speak out; get your book and your message out to the world your flock will come!

27 My sheep recognize my voice; I know them, and they follow me. 28 I give them eternal life, and they will never perish. No one will snatch them away from me, 29 for my Father has given them to me, and he is more powerful than anyone else. So no one can take them from me. 30 The Father and I are one." **John 10:27-30**

I bet you have never heard that scripture through the eyes of a K.B.O. before. I am telling you, for some of you people are literally dying for your help. Walk with your head held high. Know that God has ordained you for a time such as this. Know that God himself wants to introduce you to 'his little flock' and have you be his hands and feet.

Remember, **it is NOT about you**. Walking with the double CC mentality (above) will kill, steal and destroy your business. Hmm, this sounds suspiciously like a tactic of the enemy doesn't it?

So let's put on our focus music in the background; clear off our desk; get a clean pad and paper and begin to find out just who you are to serve!

When you take time to work through this process, there will never be an issue in seeing, knowing and finding out exactly where your little lost sheep is. This exercise is designed so that you can leave your growing flock in God's hands to go after the tiny one with the focused heart of Jesus!

Here are the following steps to help you get close and personal with your sheep. Even if you have an idea who your target market is, I implore you to go through this process.

I have been told that this process is a great process to walk through if you are looking for other types of partners in your business, not just your perfect target market. For example, real estate investors love this because they have 3 levels of partnership. They have one, their perfect buyer, their perfect seller, their perfect investor.

Shall we begin with your perfect partnership?

Walk with me through this process and write down all of your answers:

What is my main core message?
What is the vision behind the product or service?
In my ***"6 Months To Best Seller Campaign***" we talk about creating an 'acorn'. Simply put, it takes less than 30 seconds to say – and it sums the whole synopsis up for the book in one quick swoop.

I teach it to our graduates so that they can make it easy for radio or TV announcers to give a 'snippet' and attract listeners (aka: their sheep!).

For example, this book – as you most likely have seen already has a 30 second acorn:

"It's a perfect balance between spiritual truths and real world marketing strategies designed to increase BOTH your bank account and your capacity to live."

I want you to notice a few things:

1. My acorn has **language specific to my perfect target** market - Kingdom Business Owners who understand that their business is their ministry. It captures their ears because they are interested in funding kingdom purposes! Right?

2. My acorn also gives a sentence or **sneak peek** of what it inside the book. You can really get a feel and a sense to it.

This works the same with your core message of who you are. What is your particular brand? A good rule of thumb for this, although we can't get into too much detail here, is to ask yourself what gifts you consistently bring to the table. Get clear. Write an acorn.

What does my product or service DO for my partner or client?

What problems do you solve? Why do they need your product to succeed? What is it about you/service/ product that makes a difference in their life?

Now for the million dollar question: **When I created this product/service who did I do it for?** It could be a friend, a current client, you! Who comes to mind when you think about your perfect client?

The A-Z Approach to Find The Perfect Client:

It's time to use your imagination and creative side now. Ask the Lord for some help with this. Picture in your mind the person (can be a made up person) that this is perfect for.

Imagine and write down:

a) What they would say to you.
b) How would they react?
c) What questions they would ask you.
d) How do they treat you?
e) Do they respect you and your time?
f) If so, how to they show their gratitude and/or respect?
g) What are they hoping to get from you?
h) How do they like to receive the information?
   - e-books
   - e-mails
   - audio
   - visual

- hard copy books
- seminars
- hands on
- phone
- all of the above
- other ways?

i) What types of music does he/she listen to? Why?
j) What types of learning do they indulge in? Why? What are they looking for?
k) What characteristics do they have?
l) What do you notice about him/her?
m) Is this person that you are envisioning a male or a female? Please don't get caught up in this question by saying, *"Kathleen my product is for everyone!"* Just for now, answer the question by 'who' popped up on the screen of your mind. Male? Or Female?
n) As crazy as this sounds, give this person a name!
o) How old is he/she?
p) Married?
q) Children?
r) Work?
s) If so, where? Why?
t) Beliefs?
u) How much does he/she make?
v) What things does he/she like?
w) Where does he/she hang out?
x) Where does he/she congregate?
y) What problems does he/she have that you can solve?

z) Why is solving these problems SO important to their walk with Christ?

Take the time to draw the person out, yes, you heard me right! Crayons, paper the whole nine yards. It is a good visual as you think about all of these things you just wrote out.

From now on when you are working on your products or services, I want you to talk directly to your new perfect partner. Every sales letter you write every blog post you write every tweet you make.

If you take the time (and you can continue to expand this), this process will show you:

1. Who to market to.
2. Where to find them.
3. The fastest medium to reach them.
4. What problems you are here to solve and why.
5. What your price point should be?
6. How to help them individually?
7. Who/How to gear your marketing campaigns.
8. How easy it is to focus and have clarity when creating products and services.

9. Tweak your current product/service to make it more desirable.
10. Say NO! to people who are NOT your perfect client.

And so much more….

Next step, partnering with the media!

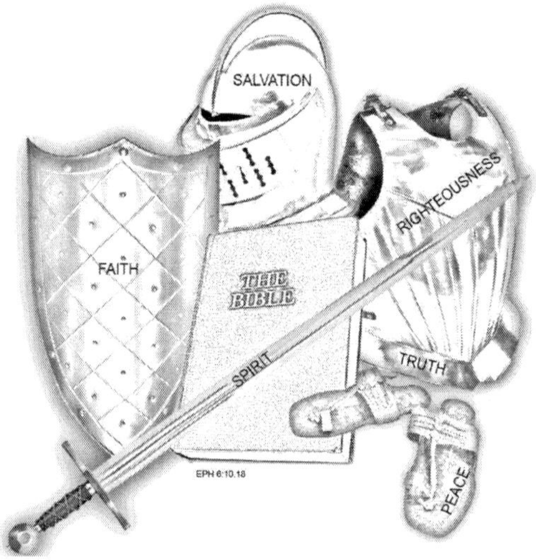

(c) 2014 Kathleen Mailer - KBO

CHAPTER NINETEEN

Media Moves Mountains

The Double-Edged Sword, Media, can truly move mountains! When 'fame' strikes, you want to be sure you don't get caught unprepared.

In 1999 when I wrote my first book, "Breaking Through Your Business Barriers! An Entrepreneurial Handbook" – I made a mistake that potentially cost me thousands and thousands of book orders. In the end, it was worth it, but only because I learned from it and never looked back.

I had been in interview after interview. The media personalities were very gracious and I ended up being interviewed on many TV platforms, radio, newspapers, AND… my international win at the time… Woman's World Magazine.

When Women's World came out with the tiny little article they did about me and my book – it was at a time when the internet was just taking off. Websites were not widely spread, and were VERY expensive. I hadn't put one up yet and was waiting for some more money to come in to do it. BIG MISTAKE.

In the article, they talked about my book, and some tips that future savvy business owners could put into practice. They had my email address in there, but they did not put my phone number in. Instead they put a 1-800- number for a business development centre down in the USA. Let's be clear, I had NO 1-800 number yet and NO website. I also didn't have credit card processing at the time either. I don't want to 'date' myself, but yeah, it was not as easy to get these things as it is now! Are you still with me?

The day the magazine came out I got over 5000 emails. People were asking for my book like crazy! The fact that most of the emails came from the USA made it difficult to receive payment. The book wasn't in Chapters yet, nor was there such a thing as Amazon then. All of this was done via email and phone calls.

Once it died down (about a week later), I decided to venture out and check in with the 1-800 number that was given in the magazine. My call went something like this, "Hello, my name is Kathleen Mailer and I …."

"Kathleen Mailer!!!! KATHLEEN MAILER!" (sounds kinda grumpy) "The lady that wrote that, that, that (stutter) book on business?"

I wasn't sure I should say yes! This was not the response I was used to. Most people, in my experience, were kind and excited to meet an author. This lady didn't sound like she felt like that at all!

"Yes, that is me." I managed to stammer out.

"Why? Why did you give that reporter our phone number! It has been crazy around here! We stopped tracking phones after the 10, 000th call! NO JOKES! That is NOT an exaggeration!"

Well, I was gob-stopped to say the least! I apologized and explained that I didn`t give them that number at all. This was done on their own research. I hurried off the phone and didn`t even try to see if they took messages or if people left their name. (Smiles).

THAT is the power of media and it is only one example. I have had the privilege of filling up workshops with a 3 minute interview ($129 per ticket and filled 2.5 seminars up – with 100 people in each one). My experiences are minor compared to some of wonderful stories I have heard from other friends who have received platforms from Oprah to a specialized small radio show.

The important thing is that you are ready when God opens the floodgates. Media is a powerful marketing tool and it can help you reach the masses.

In this chapter, I am going to give you a list of the things you will need to pull together so you are ready when information strikes. This is by no means an exhaustive list. I recommend you delve deeply into this subject. With our K.B.O. Monthly Mentorship, we actually go through each piece I am listing here and develop it into something spectacular.

Here is what you will need:

1. **A Website:** YEAH! On your website you will want to upload high quality photos, the rest of the press kit we

have below, and any media coverage you have gotten. Make sure, as I said earlier, that you have a way to capture names AND orders. Your business is ONLY as valuable as your database! MRB's know that people are their most valuable resources.

2. **An Author Bio:** You actually want 3 lengths. 1 is a small sound bite that can be said in 30 seconds or less for the quick introduction for you. 1 that is slightly larger and can double as an introduction when you are speaking. 1 that is a little longer, telling your story a bit more. Be sure to have a high quality picture in your bio.
3. **A Book Review page:** If you are an author, (I hope you are now or are planning to be one soon!), this valuable page should have some testimonials.
4. **F.A.Q.** – Frequently Asked Questions are very important. List around 10 of them. People come to you for advice, what do they ask? Why are you the expert?
5. **Good idea to have a demonstration in your back pocket.** TV episodes love to 'show' people who you are and what you do. If you have a good demonstration in your back pocket, they love it! This is often what gets you booked on the show! If you cook? Demonstrate something simple and quick. If you are an inspirational speaker, what 'story' can you demonstrate?

Let me give you an example. One of our author/partners wrote a book called, "Tammy In Her Jammies". I got her booked on a morning TV show and had her show up in her one piece pj's. The story had a moral to it and she was able to deliver it quickly. It was a SMASH hit!

6. **Press Release:** This is where the magic happens! You need to capture your interviewer/producer with the quick headline on the page. You must have a great press release in order to get through the first phase. You want the interviewer/writer/producer to touch base. Remember, when you are writing the press release, you are 'helping' the reporter get his/her job done! If you can help them, they will help you!

Components of a Press Release:

1. *Top left hand corner:* write the words, in all caps: FOR IMMEDIATE RELEASE if you are sending it out and want to get booked within the next 2 weeks.
2. *Top right hand corner:* Contact - Name, Phone Number, E-Mail Address
3. *Press release* is ONLY one page long (or less) – no longer!
4. *Headline:* Set bold and centre it.
5. *First paragraph:* Set the city/town you want to reach and put it in brackets. An example, you start your first sentence with, (Calgary, AB), and then type your sentence in.
   This paragraph gives a quick explanation as to why they should listen to you – in my case I could say something like,

   (Palmdale, California) Kathleen Mailer, the International Business Evangelist, is in Palmdale today helping Christian writers become published

authors! According to Mailer, it is as easy as planting S.E.E.D.'s ™.

6. The next paragraph goes on to explain a bit more.
7. The third paragraph gives more details
8. The contact paragraph is the last one.
9. End of the page type and centre the symbols: ###

I have given you an example of a press release to help you visualize it a bit better.

How to reach out to the media:

1. *Create a media list:* This is a contact list with the producer/reporter's name, phone number, email address, and fax number.
    - Make sure you ask the receptionist HOW the person you want to touch base with likes to receive press releases. Some like it sent via fax, others via email.
2. *Send out your press release* via the preferred method.
3. *1 day later,* contact each person. Be sure to be kind and courteous. If you get them on the phone when you call, ask if they have a quick minute before you ask the following questions.
4. "Do you have any *question*s for me? Would you like me to send you a press kit? Is it something that you may consider? If not, can you tell what you may be looking for?"
5. *Book* in your interviews.
6. Always, *send a nice thank you card* VIA physical mail after they have interviewed you. It truly sets you apart from 90% of the people out there!

Obviously there is a lot to do when it comes to the press. Having a good plan and working your plan as part of marketing and branding yourself is a TOP priority for K.B.O's.

FOR IMMEDIATE RELEASE

To book an interview:
CONTACT: Linda Olson
PH: 123-456-7899
E-Mail: Linda@sample.email.com

85% of people have either thought about -OR want to write a book!

(Palmdale, California) Kathleen Mailer, the International Business Evangelist, is in Palmdale today helping Christian writers become published authors! According to Mailer, it is as easy as planting S.E.E.D.'s ™.

"The trick to fast, easy writing is getting an outline down-pat so that you can just fill in the blanks when it comes time to write that book! With my S.E.E.D. Formula I can guarantee that you can have a complete working outline and title in less than 5 minutes." says Mailer.

She is giving a **FREE talk** today at the Hilton Gardens Hotel that speaks to K.B.O's – her term for Kingdom Business Owners - ***"Add A Book To Your Business & Double Your Income."***

"I won't hold anything back. I will tell you why you need to write a book; dispel the common myths around writing, publishing and marketing; and discuss the ins and outs of the book business."

Mailer is the founder of 'A Book Is Never A Book Boot Camp' – where graduates quickly learn that their talents, gifts and abilities collide with destiny. www.ABookIsNeverABook.com

Kathleen is a fun, effervescent interview. To book her on your next show or receive a press kit - feel free to contact Linda Olson at: 123-456-7899 or email her at Linda@sample.email.com. You can check her website: www.KathleenMailer.com for more about Kathleen

###

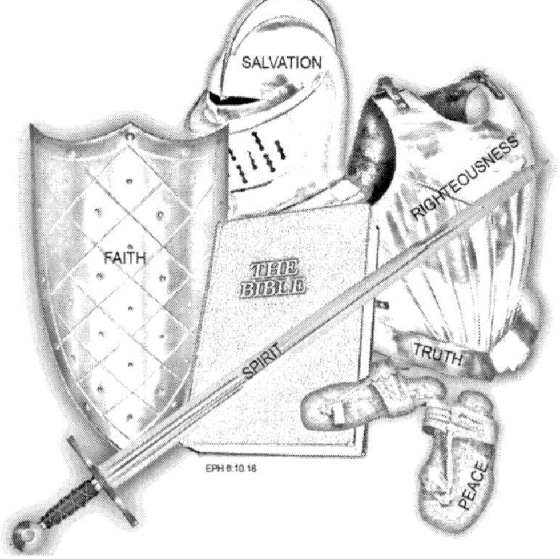

(c) 2014 Kathleen Mailer - KBO

CHAPTER TWENTY

Create A Landing Strip For The Holy Spirit, A Successful On-line Store-Front

It's time to make some money! Now that you consider yourself a leading expert (at least I hope so) in your field, it is time to brand YOU! Yes YOU! People need and want your message, so we will have to create the brand behind all of the brands you will create.

Everyone knows you need to have an effective website in order to create cash flow; showcase your talents, products and services; as well as make it easier to systemize your business.

A fruitful website will become a lead generator as well as a delivery system to feed and fatten your sheep.

Here are some check points that I go through with K.B.O's who have enrolled in our Monthly Newsletter, *Predictable Profitability* ™. Be sure to take your time and check off the items you have now, and begin to incorporate the other items as you go. Slow and steady does win the race. If you have all of these things in place, you can then grow your marketing and not have to duplicate the work. It will save you time and therefore money to give to the Kingdom purposes you are called to.

11 Essential Components an MRB Needs To Position Him/Herself to Prosper!

This is by no means a complete or detailed list of how-to's. What it is - is a guideline to ensure you don't miss a step or two. Through our K.B.O Monthly Mentorship Program, each of these steps are done with a reputable web designer, and all you have to do is give them the information they need to plug in.

When you interview your web designer, ask them directly, 'Tell me what you would do to make my site successful.' If they have grand and BIG ideas that won't keep your site 'simple' and to the point, respectfully walk away.

1. **Domain:** Branding you – your name dot com - meaning… www.YourName.com

Example: www.KathleenMailer.com and/or the name of your company: www.TodaysBusinesswomanMagazine.com - This is vital to growing your business and the search engines for finding what you need.

Apart from your business names, you want to brand any workshops/books/positions or coin phrases that you use to build a brand. Example: www.PrepareToProsperBook.com, www.ABookIsNeverABook.com

You can have several domains (usually costing a small fee) that can point to your main website that is set up with the rest of the components in this Chapter.

There are several domain providers but PLEASE note they are not created equally. You do NOT have to pay an arm and a leg for most of the domain names you are looking for. Please ensure you are not being bombarded by people who are buying up domain names and selling it to you at a premium. (While there are places for this too… right now, that isn't what you need.) We currently are using Vox Domains and/or GoDaddy – for a great price.

2. **Capture Leads:** give your flock value and fatten them up with a continuous flowing note from you directly. A good example is my 7 Ways to Use Your Knowledge to Create Wealth newsletter. When my guest signs up on my website, with their email only - they receive a great newsletter designed to get them thinking, writing and implementing the different ways they can expand their business. (www.KathleenMailer.com) It is on the first page and our job is to entice them to stay with us a little longer. After all, as an MRB, you NEED to make sure you take care of every lamb God brings your way as best as you can.

This is an excellent way for them to 'experience' a bit of you – so that they can decide if you are right for them. It is the best way for you to continue to give them a hand up – and share the fullness of your message.

Usually this is a FREE BASED program. Later you will take them deeper and ask them to purchase something from you, when their commitment level deepens with you.

It doesn't have to be the written word, it can be audio or video. **www.ABookIsNeverABook.com** gives 3 FREE VIDEOS away – when it comes to writing, publishing and marketing your OWN how to book. Again, it gives our guests (Christian writers who want to be published authors) a chance to experience my style of teaching. After the videos you get a clear picture of who I am and you get to 'experience' the Holy Spirit working through me. Then, we ask you to go to the NEXT level and experience our boot camp that comes only once per year.

3. **Delivery Method For Automation:** of said lead capture and other products you want to be able to reach out on a regular, consistent basis. There are several of them in the market. I am currently running with Aweber, but I am exploring a few other programs that I know will work best for my growing flock.

4. **About YOU page:** You have to have a bio of who you are on this website. It will help people to understand your story and then God can get the glory.

You want 3 levels of bio:

- Short 2 or 3 sentences of introduction, for Media Interviews
- A little longer for an emcee to introduce you to his/her guests.
- Again longer than that – to have a little bit about your story (so little) but enough so people will enjoy getting to know you better.

5. **Professional Photos:** Be sure to have your best 'face' forward on your website. Also, you want to make sure there are some 'downloadable' places so that media and event coordinators don't have to 'ask' you for pictures. It will save you time and money.

6. **Media page:** FAQ's for the media, book review profiles, postings of other media you have been on. This helps the interviewer find out what kind of guest you are and if you fit for their audience. See more in our Media chapter in this book.

7. **STORE:** You HAVE to have a place where you can sell your products and service in the store and people can buy from you ON LINE. With a 'buy now', you don't have a store. The whole purpose of the website is to bring in cash flow and help you set up a system of delivery that makes it easy for your flock to get to you.

8. **Blog:** Again, this is really good to use to 'feed and fatten' your sheep. It is vital to marketing your business and your message.

9. **Inexpensive Web Hosting:** This is where people can 'get' you. Use a provider that is reasonable and makes it easy for you to have your monthly hosting done through them. We have recommended *Weebly* for many of our authors over the years. The prices are reasonable. For me, I find creating the websites easy … so I know almost anyone can do it.

That being said! If you can farm out this part and it is easier for you to have someone who knows what they are doing… I recommend you compare your time value (how much you can make doing your top priority business tasks) to that of someone else. Seriously! I have found, even in my own life, developing your own website can be a time waster! Make sure you weigh the 'pros' and the 'cons'. Make an informed decision. You have everything now at your fingertips in order to do so.

10. Search box: It is a great tool to have to help your visitors navigate your site.

11. Contact Us: On every page give the opportunity for people to find you on your social media sites, email you easily, call you – you need a phone! Some people still love to hear the sound of your voice. It is very important to be able to have this option as well.

12. Get in the "know" about 'SEO": Search engines are great for marketing and essential to make sure you can grow your business. Get an SEO specialist to help you understand this concept and get things in your website ready to market. This is not something you need right now today, but something you can work toward to get better and better at getting yourself out there, in a very big world!

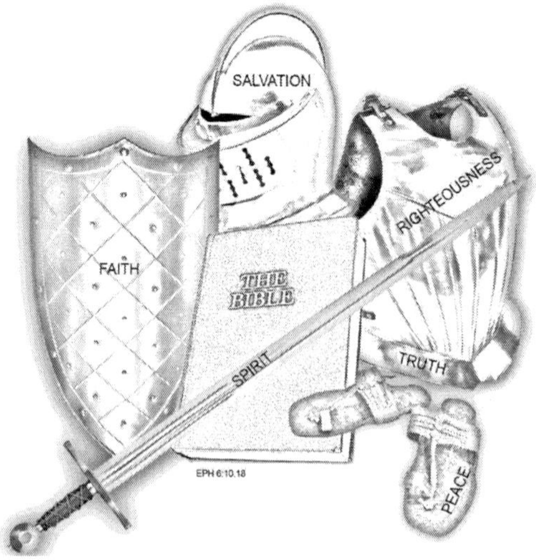

(c) 2014 Kathleen Mailer - KBO

CHAPTER TWENTY ONE

Relationship Marketing, Feed and Fatten Your Sheep

Encouraging, edifying and building up your flock are your number one priority. You can only do that through great communication! That means having a few things in place to ensure your success.

This is a long chapter and a good check list. I suggest reading it through, then going back and checking off the things that you have in place.

After you have done that, go back and list, in top priority to you, what you need to work on next.

Marketing is a work in progress – it isn't something that is done all at once. One of my K.B.O. graduates came to me in tears. She told me that she will never be able to learn all of the technology she needs to in order to succeed. This business of marketing just seemed so overwhelming.

She was beating herself up because it took her so long to 'get' this stuff and she had so much fear on top of it.

I told her, as I will tell you now – it is a journey, NOT a destination. Like every relationship, it takes time to grow, nurture and share. Think of it as getting to know a new best friend. Think of it as learning to tie your shoes.

Would you yell at a child, if you were teaching him to tie his shoes and he didn't get it the first time? Of course not! Then don't do that to yourself either!

Remember, K.B.O's are life-long learners. We must be open to learning new things, focus on getting better, stronger, faster and more systematic. We have a lot to do in the world, and if we try to do it all at once we end up doing nothing at all.

Let's begin our checklist,

Social Media:

Facebook, Twitter, Linked-In and many, many, more. You will get advice that one is better than the other. While it is true, each one has its merit and it depends on what your goals are as to tell which will work best for you. I find - these top 3 are very important at the to have at the moment. Of course, this can all change as the years go by.

My point is, get up on the main social media platforms. If you don't know how, or what to do to use them effectively, take courses - there are many good ones out there.

9 Quick Social Media Ideas:

1. Post questions geared to help your audience think.
2. Post pictures (very important for visual).
3. Post your blog links (we will talk about this further down).
4. Post cute, funny jokes. People love them.
5. Post inspirational quotes.

6. Post tips, tricks and techniques that you use in your business or that your clients can use.
7. Post other interesting articles, blogs, tips, etc. which you found useful and share that with others.
8. Get involved in some 'groups' and share with your new friends.
9. Always take time to 'like' or 'comment' or 'share' others posts and links. That is why they call it social!

I have given you some gifts to get you started in the next section of the book. I hope you like them.

Blogs:

You must have a blog or two! Blogs are journal entries that will help you connect with your audience. Here is a great place to expand on those tips you share, give an example or two to help further explain the point you are trying to make.

Blogs are great when shared. Be sure to have a good visual of a picture to help capture your reader's attention. Be sure to invite your audience to share it with others on the social media sites they frequent.

Make sure they are helpful and evoke some emotions. Those emotions can be excitement, peace, joy, laughter, courage, strength. Be sure to leave your readers in a better place than where they started.

As a rule, a blog should be short and to the point. You don't want to have a super long blog – although there are some who feel that is important. Remember, we live in a busy world. Do you want to read a 5000 word essay? Or would you put that off to the side, even if you are interested, for later? Guess what? Later NEVER comes.

Articles:

Articles, like blogs, make a huge difference in your flock's life. Like a blog they should have a point to them. Be clear and concise. Always have a small word by-line at the end that states your name, business name and email or website. Usually magazines, newsletters and the like are happy to afford you with this 'shout out' space.

Be sure that the articles are newsworthy and valuable – this isn't the time to 'sell' your product/service. It is a time to invite new people into your sphere so they can get to know you a bit better.

You can write articles and post them for free on Ezine.com (and others… just google "free articles"). You can also send inquiries (watch writer's guidelines) to magazines, newspapers and other printed material.

Some venues are paying so you can make some extra cash, others not so much.

Videos & Audios:

These are really great to put up on your website. Give them away for free to capture names. You can even package this right and make money on them. If you don't have at least some video and some audio on your website, please consider putting something up.

They are easy to 'share' on social media platforms and your audience can now 'listen' to your voice or 'see' you in action.

Remember there are many ways people absorb information. Some are auditory, some visual, some love to read. You want to be sure you have all of the above in order to best help those you are called to Shepherd.

Radio:

Radio is still very important today. Many people listen to blog talk radio. www.blogtalkradio.com covers so many important topics. Take a stroll through the internet. Check to see how many radio shows have your perfect target market. Try to get on to the radio show in an interview.

What I also want you to consider is possibly becoming a radio show host yourself. A radio show is a great way to attract quality leads, and it is an excellent way to connect/educate your flock.

TV:

TV, too is now largely on the internet. While mainstream TV is a great place to get interviewed, internet TV shows are even better! This will help you reach your flock around the world in one swoop. It is also easier than ever to air those segments over and over again. More play time, means that you are 'more in play'. That is good for you AND the TV show experts.

Newspapers & Magazines:

While getting interviewed in the newspaper is very important, so is writing articles as we discussed above. I want you to think in terms of getting a weekly or monthly column. This will give you even more credibility and you become a 'stable' in your reader's world. They can count on you. It shows you are not a fly by night but a here to stay kind of person.

E-Zines:

This is for you and others. Again, an E-Zine or Newsletter can help keep your flock happy and satisfied. Good content should be easy for you to find. Think about inviting other 'partners' into your world. You can have inserts from your clients in here, too. OR, you can interview your clients to help others find answers to questions they seek. It's a great way of building up steam and giving the people what they need.

There are obviously more things you can do to feed and fatten your sheep. While you may have thought/heard about most of the above, here are a few you may not have thought about.

Voicemail:

It is something you can share with others to encourage them. You have 'free' reign. Don't be the same as everyone else. As a matter of fact, I am telling the truth here: People phone me and leave a message saying, 'I am just calling to hear your voice Kathleen. Don't bother calling back. I LOVE your voicemail."

What tip can you give your callers? What encouragement? How does your voice sound? Are you bland and boring? Blah blah blah. OR, are you exciting and just the sound of your voice changes everything. Upbeat, happy … ready!

Your business card:

Use both sides of the card always. Have the pertinent information on it… sure…. Just make sure your picture and tagline are on the card. Pictures really are worth 1000 words!

E-Mail signature:

Give more information. Encourage your readers to find out more. Give a call to action. Give them a thought for the day or something to entice them to ask questions.

If you have all of these things in place, BRAVO! I am still working on mine! Pick one and decide that you are going to get better, or put a better system in place for handling it. OR, change it up a bit so that it doesn't go stale.

Stale food is no way to feed and fatten your sheep. They won't be fooled. If you don't keep recycling and refreshing, your sheep will be 'outta here'. Why? They will see that the grass is greener on the other side!

CHAPTER TWENTY TWO

Make $500 in 30 Days; Acquire a FREE International Conference Centre.

I have to set a disclaimer here first. Not everyone who sets this up makes money. As a matter of fact, many of my K.B.O's don't use it for a money making platform. Rather, they use it to generate leads.

However, I want you to realize that it is an excellent income generator if you want it to be. Let me tell you a little story:

When I wrote my book: *How To Write & Publish Your Own Book: From Conception To Bookstore In 90 Days!"* I decided to do a virtual book signing.

I had already done book signings at Chapter's bookstores across Canada. I was graciously invited to many bookstores and other venues to do book signings. While this was great and lucrative, I longed to make a better, higher purpose for my time and effort.

That is when I created a book signing on the phone! That is right! On the phone! It is very exciting to do this. Also, it is inexpensive for some of you who do not have a lot of cash flow at the moment. (Soon to change I hope!)

Here are my EXACT steps. I hope you can duplicate them for yourself: Remember, my results are not the 'norm' for many of my K.B.O's (although some have done it) – I just want you to see for yourself how this is done. Ready? Set? Go!

1. I ripped a chapter out of my book: I knew that many people wanted to know about the self-publishing aspect. So I called my 'talk': "13 Steps To Self-Publishing – Get your Book Out of Your Hands and Into the Hands of Your Reader".

2. I set up a page on my website to place an order and sell the "talk". I GAVE my book away to every person that signed up. Are you getting this? My book is $39. They got it free when they signed up for the $79.00 1 hour talk. Do you see what I just did? I got $79 for my book instead of retail $39! This is the type of thing we talk about in the "A Book Is Never A Book Boot Camp"! - anyway… let's move on.

3. I signed up for my FREE CONFERENCE call centre - google those words and find one for yourself.

4. I had 100 people on the call. Go ahead and do the math! I will wait for you. That is right, $79 x 100 people… $7900.00 for a 1 hour talk.

5. I got a cup of tea, my head-set, a quiet lounging chair and my book – and I taught for one hour. It was wonderful.

6. I then opened the floor for questions (15 minutes) OR they could send me an email. I had everyone answered within 1 hour after the call.

7. All of the books were mailed out, and while I did that I sent, information on the writer's workshops I was doing at the time.

EVERYONE was happy!

Just think about this: If you could do this once a month, would that change your financial picture? How about once a week?

Once you have a system in place, you can most definitely do this on a consistent basis. In the next chapter, I will take you a step further so we can secure your financial future.

The good news is that you don't have to invest money into booking a room to hold your workshop, you don't have to travel (good for K.B.O's with kids), and it saves you time and effort.

Don't forget to record it!

Upside, you can do this while you are on vacation almost anywhere in the world! The ease is incredible.

Downside, it is long distance for your people to call in. However, most people have a free long distance plan OR they have cheap Skype plan they can use to connect.

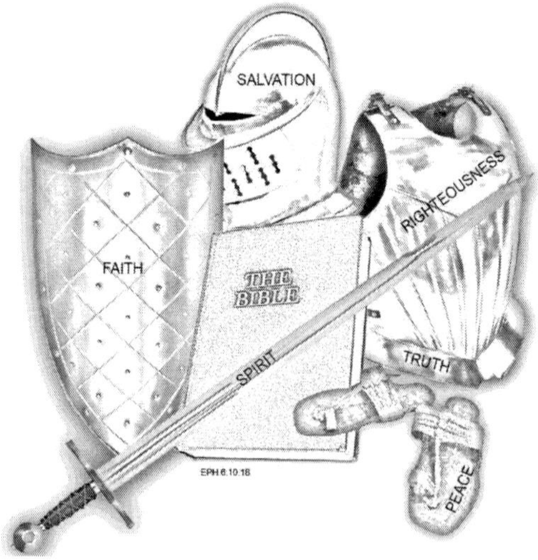
SALVATION
FAITH
THE BIBLE
RIGHTEOUSNESS
SPIRIT
TRUTH
PEACE

CHAPTER TWENTY THREE

Enlarge Your Territory & Secure Your Finances - Create a Monthly Fee Based Program.

Residual Income Is Your God-given right!

I can't say it enough, "God gives us a business so we can go out and DO God's business!" In order for us to do that, we need to have money coming in on a regular basis to take care of our own personal needs for our family and our home. It also means, that we need to have income coming in so that when God calls us to any mission opportunity, ministry opportunity, project, partnership and the like - we can make informed decisions to move forward.

When the Lord gave me the Today's Businesswoman Magazine, I was singing his praises. My husband and I were going through a very hard few months. We had 6 significant deaths in eight months and family members counted on us to help them during their transition to be with the Lord OR we were dealing with someone who had tragic circumstances around the death of a loved one.

I was praising God, because he had given me the idea of residual income YEARS before, when my mother and father had passed away. This residual income became a base for us, allowing my husband and I (me 34 and him 36) to retire from his J.O.B. and find his passion and purpose. That was IF we stayed at the same standard of living we currently were at. Debt Free, Financially Free in Jesus name!

This residual income and his provision is what walked us through the hardest few years of our entire lives… financially we could NOT work or build our business. Through it all, God's grace and provision prevailed – and that was my heart song the morning he asked me to 'step up my game' for him.

He wanted me to ensure that his 'girls', everywhere, shattered the shackles of poverty! He wanted me to teach them how to build, save, grow, share, and live a Godly life that HE, Jesus Christ, fought for and died for. It means a life of abundance for you and for me.

What is residual income for K.B.O.'s?

Simply put, for a Christian business person, residual income is income that comes into our household on a regular basis with little to NO extra effort.

This effect can be added to our business through several different platforms:

1. **Multli-Level Marketing companies**: If you are good at relationship marketing, this is a great avenue for many. Often, there is great quality education, mixed with outstanding product. The key to longevity: align with a

company that carries the passion on your heart. Ask yourself if it fits within your purpose for the ultimate outcome. If you have great leadership skills and you can share your vision, then this may be an excellent opportunity.

WARNING: Don't jump in quickly; prayerfully take time to consider the pro's and con's. The scriptures talk about, 'counting the costs'.

- Are you willing to put the work in to build a business?
- Are you willing to persevere?
- Are you TEAM oriented?
- What are you giving up to achieve this dream?
- Are your leaders people whom you trust to a) give you advice, b) uplift you and encourage you, and c) be willing to train you?

If you are not willing to work on those things, perhaps you should just become a customer and lovingly refer people to the person who invited you. You will be happier and you won't WASTE time and resources (yours and others').

2. **Real Estate:** There are many different real estate opportunities. The key to residual income is to make sure they provide CASHFLOW. Set up this business like you would other businesses to make it so that you have little 'hands on' time every month and come out with POSTIVE cash flow.

WARNING: Without proper mentorship and/or education this can be a costly and devastating endeavour. Sometimes, it can throw you completely off your mark. While there is risk in everything, real estate (if done right) can be enjoyable, exciting and highly profitable. If you are thinking about adding real estate to your portfolio get expert advice. God is a God that blesses us in the 'land he has given us'. I believe as we move forward into the end of times those who are now homeless, will own their homes in Jesus name. I believe K.B.O.'s will acquire more real estate in more creative ways than ever before, stewarding the land for God and HIS purposes and plans.

3. **Information Marketing:** This is the place I would like you to explore further with me! One thing that I pour out to K.B.O.'s everywhere around the world is that you have everything you need right at your fingertips. Residual income is no exception!

Because this is much easier, and usually much more affordable to implement, this quarter I would like you to work on creating RESIDUAL INCOME by creating programs to help people in the world, help themselves.

Here are two ways you can implement this strategy.

Before I release that information to you, I want to go on record saying that it is HARD WORK to create the content, put the systems in place to make it automatic and find the team to manage what you don't want to/can't do. That being said, when you plan and purpose it – you can find freedom! It MUST be consistent. You must persevere. You must find the right mentorship to help you implement the systems. You then will have success.

a) **Create a monthly newslet**ter with content that your 'flock' (those that God has chosen for you) want to read, learn, grow and understand. Make it full of meat and potatoes. Put a dollar value on it. Even if it is only $9/month to start! If you get 100 people, that is $900/month! If you don't want to create all of the content yourself, think about people you could interview to bring value. Start researching on the internet and ASK experts if they would spend some time with you – to give sustenance to your flock. Many people are happy to help if you just ASK. Scriptures tell me: (A – Ask, S – Seek, K - Knock – and it will be opened to you.)

Take time now to list some main theme topics you could cover that your flock would like to have.

Ask yourself the questions, 'Whom do I serve? What do they need/want? How can I better serve them through a newsletter? What skills/systems/tools do I need in order to see this through?'

b) **Create an audio program or radio blog.** Use the same premise as with the newsletter above and start your own radio program with solid meat and potatoes. www.blogtalkradio.com is truly an excellent resource to find out HOW you can create income from a radio show. This leads to advertising dollars as well as building a portfolio of great material to serve your flock.

Something to think about: you could gather these and then transcribe them. After that, you have the same information recycled. You can sell BOTH. Some people learn through audio, some through reading. Some like both. Package them together and charge a bit more per month – making it easier for you to create income with little effort AFTER your original set up.

Go to the website now, do some research. Ask yourself the questions, “How can I put this into practice even now? Is there something I could do to add value now to those whom I serve?” Pick something and start to work on it.

Remember in the previous chapter I showed you how to create an audio and sell it? Why not do that once per month. Think about it… using the example we used there…

100 people x $79/month x 12 months of the year = $94,800.00/ year PROFIT…that means… no expenses! Once you have recorded this, you can actually start any new people at the beginning without using any extra time.

Make this an automatic download and continue to bring people in each and every month.

It doesn't matter if it is $9/month, $49, $79, $97, or $129/month. This system makes sense. Think about systemizing your resources. How will that provide for your future?

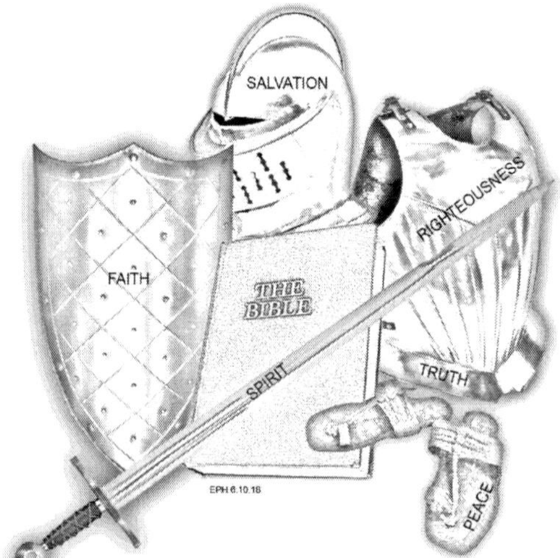

(c) 2014 Kathleen Mailer - KBO

CHAPTER TWENTY FOUR

There Is Power In Your Testimony, Speak Up! Speak Out!

This is one of the most greatly feared actions on the planet yet it can be one of the most rewarding!

As an MRB you will have to learn how to communicate in this way no matter what. You are called to 'speak into' the lives of your sheep. You have to do this to give them a hand up – not a hand out - and make an impact in their world.

I make a lot of money speaking. I sometimes get paid a fee, an honorarium, and also my back end sales.

Back end sales are when you can sell your book, product or service as a result of speaking. Always be ready to have your immediate income at hand when you go to networking groups, speaking engagements, and interviews.

Here are some tips to help you with getting ready to speak up! And Speak out!

1. Have a **'canned' speech ready**, usually involving your testimony. Let this talk be something you can do in 15 minutes or expand to 30 minutes. I am blessed because I have a topic that can also expand to 45 minutes up to 90 minutes. I am always prepared.

2. Make sure the **benefit** of what you offer comes through in the **title.**
   Don't Ever Get Caught In An Economic Downturn Again!
   Systemize Your Resources ™ & Create Predictable Profitability ™
3. Always **speak about what you truly know**. It makes speaking easier.
4. Always **have your back end in mind and on hand.** From this topic, depending on the crowd, I can sell whatever product/service I want to that day. I can sell my Today's Businesswoman Subscriptions, or this book (a few of my books actually), I can sell my boot camp tickets, and I can sell my Aurora Partnership Program (helping writers become published authors).
5. Watch the experts; **get a mentor** to teach you the ins and outs of speaking and using it to create income.
6. Make sure **you look the part**. Are you dressed and do you handle yourself in a way that shows people that you know what you are talking about?
7. This should go without saying, but if you are **going to speak don't drink** alcohol. There are so many reasons for abstaining that I won't get into here. Just know that even one glass of wine is not a good idea.
8. **Practice** your canned speech as much as possible. Practice doesn't make perfect in this case, it makes you prosperous!
9. Be sure to **know your audience**, what they like, what they don't like. Know what kind of language to use, and what not to use! I am not talking about foul

language. That is never acceptable – I am talking about 'lingo' or particular quips that your audience uses. For example, if you are speaking to young men in the skateboard community, it MAY be ok to say, 'whatsup, dude!' Maybe… smiles… I am not sure about that. But can you imagine if you are sitting with a group of 80 something Christian women, talking about a serious subject and you came up with that same sentence? No, I can't imagine it going well either.

10. Look at your audience. Look around the room. Look people in the eye as you are speaking. **Make it personal.**
11. **It is ok to be funny**, as long as it is you. Don't try to tell a joke that is inappropriate OR that is hard for you to get to the punch line. If it isn't you, be yourself. **Just be yourself!!!!!**
12. If you **mess up, 'fess up'**. Just say, ooops… or make a comment, or start again or whatever. You don't have to be perfect.
13. **Stay on time!!!** Do NOT go over your time. If you are on a platform of many speakers do your best to catch up on time when you go up to speak if the event is going over the set time limits. Staying on time will get you back in the door. Going over usually means you are 'done.'
14. As I have said over and over again, **your business isn't about you!** Think about the message you want to share with the hearts of your perfect audience. What do you want them to walk away with?

If we follow our Lord and Saviour, we see that he spoke anywhere and everywhere he could. He had to get the message out into the world. I know you wouldn't be reading this book if you didn't know that you need to do this.

You can do this! Start fresh and small and work your way up. Speak for free at first to get practice – then start to be more specific about making money with the platform.

The biggest piece of advice I can give you about this: Have fun with it. God is good! He's got this!

CHAPTER TWENTY FIVE

Increasing Your Faith While You Build Your God-Sized Dreams

If your faith is dwindling, then pray for more faith. If you can't believe that you can receive more faith, then pray for faith to believe for more faith! **Kathleen D. Mailer**

As you work toward your God-sized dreams, you will notice that there are different stages on the journey to success.

The wilderness stage is one that occurs after accomplishing every minor goal, on your way to bigger and better things. At this stage, you seem to wander around in circles, wondering what you should do, who you need to meet, and generally feeling as if you've come as far as you can. This is when many people quit. They cannot persevere because they don't realize it is only a stage.

I liken this situation to a PROMOTION. Do you remember what it was like to graduate? Generally people are happy and celebrate this most important milestone in their lives, but they are also a little sad at what they need to leave behind. Looking forward is exciting, but the unknown can also be something you fear. Faith will help you move beyond these milestone moments and bring you into your promotion, stronger and more confident. You just have to learn how to bring MORE FAITH into the picture.

You may also notice at this stage that you begin to doubt that it was God who brought you to this place. Perhaps you "heard wrong", and this wasn't from Him, but from your own selfish desires. Let me stop you right there. God called you, all right, to this place! Don't you EVER forget it! You need to realize that - yes, this is just a phase, and then take action to move yourself past the obstacle.

Let's work together now, so you can understand that what you are facing is just a bump in the road, and not a mountain.

Here are a few things you can do to increase your faith.

1. **Reading the Word:** Reading stories in the Bible in which God appears is not just for enjoyment. There is a supernatural element in what God puts on your heart as you read. It is a gift from the Holy Spirit, moving into your life and enlarging your faith cup.

2. **Confessing the Word:** What do you confess? If you have been reading our magazine for some time, you KNOW how important this is. If you confess lack and frustration and give testimony to how your bills are piling up, you are overdrawing your bank account of faith. This is where hopelessness and despair come from - a LACK of Faith. When you start to confess God's promises, you start to believe it and REMEMBER who you are and what He has called you to do.

3. **Praying:** Ask God for more faith! Yes, you can pray and ask God to increase your faith so you may absorb the wisdom and discernment you need to do what He has called you to do. This is depositing FAITH into your faith cup, and creating a greater perspective. With more faith, you can give more. It is the Law of Sowing and Reaping.

4. **Forming a prayer team:** Pray daily with a prayer team. You need to be present for this. This is not your intercessory prayer partners; it is your own group that believes in you and what you are doing. Together you can build faith by confessing the Word and reminding each other of the blessings God is putting in front of you. Too many times we talk of lack and don't see the abundance. Talk of lack creates lack - talk of faith encourages growth in faith.

5. **Asking for a revelation:** Ask the Holy Spirit for a revelation, something that will help you realize what He is doing - a sign, a wonder, a miracle. Then write it down. The ACT of writing down what was given to you is significant. When you feel your faith waning, READ what you wrote. Sometimes it is a scripture; read it over and over, and try to remember what it felt like when you received it. It will increase your faith.

6. **Creating a to-do list:** As crazy as it sounds, a to-do list can help you increase your faith. When you start to check items off your list every day (after asking God to

prioritize them), your faith will naturally increase. Ask yourself: "Can someone else do this job?" If the answer is YES, ask that person and cross the item off your list. This will build faith in your abilities and you will be able to see the path in front of you.

7. **Writing your testimony:** HOW did God call you into this business ministry? WHY are you doing what you are doing? WHO are you called to help? WHAT part of your history is He using to change lives? WHEN you are in doubt and wondering if you are doing the right thing, bring out the testimony. It will not only increase your faith while you write it, but also help fill your faith cup for when you need it. It is also transferable (give it to another and increase his/her faith to trust God too).

8. **Requesting testimonials from clients:** You heard me right, get testimonials from your clients! Read them often. You should use them in all of your marketing, but you should also read them when you are feeling down, when you need to make it to the next level, when you need to increase your level of belief that you ARE walking the right path. Thank GOD for clients! Their acknowledgements are heavensent.

9. **Seeking mentorship:** Seriously, get yourself a mentor. Get someone who has done, in some way or another, what you are trying to do. Getting a mentor will help you cut the time it takes for you to get from A to Z, and

it will also serve as a gentle reminder that you can do it - if they can do it. Mentors will remind you that every stage is normal and help you with self-motivation. A good mentor will increase your faith. Make sure they are on the same journey as you, and that their motives are to see you succeed! *Today's Businesswoman* Fall 2011

10. **Getting proper sleep:** A no-brainer. When you get tired and worn out, your level of faith will wane. You will feel you can't do what is required. You will forget that it isn't by your power or might, but by His strength that things get accomplished.

    If you get really tired, then you are working on your own strength. That spells disaster on many levels. If decisions need to be made when you are weary, table them until after you've had a proper night's sleep. It is true, things do look better in the morning, AND your faith in yourself and others will grow.

11. **Looking after your health and nutrition:** You have to "feed" your faith level physically too! It isn't just spiritual. When you feel good and have energy, it is much easier to believe that you can accomplish what God is calling you to do. If you want to increase your level of faith, look at your health and your nutrition.

12. **Cultivating the right friends/family:** Friends and family can be such a Godsend when you are feeling

down. Make sure they are the RIGHT people, or your situation can become much worse. Many family members and friends like to sow strife in your life, and remind you that they told you so. THESE ARE THE WRONG PEOPLE to go to.

K.B.O. – Stacey, talked to me at a time he described as the very end of his journey. He was so discouraged with what he was trying to do that he was ready to throw in the towel. That meant throwing away his business, his family, and his friends!

I asked, "When you started to feel discouraged, whom did you talk to?" He answered, "I am really close to my Dad. He told me that what I was trying to do couldn't be done. He told me that if I thought that Jesus could help me build a business, then he had some 'alien stock market bonds' to sell me."

When we cast out the "spirit of stupid", (just kidding, those were HIS words, by the way), he saw that he was almost bankrupt spiritually. Others can deplete your faith cup, if you are not careful!

13. **Attending church:** I will say it again, doing "home church" while watching some great ministers - they are great, I won't deny that - does NOT constitute church. God did NOT call us to the TV. He called us to commune with one another. That means OTHER

BELIEVERS! The more BELIEVERS you are in contact with, the more you can BELIEVE.

Of course, I know there are many churches that try to pull you down or don't believe in the business ministry. To this I say, ask God to help you find the church that you fit into. As an aside: before you go to another church, ask yourself if you could possibly be the problem. Really look at the situation in the church and see if you have issues. Get them settled before you go to another church.

14. **Praising and Worshipping:** Ahh, yes. Praise and worship music can lift you to new heights. There is a "spiritual deposit" that takes place, just as with the giving of testimony. If you think about it, all songs ARE a form of testimony. Am I right? This will help you change your frame of mind, and level of faith.

15. **Business Success Exercising:** Those good ol' endorphins, bringing you to the next level in 20 to 30 minutes of exercise. There is a reason that so many experts advise sufferers from depression to exercise daily. It will bring you so many benefits. Decisions are easier to make because your head is clearer. Your faith level rises as you exercise and pray. Exercise will almost always increase your faith cup.

16. **Writing down prophecy:** If you had an anointed prophetic word put on your life, write it down! Date it! Read it. When your faith starts to wane, start reading it aloud. Ask God to restore your faith and your desire.

17. **Writing down goals:** Always, always, in all ways, write your goal down and read it. Every achiever knows this is the secret to success. This is so because it helps to remind you to have "the plan" in your life. Let it lift you higher!

18. **Creating a dream board** - This is a picture of your goals, even if you have to get out the crayons and white paper and draw it! Find your inner artist and do it. You will see things change right before your eyes. Get it right and increase your faith.

19. **Using team reminders and accountability:** Yes, your team will keep you accountable and on track. They will even ask you the tough questions when they see your level of faith shaken. They will ask you to look at what you are trying to accomplish and help you "get Business Success together". You rely on them, and THEY rely on you. There's nothing like the pressure of making sure your team's level of faith increases - but it works!

20. **Sharing your dream:** The more you share your dream, the more your faith increases. Practice your sales spiel out loud daily, and tell it often. The more

people you share your dream with, the more will come on board. The clearer you are about what it is you want to accomplish, the more easily communication happens. When you have so many people wanting to link arms with you and do something huge, your faith in what you are doing will increase. Sometimes others will have more faith in you then you do yourself. Stop and think about it and share your dream out loud once again. You will see your faith rise above the stars.

I think of Abraham in the Bible, when God tells him to go out and count the stars. Imagine, counting 1, 2, 3... 4,569... all the while he is in awe of God's creation. God reveals to him what the stars mean. OH sure, Abraham had all of the reasons to tell God that what He was talking about was impossible. He also had to wait so long that he could have given up on God, saying, "I was wrong; it must not be God's will. It was my own wishful thinking."

Sound familiar? If your faith is ebbing because God's promises have not come about yet, think of all the other things He has done. Read about Abraham. Remind yourself that you should enjoy the stage you are at, no matter what... and increase your FAITH.

So faith comes by hearing (what is told), and what is heard comes by the preaching (of the message that came from the lips) of Christ (the Messiah Himself). **Romans 10:17**

SECTION THREE

BONUS AND BLESSINGS

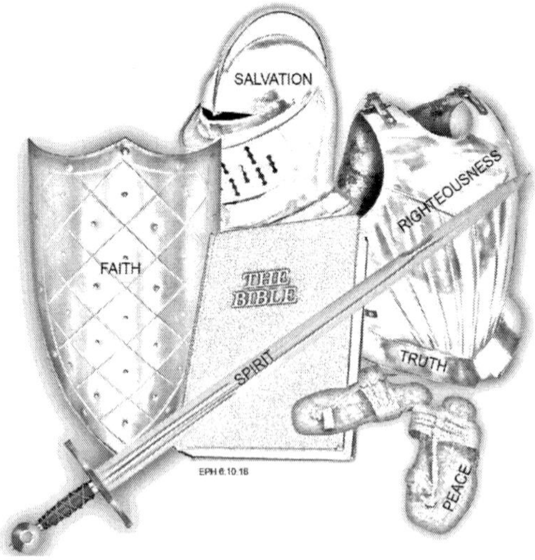
SALVATION
RIGHTEOUSNESS
FAITH
THE BIBLE
SPIRIT
TRUTH
PEACE
EPH 6.10.18

CHAPTER TWENTY SIX

'Mailerisms' To Build Momentum

This chapter is really created for my K.B.O. students! They have been asking me for quite some time to create a book filled with what they coin as 'Mailerisms'. I laugh at the term but do want to oblige and honour them today.

These quotes cover a wide range of topics in every area of life: faith, business, relationships and inner growth. They can be used for many purposes.

I am most excited about the social media aspect. So excited that I went to the next level and created a few jpegs. They are set up for you to use as a FREE RESOURCE on our website at: www.PrepareToProsperBook.com.

You are welcome to download each of the jpegs and use them on any platform including Twitter, Facebook, Linked-In, Instagram, Blogs and more.

Here is another thought you might like to explore: Why not start a journal and use these for mediation purposes?

1. Simply write the quote at the top of the page.

2. Now answer the following questions:

(a) What does this quote mean to me, in my life?

(b) What example can I give from my life that demonstrates this.

(c) How will I incorporate this knowledge today, and change the direction of my thoughts, habits and/or beliefs?

After you have done this for 30 days, why not take this collection and create a book! You have everything you need to make an impact on someone else. Go ahead! Get started today!

You can use them in your speeches or as a 'call out' in your book. These little quips are snappy, thought provoking, and make a Holy Spirit-filled impact. It is a way to start or end a major point. Impact your audience and they will come back for more.

When you do use these quotes, it is important to remember to copy them EXACTLY as shown. This ensures you don't have any copyright infringement issues to deal with. If you are writing it in a book, here is an example of what that would like:

When you use a quote in writing, make sure it's in Italics and remember to credit the author.

For example:

"*God gives us a business so we can go out and do God's business.*"
Kathleen D. Mailer, International Business Evangelist

May you be inspired! Let's begin….

"Your history is really, His-story!"
Kathleen D. Mailer
❄❄❄

"There is a fine line between expressing extraordinary faith and telling a bold faced lie!"
Kathleen D. Mailer
❄❄❄

"The Hell you have been through is really the platform to your purpose."
Kathleen D. Mailer
❄❄❄

"God doesn't want PERFECTION, he wants PURE-AFFECTION."
Kathleen D. Mailer
❄❄❄

"Choosing not to choose is the deadliest choice one can make!"
Kathleen D. Mailer
❄❄❄

"God gives us a business so we can go out and DO God's Business."

Kathleen D. Mailer

❄❄❄

"Set backs are just stepping stones to success."

Kathleen D. Mailer

❄❄❄

"The people shall perish from lack of ... perspective."

Kathleen D. Mailer

❄❄❄

"Transformation happens at the intersection between revelation and action."

Kathleen D. Mailer

❄❄❄

"Never look at a closed door with sadness, contempt, frustration or failure - remind yourself that you have graduated and now you are ready for promotion!"

Kathleen D. Mailer

❄❄❄

"Change is GOOD, but ONLY JESUS can make you change for good!"

Kathleen D. Mailer

❄❄❄

"The antidote to a victim mentality
is to simply take responsibility."
Kathleen D. Mailer

❄❄❄

"Aiding and abetting someone with a victim
mentality is NOT compassion – it is a toxic and colossal
waste of time, energy and resources."
Kathleen D. Mailer

❄❄❄

"Words are very REAL Arrows of intention.
They will hit their intended target (mission accomplished)
and bring back to you (like a boomerang)
what you sent out."
Kathleen D. Mailer

❄❄❄

"Making money isn't just a 'nice dream'
for those called into business!
It is your moral obligation!"
Kathleen D. Mailer

❄❄❄

"A Book is never a book! It's your sales force!"
Kathleen D. Mailer

❄❄❄

"God is calling you.
How will you respond?"

Kathleen D. Mailer

❄❄❄

"God is raising up women to BE SOMEBODY and DO SOMETHING HUGE with their lives! Believe it!"

Kathleen D. Mailer

❄❄❄

"It's not your accomplishments that matter, but rather what God is accomplishing though you!"

Kathleen D. Mailer

❄❄❄

"The greatest feeling one can ever have is to have PEACE amongst the CHAOS."

Kathleen D. Mailer

❄❄❄

"It's the rehearsal that brings forth the miracles of success. Don't forget this step when you PLAN for your DREAM."

Kathleen D. Mailer

❄❄❄

"At the end of the day, you have to ask yourself, 'Who did I serve?' If the answer is, 'no one', then you are NOT doing business God's way!"

Kathleen D. Mailer

❄❄❄

"I declare by faith, right now, that your breakthrough is just an open door away!
So open the door the Holy Spirit tells you to!"

Kathleen D. Mailer

❄❄❄

"Your business IS your ministry! Act like it!"

Kathleen D. Mailer

❄❄❄

"A book is Never a Book,
It's the 'VOICE' that goes before you
telling your perfect client
'Get ready here he/she comes!"

Kathleen D. Mailer

❄❄❄

"I declare and decree that you have the
RIGHT to residual income so that
you can live your life on God's Terms!"

Kathleen D. Mailer

❄❄❄

"Living as a K.B.O. has so many rewards. One of them is that the Lord will provide ***your*** *daily needs WHILE you build His business into the empire that will move nations!"*

Kathleen D. Mailer

❄❄❄

"It's the season we all have been waiting for!
It is the tipping point separating the hard labour
over the summer months and into the harvest of plenty!"

Kathleen D. Mailer

❄❄❄

"It's time to take a stand! What will it be?"

Kathleen D. Mailer

❄❄❄

"How Great is Our God?"

Kathleen D. Mailer

❄❄❄

"Taking responsibility for your life is
NOT the same as taking blame!"

Kathleen D. Mailer

❄❄❄

"A God-incident is NO accident"

Kathleen D. Mailer

❄❄❄

"When your love for others is greater than your toolkit,
it's time to get a mentor!"

Kathleen D. Mailer

❄❄❄

"Apathy shows up in avoidance and creates a deep annoyance in your life and in the life of others you walk with in your journey."

Kathleen D. Mailer

❄❄❄

"Good enough isn't God-enough.
Be An Expert!"

Kathleen D. Mailer

❄❄❄

"The devil isn't anything much, but he is persistent."

Kathleen D. Mailer

❄❄❄

"Failure is a success marker that marks the graduation line of one season and the start line to your new promotion."

Kathleen D. Mailer

❄❄❄

*"**Your Book:** Your seed that is planted.*
It's 'soul' purpose is to reap a harvest for the Kingdom."

Kathleen D. Mailer

❄❄❄

*"**GRACE: G**-God's... **R**- Release... in your...*
***A**- Actions through... **C**- Christ's... **E**- Empowerment"*

Kathleen D. Mailer

❄❄❄

*"**EXCUSE:** When you **EX**- EXit ...*
*your **C-** Calling ... you need to **U-** Understand....*
***That** is when **S**- satan.... **E**- Excels"*
Kathleen D. Mailer

❄❄❄

*"**CARE: C**- Create loving .. **A**-Actions....*
*that **R**-Raise.... their **E**- Expectations"*
Kathleen D. Mailer

❄❄❄

"When the Bible says God is your portion deliverer,
it doesn't mean 'rations'!"
Kathleen D. Mailer

❄❄❄

*"**World VS Kingdom Business**:*
One works on the pressure of performance,
the other through the flow of grace."
Kathleen D. Mailer

❄❄❄

"Self-discipline is not about inflicting pain, guilt and shame.
It is a deep act of loving who God created you to be.
When we can lovingly correct our steps and move on,
we easily rise to the platform of excellence."
Kathleen D. Mailer

❄❄❄

*"**Sab o tage** (self) Flesh; **sat an oge** (enemy) Spiritual.*
Two unseen forces formed against you at birth to destroy
YOU and your calling."

Kathleen D. Mailer

❄❄❄

"Thinking that a situation is impossible is
really a figment of your imagination."

Kathleen D. Mailer

❄❄❄

"The truth is nothing is ever 'the end'.
It is a FRESH new start!"

Kathleen D. Mailer

❄❄❄

"God uses your desolate wasteland experiences
as a marker to your success.
The fruition of your dream is just around the corner!"

Kathleen D. Mailer

❄❄❄

"Failing to launch is the only thing that
has a 100% guarantee of failure."

Kathleen D. Mailer

❄❄❄

"Gifts are a double edged sword.
They can be used for blessing and for cursing.
You got to learn how to manage your gifts."

Kathleen D. Mailer

❄❄❄

"When we start to confuse the two words,
***Busyness vs Business**, we NEED to get a new perspective!"*

Kathleen D. Mailer

❄❄❄

"Marketing is your highway to selling.
All selling is, is sharing your story."

Kathleen D. Mailer

❄❄❄

"Don't let FEAR rule over your ability to make a definite decision on the action that will greatly impact your future success!"

Kathleen D. Mailer

❄❄❄

"If an unmanageable problem threatens to
consume you, turn and help another.
Only then can the unmanageable become manageable."

Kathleen D. Mailer

❄❄❄

"When you unfairly judge something,
you are giving it power over you."
Kathleen D. Mailer
❄❄❄

"God never puts anyone in a place which is too small to
grow into something amazing."
Kathleen D. Mailer
❄❄❄

"Never let go of the God-given dream on your heart
until you're ready to wake up and make it happen."
Kathleen D. Mailer
❄❄❄

"Thank you, God for being in my life.
As for the multitudes who don't know You,
that deeply saddens me.
Millions claim to know all about You,
but have no idea who You truly are, that breaks my heart!"
Kathleen D. Mailer
❄❄❄

"If you truly don't want to walk on water,
then don't get out of the boat!
Move it on over so someone else can take a turn."
Kathleen D. Mailer
❄❄❄

"Reputation is what others think about you.
Character is who your family knows you to be.
Which rules and reigns in your life?"

Kathleen D. Mailer

❄❄❄

"When SHIFT HAPPENS in your life –
MAKE MONEY, write a book!"

Kathleen D. Mailer

❄❄❄

"Being HUMBLE: Standing in AWE of His greatness
while never diminishing your own beauty
OR relinquishing your own self-respect."

Kathleen D. Mailer

❄❄❄

"Clear focus and vision of where you want to go will
help you generate a successful map of how to get there."

Kathleen D. Mailer

❄❄❄

"True prosperity is the complete alignment of your
HEALED belief system,
thought process, vocabulary, and faith-filled action."

Kathleen D. Mailer

❄❄❄

"If it isn't relevant to the conversation, don't say it.
Too much talk only amounts to noise."

Kathleen D. Mailer

❄❄❄

"Saying it once to someone who can give you proper perspective is explaining.
Saying it over and over again to anyone who is listening is complaining."

Kathleen D. Mailer

❄❄❄

"Transform your thoughts, manifest your dreams.
It's the way of the Lord!"

Kathleen D. Mailer

❄❄❄

"You are always under surveillance."

Kathleen D. Mailer

❄❄❄

"The antidote to a victim mentality is to simply take responsibility."

Kathleen D. Mailer

❄❄❄

"Making money isn't just a 'nice dream'
for those called into business!
It is your moral obligation!"

Kathleen D. Mailer

❄❄❄

"God is calling you, how will you respond?"

Kathleen D. Mailer

❄❄❄

"Overwhelm is God's set up for breakthrough!"

Kathleen D. Mailer

❄❄❄

"If you do your best, God WILL do the rest."

Kathleen D. Mailer

❄❄❄

"People are hungry for something more in their life,
and when they encounter Jesus through
your business ministry –
they step up and step out in Faith."

Kathleen D. Mailer

❄❄❄

"Pressure of performance vs flowing with grace
is what separates the workaholics
from the true success builders."

Kathleen D. Mailer

❄❄❄

"Your journey toward the fulfillment of your dreams should be about progress and not perfection."

Kathleen D. Mailer

❄❄❄

"When your hearts out-grow your current level of understanding, God's promotion is in your immediate future!"

Kathleen D. Mailer

❄❄❄

"If you alter the confessions of your mouth, you will transform your life!"

Kathleen D. Mailer

❄❄❄

"Books don't just generate income... they leave a legacy for years to come!"

Kathleen D. Mailer

❄❄❄

"After you write a book, you then can speak from your healing and not your hurt!"

Kathleen D. Mailer

❄❄❄

"Are you hoarding your story?"

Kathleen D. Mailer

❄❄❄

"Writing a book isn't just a product to sell,
it is your moral obligation."
Kathleen D. Mailer

❄❄❄

"Being a victim is a perpetual state of being.
Being victimized means you may have been knocked down-but you don't stay down. You get up stronger, more vibrant and more relevant to God's purposes and plans."

Kathleen D. Mailer

❄❄❄

"Thanks to Jesus, I went from messed up to blessed up!"
Kathleen D. Mailer

❄❄❄

"Money is NOT the root of all evil, it is a vehicle in which we can serve mankind and set captives free!"
Kathleen D. Mailer

❄❄❄

"Setbacks are the stepping stones to success."
Kathleen D. Mailer

❄❄❄

CHAPTER TWENTY SEVEN

Interviews With The Experts From Aurora Publishing Learning Center

The following interviews were transcribed directly from a radio-interview on Aurora Publishing's Learning Center.

We hope that you will be blessed, inspired, and motivated by each conversation to take action and implement it into your business today.

Our experts would be more than happy to hear from you, should you have any further inquiries about this discussion or their services.

We would also like to note that these interviews are not 'formally' edited as to preserve the interview 'feel' and 'voice'.

Please enjoy,

Warm regards from the team at Aurora Publishing

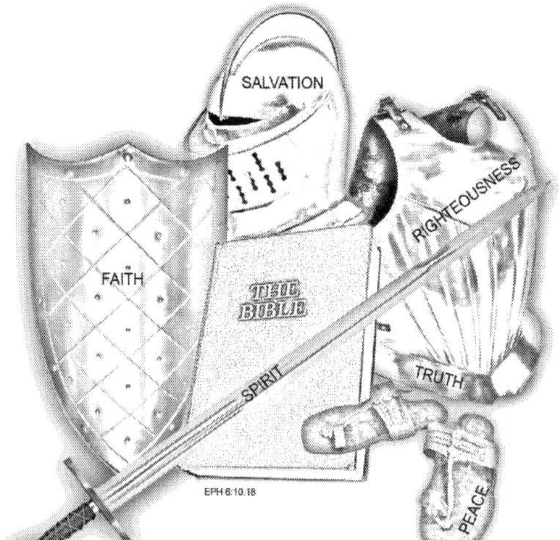

(c) 2014 Kathleen Mailer - KBO

CHERYL SCOFFEILD

Interview With An Expert From Aurora Publishing Learning Center

We are rockin' here at Aurora Publishing Learning Center, where we help turn Christian writers into published authors.

Yes, this is Kathleen Mailer again, and I will be your honoured host today. I get the privilege of connecting you with another partner of mine, Cheryl Scoffield. She's the author of ***'Follow Up Secrets How to Harness MORE Sales Opportunities In 5 Easy Steps'.*** She's also the CEO of, KickStart Your Company - and truly is one of the best connectors I know!

I know I will be taking lots of notes in this session that we have together and I suggest you do the exact same thing. Make sure you have a pen and paper handy so you can jot down all of these amazing nuggets of wisdom. What this woman has to say is pure gold!

I know so many of you that are listening here already have your pre-launch copies of my book, ***'Prepare To Prosper, Taking Your Business to A Higher Level'***... Just a quick side note on that - thank you so VERY much for purchasing those books and for being such a treasured blessing in my life. If this is you, grab out your working copy - remember I suggested you purchase three books when you have a life changing book? Number one to give to a friend, ***because a lifestyle of giving gives your life, style***... let me say it again: a lifestyle of giving gives your life style; and of course two books for yourself.

One of the pair is for your READ ONLY success library and the other is your working copy. This is where you have my permission to highlight it, write it in, dog ear it and make it as a resource you can use over and over again. Today, you will want to write down the God given ideas that come as you HEAR from my good friend, Cheryl Scoffield.

Cheryl I want to take this moment to acknowledge you and welcome you to the call! THANK YOU so much for stepping away from your incredibly full schedule and sharing with our K.B.O's around the world.

Cheryl response: *Oh, great, Kathleen, it's a pleasure to be here. I am so blessed to have found you too to help me to get my book published. Thank you.*

KM: Oh, it was a pleasure! You know Cheryl, one of the most exciting things that impressed me from the first time we met is your passion to help organize the marketing end of our business into systems. YOU AND I BOTH have talked about this, right?! We see it as the way that K.B.O's really need to position themselves so that they can have more money and more time.

As a self-proclaimed Follow-Up Specialist, you teach us how to turn your stacks of business cards into MORE sales opportunities.

AS a matter of fact, doing this for yourself actually helped you create your own program, right? I think it's called 'The Business Growth Positioning System'. Can you tell us a little about that?

Cheryl response: *Yes, it is exactly a way to get organized because I found that myself, I would keep going to a lot of networking events. We have all heard that advice, you know: " get out there and meet people to find new clients. That you need to grow your business". Then, when I heard the statistics that said 48% of business professionals who attend these meetings will never follow up after they exchange business cards with you. That's crazy, isn't it?!*

KM: Yeah, absolutely.

Cheryl response: *Especially when you consider that 80% of sales are WON on the 5th to 12th contact. So we're just not following up long enough. Let's get organized so we can get those business cards off our desk and they can stop being a burden. Every time we see them, we think to ourselves "Oh, I've let myself down." Let's wash that out of our hair!*

KM: Sounds good to me! I know you have a mission to show business professionals you know how to do that. I think you said something about how you can multiply your marketing results by "x" amount of time. What was that?

Cheryl response: *By nine times! In fact that methodology, the business growth positioning system, it shows you how to multiply your marketing results by NINE times. That's a statistic that I picked up from Forester Research.*

KM: Wow. I mean I just… is everyone getting this down? That following up and doing it the right way – the way that Cheryl teaches it, is that it can multiply your marketing results by NINE times! So if you take a minute, let's get through the math in our heads. Think about last year. Think of how many clients that you had and then multiply that by nine times. What if you had nine times more clients this year then you did last year? How different would your life be?

Cheryl, one of the things of course that I do, is teach the KBO mentorship night (Kingdom Business Owner's Membership Night) and in there we talk about Daniel and how he was ten times greater than the others. We started talking about what your life would be like if you had ten times more? Ten times more clients, ten times more time, ten times more giving power, ten times more relationships; and here you are today saying if we follow this advice that you are going to give us and you are going to give us a few little nuggets, right?

Cheryl response: *Yes*

KM: Ok, so if we follow your advice, we can have nine times our marketing efforts. That's just incredible when you sit and think about that! 9 x more. That's awesome, thank you.

Cheryl response: *That's the power of focus.*

KM: Yeah, it sure is! It sure is. You know what? I would love to hear some of these keys that you have for us with regard to making that stretch because I have no idea how I could even fit that into my mind right now. I am just so blown away here.

Cheryl response: *Well, great! You know I am a really research based person. If you get to know me, I am very organized and I always like to make sure that the information that I'm giving out is based in fact. That I actually went out and I researched it myself. Here are my top three tips that my research revealed. There are two main reasons why people don't follow up. First, it's limited time. You know that's why many people only follow up with the obvious, easy sales. You know who they are... they're the ones who look you in the eye and say they're ready to do business. Second, the reason why people don't follow up is because they hate feeling like a pest. I mean who wants to follow up to the 5th to 12th contact if the only conversation you have is, you know, well, "I've shown you my product or service and now I want to know – are you ready to do business?" I mean, that conversation can become really boring, really fast. Wouldn't you agree?*

KM: Oh, absolutely! And you know what? Those two key points are exactly bang on! I think we can attest to that. I want to make sure everyone got those things down. Two reasons why people don't follow up: Number one, limited time. They just don't have enough time. Number two, is they don't want to be a pest and you do have to keep calling up, plus you don't want to sound like a boring record of "I showed you my stuff, do you want to buy?" OK, keep going, I'm writing all this down.

Cheryl response: *Perfect, So there are three ways that you can follow up that I discovered over the years that will not only save you time, but also prevent you from feeling like a* *pest and when people see you coming. They will never think to themselves, 'Oh no, here she comes'. Right.*

KM: Yeah, met a few people like that in my life.

Cheryl response*: I know.*

KM: Ok, Number 1

Cheryl response: *The first one is: become a detective. When you're out meeting people, put your thinking cap on and become a detective. Get out your pen and paper. You know everyone is looking for information to fill in the gap from where they are today to where they want to go. So, as I say, carry a pen and paper with you or you can easily use the recorder on your smart phone if you're better just making auditory notes. What you want to do is capture the questions that people are asking you on a regular basis.*

It could be questions about your business - what you do specifically, about where you go generally. You know you've got three areas of expertise, right? Your own area of expertise, the people that you are connected with and the information, that you know where to go and get that information - where to find that information. So pull out of your thinking cap, get out your little detective pack and your book and when people are asking you these questions, make sure you are writing them down and keeping a catalogue of them, because when you get back to your office you are going to share from your expertise, or from your resources, and the insights you've gained from being a business professional and you are going to develop standard answers to the common questions that you are asked.

KM: Wow.

Cheryl response: *So you are going to carry a pen and paper, record the questions that people are asking you and when you get back to your office, you are going to take from your area of expertise and write answers to those common questions. Having these questions will mean you will never feel like a pest because when you're following up you are helping people. When you are following up to share information, it helps people reach their goals. That's what they mean when they say you are adding value to someone, that's what you are doing. You are adding value; you are following up to share something that you have learned. It's a great way to build the know, like, trust you factor, super-FAST.*

KM: That is an awesome point. I just want to interject here. You know one of the things I talk about in my book – Prepare To Prosper – is that we are master relationship builders. This just goes right along with that. How can you help build relationships and be a blessing to others? This is exactly what I am talking about! That's awesome. OK, I'm ready for number two.

Cheryl response: *So number two is: now that you have those answers to their questions, you need to create systems. There is no point in continuing to spend time reinventing the wheel all the time. If you've invested your time to develop a great answer - why keep this information locked away inside your* *sent folder? Dig it out! Dig it out and think of ways that you can reuse it - various social media platforms - because if that person that you have met in person is interested in the answer to that question, I'm sure there are lots of other people who are interested in that answer as well. So, expand on that answer. Maybe you can repurpose it into something bigger like a talk where you can stand up for a few minutes (or twenty minutes) in front of a group where you are going to promote your business. Especially if you have intellectual property, that it's your expertise and is in your head. It's not tangible and people need to see it. They need to see an example of it.*

KM: Mhmmm, true.

Cheryl response: *Many of the messages I use on a daily basis are simply modified from messages that I know are already working in my business. Here's an example: I use a standard thank you message. If you were to connect with me via a message on Linkedin, it offers you some helpful information and it directs my new connections to my website where I'm building my list.*

KM: Brilliant stuff! This is awesome! So is everybody getting these great little gems down? Because I mean, what she's sharing here today can change everything for you, from this moment forward. These are some action steps. She's giving you lots and lots of actions steps for you to take, even today, right after we are done on this call. OK, so, Number 3, what's number 3?

Cheryl response: *I know you have heard this before, but you have to start zeroing in on your target market. I know you have heard it many times before, but it's a key to your success. A lot of people that I meet believe their products or services are for everybody. For everybody. You know. How many times do you hear that?*

KM: You know if I could just interject... one of the things that I always say is if you are 'selling everything to everybody, you will sell nothing to anyone unless, of course, you are a toilet paper manufacturer'. I know that isn't grammatically correct BUT it really hits home.

Cheryl response: *Exactly.*

KM: Oh dear. Ok, target... zero in on your target market. Ok, keep going.

Cheryl response: *That's right. Once you start to get clear, and here's how you are going to get clear: you know in the beginning you are going to get clear by understanding who is asking those questions? Now that they are asking those questions and you've got your questions, you can start looking at them, finding out who they are. See, if you can, similarities between the type of people who come and ask you those questions. Are they all independent business owners, are they all lawyers, are they all accountants? You can start to see those similarities. It's going to help you get a clearer definition of who your target market is. You can ask yourself questions like, 'Who is buying from you?' Are they doctors, are they lawyers, are they old, are they young, maybe they're* *single, they're married, they have children or they don't have children.*

Another one is: what are they buying? Is it your product? Is it a service? Why are they buying it? Are you helping them to save time, make money, be healthier, solve a specific issue in their business, or maybe they are simply looking to build relationships. Some of the people that you meet are not going to be your clients. They are going to become strategic partners. I think those are the ones, that's the money, where people leave money on the table all the time.

KM: Right. Absolutely right.

Cheryl response: *So you just figure out finally why they are buying from you. Maybe it's simply because you are friendlier and you bring a sense of fun to your work. Maybe it's because you've become more knowledgeable about your topic than your competitors. Start noticing. Don't just, you know, blindly go to the networking, then come home with a pile of business cards, and keep doing the same things you are doing. Start to actually take a moment to stop, look back and see "what have I learned", "what can I learn from what I've done in the past".*

As you become more clear about who you serve, talk it up. Tell your stories and be specific about clients you have helped. How your products and service helped them to reach their goals. Where were they?

It's like those power stories that you hear that people tell with their resume. What was the problem, where were they when you met them? What was the problem they were having? What actions did you take? What were the results that they got? When people are giving you testimonials, make sure that you include those three stages. People want to see that the work you do brings a transformation to your clients. That's what they are looking to see. Where were they, what happened to them, what journey were they on and what were the results that they gained?

KM: WHOA… that is a TON of information! Wow! You know, sometimes we can get a little overwhelmed with all of this. Is there a way that someone can take this information, maybe touch base with you? How can you help us to kinda get to the next level? Because I'm a firm believer that while it sounds simple, (the truth is very simple), but it can seem so overwhelming to start with. Is there something you can do to help us get to that next level?

Cheryl response*: Actually, the one thing I tell my clients all the time is "how do you eat an elephant?" "One bite at a time". That's right; you're right, just pick one thing that I've said and start there. On my website, Kickstart Your Company I offer a progressive series of online learnings and I would love to offer that as a gift to our listeners. You can...*

KM: Wow, thanks!

Cheryl response: *You're welcome. You can access the information by going to my website, as I mentioned Kickstartyourcompany.com and there you are going to find a Business Growth Strategies Report: 'You've Worked The*

Room – Now What?' It's 3 Essential Follow Up Secrets To Skyrocket Your Sales! Once you have downloaded that, you receive your report and then I'm also going to send you an invitation to attend the Webinars that I produce and that will help you to get started creating your own signature follow up marketing system.

KM: Wow, thank you! That is just amazing! So folks, you got that? I am going to have her give us her email address and her website again, so make sure you are getting this down. Could you give that contact information to us again, please Cheryl?

Cheryl response: *Sure, my name is Cheryl.* Cheryl@KickstartYourCompany.com. *So you are going to go to* www.kickstartyourcompany.com *and download your Business Growth Strategies Report that's called "You've worked the room – now what?"*

KM: That's awesome, thank you very much! I just... I don't know about the rest of us here, but I feel full. I feel like I really got a tonne of value here today. I am so grateful that you took the time to be with us. Thank you, Thank you, and Thank you! Maybe before we kind of end our night together, could you please give us a word of encouragement in regard to your message?

Cheryl response: *Sure, you know, Kathleen has mentioned, it can seem overwhelming. There's a lot of information, good information. It's simple information, but it does mean you have to take action. You have to begin. Just choose something that is easy for you, pick the one you like the best and start* *there, that's fine. As you are progressing, take time to notice the progress that you've been making. Often, progress is so incremental and it's easy for the small steps forward to go unnoticed. Take time to acknowledge the progress that you are making and take time to notice: who do you love? Build yourself up. Who do you love and who loves you?*

Congratulate yourself and others in your circle for the all of the effort that you're putting into building your business and point out that they are helping you and you are helping them. Its hard work and much of what we do as business professionals, it is done alone: you know a lot of it is internal work, right? You have to find it within yourself. Kathleen and I are always saying that. It's work! You know it, but it's wonderful to give and receive a HIGH 5 and to be recognized for all you do. There's not enough recognition going on, so start recognizing yourself and others.

KM: Thank you so much, thank you! Thank you! May God bless you and keep you and I pray for prosperity and productivity over all you do. I ask that the Holy Spirit open divine doors for you so that you can reach out and find the partners who are meant to work with you. Partners: we don't call them clients because it really is a partnership. It's between you and someone else and together you give God the glory. So in this moment, I ask, Holy Spirit, that you bless this woman, that you increase this woman and that you multiply this woman for all the good that she is doing in this world. And for you listening out there, I pray that you will find within you those actions and steps that you need to take and that even now, even as we speak, there's one little action that's popping up into your mind and that as we close this call today, you will immediately take action and put that into your plan, right now. In Jesus' Name.

Thanks so much for listening everyone, thank you for coming in to the calls today. As I said, until next time, I pray for productivity and prosperity in your lives.

Remember we are now prepared to prosper. Let's get out there and take our business to a higher level.

MARGIE MCINTYRE

Interview With An Expert From Aurora Publishing Learning Center

We're having a great day here Aurora Publishing Learning Center, where we help turn Christian writers into published authors.

My name is Kathleen Mailer, and I am your host. I truly love to bring you incredible wisdom from incredible 'Life Enhancers' around the world. The truth is the wisdom we bring to our business, is really what we bring into our WHOLE life.

Like I said in my book, Prepare To Prosper, Taking Your Business to A Higher Level – we are a K.B.O, fully created in Christ. Our business IS our ministry. Our family is our purpose. Our walk with HIM is ultimate. Our health is imperative. We can't separate one from the other without being out of sync with our Creator.

Many of you listening today may actually have purchased your pre-launch copies, or a bundle of my latest book and you are reading along with us from the reference section of the book. BRAVO! That is so fantastic. Don't be afraid to highlight important parts, make notes in the book and really have this book as your REFERENCE book, your go to book: the thing that you go back to time and time again because you will find that having that it right there on your shelf will bring you success. This will also really help you really remember that WISDOM must be shared.

That is exactly why I always say; buy three copies of any life changing book. One for a friend that really needs the information (a gift of wisdom tops everything else EXCEPT our salvation in Christ), and get two copies for you. One for you to 'READ ONLY"... and one that's a "WORKING COPY". Seriously, it's the way to go. I have shelves full of my working copy books that no one gets to borrow. The same book will don the shelves of my read only library - those ones I share with people. Your working copy is something that you will have with you and that way, the information really SOAKS in, because you can LISTEN (which is what we are doing with these interviews here today), you can WRITE (by making notes) and then you READ... and that's why it's so important in order to incorporate it all.

That being said, there is another person on the call with me today who will facilitate some incredible downloads. I have none other than Margie McIntyre, author of: '*MIND MATTERS: Change Your Mind, Change Your Life!'*

I have been so incredibly blessed by Margie over the years I have known her. I am absolutely astounded at the - hmmm, how can I describe Margie? The integrity and authenticity of this woman. She has raised 4 beautiful children as a stay at home Mom. She moved on to the work place and has done a wide variety of things. I just laughed when I found out she worked in retail, waitressing, and a highway truck driving, she was with farming, Agritourism, and she even served on the board at the BC Farmers Market Association.

All of this experience, God directed, brought her into coaching and training. Right now, I know she is helping families build plans of financial stability and teaching others to understand their "MIND MATTER"- and that their MIND MATTERS. She really helps people break free from those strongholds, you know - those ones that really hold us back.

I think her favourite quote will sum up everything about Margie in a nutshell. Her quote is… *"The most beautiful gift I can give someone is the ability to change." – Dan Dyck*

And that describes Ms. Margie McIntyre in its entirety! WELCOME Margie on the call!!! I am SO glad you took time out of your so busy schedule to be with us today.

Margie's response: *Well, it's an honour to be here. Thank you Kathleen.*

KM: I'm going to have so much fun with you today because every time we get together we chit chat and the time just goes by so darn fast. We have so much to share with the world. What I love about you most, Margie is that you have a mission in your heart to help people grow in all aspects of life. What is your primary mission when it comes to helping entrepreneurs?

Margie's response: *Well, I really want to help them understand that they really can become whatever they BELIEVE they can become......but it usually takes changing* *their current mindset or way of thinking into one that will actually get them there.*

KM: That's a good thought. It's in the Bible where it says 'as a man thinketh, so shall he be'. Is that kind of where you are going with that?

Margie's response: *Totally, yup, that's right. I certainly bring that up in my book and it's probably the basis of where I got to thinking for myself. 'As a man thinketh, so is he'. It was a book I read a long time ago and then it tied in with the Bible and it just really made a lot of sense to me and has just been working in my heart ever since.*

KM: Awesome. I know that out of that, you have actually built a system that you have used for many, many years. That took you from kind of floating around in life to a life of strength, and courage and understanding. I'm not saying that means that nothing ever wrong happens in your life… it is, rather, that you RESPOND rather than REACT now.

Can you give us some pieces of advice, maybe about three of them, to build into our daily routines, that way we can make some lasting changes? Would that be ok?

Margie's response*: Absolutely! No, it something that I definitely have taken into my life and I recognize that I need to take responsibility, recognizing that it has been my choice to think the way that I currently think.*

KM: Awesome, can I just stop you right there? You know what everyone? If you don't have a pen and paper, now is the time to get it. These are credible nuggets of wisdom, so if you are following along in the book this is a highlight piece. If you are getting this just by listening, write it down on a piece of paper. I'm writing it down right here and I even have it in my book. Take responsibility, recognizing that it is your choice to think the way you currently think. Can you give us an example, a little bit of this and expand on it a little, please?

Margie's response: *Oh, um well, even just this morning my husband and I had a conversation and it got a little bit heated and he was recognizing – or he was thinking that I was saying something that wasn't at all what I was saying. He was thinking something different. I have to recognize that the things I have been saying are my choice to say. They are coming from my thinking and what he is receiving from me is not necessarily what I'm saying to him because he is choosing to think the way he thinks and I'm choosing to think the way I think. That doesn't always jive, so we need to work that through.*

KM: You need to take responsibility for that.

Margie's response: *Absolutely, and we had to work that through this morning which is what we do.*

KM:

That's just perfect, thank you. So what's another piece of nugget that we can have today, that we can – I really hope that everyone is getting this and understands how important it is that our choices about, you know, the things that are happening around us is are understood by us because of our choice. We have ability to change that choice or to continue on in that path. So what's the second thing that we should do?

Margie's response: *Well, I think that we need to start paying attention to what we think. We need to find out why we think that way and what event or events in my life make us take on that perspective? And then we need to realize that it is just OUR perspective. It isn't necessarily truth. That's been huge for me.*

KM: That sounds big. Can you give us an example of that?

Margie's response: *I can break that down a little bit. First of all, paying attention to what I am thinking. Lots of times I'm just thinking away, not even really stopping to pay attention to what's going on in my mind and that can take me down a path that can be good or can be bad, depending on what I am thinking. If I don't pay attention to what I'm thinking I can be in a bad place very quickly, but if I pay attention to what I'm thinking I can actually take that thought and change it and decide not to go down that bad path. I can go down a much healthier path by changing the way I think. And then, there are times when you don't know why you think the way you do. You have been doing some thinking about what's going on in your head and you're wondering where those thoughts came from and I have been realizing that often there is an event in my past that has kind of imprinted on my heart how I think about myself, for instance. Say, if I thought, "I'm not pretty enough" or "nobody loves me" or whatever, those thoughts can take me down a wrong path, but if I recognize where those thoughts came from, then I can start going "Oh my* *goodness, that isn't true, that really didn't happen the way that I thought it did". Then I can change my thinking, especially when we take from the Bible the way God thinks about us. We know he loves us and we are special to him and that we are fearfully and wonderfully made. We start taking that thinking into our heads and into our hearts, then we go down a much healthier path.*

KM: And your life becomes much more joy-filled and it just seems to work better, doesn't it?

Margie's response: *That's right. That's right and then we are changing our perspective. We had an old perspective of how we thought about ourselves taken from a long time ago and we just carried that same thought over the years and everything we do and think is discoloured by that old thought. Until such time that we recognize what we are thinking, or pay attention to what we are thinking. Then we can decide that thought is not a good thought to be thinking. Then we can change our perspective by recognizing the truth - that we are special in God's eyes and that we are fearfully and wonderfully made. We can have a new perspective about who we are.*

KM: That's awesome. You know, in reading your book, I would like to expound on this just a little bit. Just to give some real examples – I mean even from my life – as you and I have been talking and going through your book, I just want to give a couple examples that I can think of and you can agree or disagree with me.

Let's talk about thinking thoughts and how you can go down a wrong path with that. I was thinking when you said that – what popped into my mind is things that I learned growing up. It can be actually the way my parent's thought and I just took it on so I'm actually thinking about it – if it's right or if it's wrong. I'm just doing, I'm just thinking, the way I have been taught to think and that may not be necessarily true. For instance, when we have a poverty mindset and we are thinking in terms of poverty. There is no such thing as poverty. That's the truth, but our thoughts can make us feel that way. So if we start to worry – say about bills, I remember the Lord telling me this a long time ago. Remember we had this conversation, you and I, about how I had to change my thinking. You start worrying about bills, worry there's not enough money, and then in your mind you start thinking, there's not enough money to pay that. I don't know what we're going to do. They are going to cut off our power, they're going to this/they're going to that... blah, blah, blah, and your mind just goes down that road and you're all tied up in knots, which isn't good because your body responds to that, so it's not a healthy shot.

The Lord speaks to me in terms of changing your thinking, change your imagination. "I gave you an imagination for a purpose. I gave you that to be the creative power in your life. So, if you are going to have an imagination of lack and all this stuff isn't going to happen, change your story, change your imagination. Stop bad thinking and think about a new perspective." Think about, so let's imagine that the money comes in now. Somehow, some way, the money will come in and you can pay that bill and there is no problem. Your life is filled with abundance and health and happiness and it changes how you feel. It changes how you feel, so that changes how you act. Right? You talk about this in your book. When you change your thoughts, this changes how you feel, and it changes how you act towards yourself. I think that's kind of what you were saying in a nutshell with this thought. You know, if people could get this, just this, nothing else when we talk. Can you imagine how different our lives would be?

Margie's response: *Absolutely, that's right. That's very exciting and that's what has happened to me because I came from a bad place of bad thinking and I realized that I needed to start paying attention to what I was thinking so that I could pick out those thoughts and those beliefs and the way that I was taking myself down such a bad road. When I got that in my head and I realized "oh my goodness, I don't want to go there." I have the power to change that, like you said, with your imagination and when I got that, that I had the power to change that, and no one else did, just me. I started changing the way I thought and so now I pay a lot of attention to what I'm thinking. When I'm thinking a thought I don't think is right or isn't going to take me to a good place, I can actively change that thought and go on a better path very quickly. It's huge.*

KM: I think it's important to know too, everyone listening to or reading this should know is that it's not, it's a habit. It's not this insurmountable thing that's mystical in how to change it. It's doing it habitually. I think you are going to talk more about that later in our call here, but I just wanted to kind of interject that, too. Remember this is a habit and habits can be changed. Any of them. They can be changed. That is awesome, thank you.

Margie's response*: One other little point though, is at the end of what I was saying is that we need to realize that what is going on in our mind is only our perspective, it's not the truth. That's huge. Once you realize that what's going on in your mind is not the truth, then you want to seek for what the truth is, which comes from the word of God.*

KM: Amen.

Margie's response: Yeah, so once I got that what goes on in my mind is not the truth and that I can pull a truth from the Word of God then I can get myself thinking on that. That's God's perspective, my perspective is never the truth, and it's just my perspective.

KM: Amen, I am in such agreement with that. Whoa, it just changes everything because you have to have some measure of truth. How do you know if it's truth or not? If you don't have a measure of truth, God provided that for us. It's been around for thousands and thousands of years, right? It's been around a long time, God's truth. So that is awesome. That is a really good point. So I hope everybody wrote that down because that is a really important point. Oh Man! I don't even want to go on to number three. I think you and I could probably talk about this all day, but maybe we should go on to the third piece that you have for us today.

Margie's response: *Ok, well then, that to me is, um, it just ties everything up. We need to decide in our hearts that we want to make a change and we want to make that change in the way we think and then we choose with a purpose what we are going to think. That is the whole key. If you can do that, if you will do that, if you decide to make that change in your heart and in your thinking and you choose with purpose how you are going to think, that's going to change your life. And then the admonition to go along with that is: Just do it! Recognize that's what you need to do and then do it.*

KM: And quit whining about it already.

Margie's response: *Exactly.*

KM: I am only coming from my own experience, girl, because I remember, I look back and think about how I used to think and go – you have heard the term stinking thinking? I just want to gag. I was like "quit being such a whiner and do something about your life already." And it all starts with that thought process. Right there and then, the decision. It all starts with a decision. I am going to change my thoughts. I am going to change my mind and as your book says, change your mind, change your life.

I just want to add one more thing to this. You know you and I have discussed it before too. It is how when you change, everyone around you changes. If you and your husband are having problems all the time, and you're always butting heads, well if you change, don't worry about him. You change yourself and if you change then he changes, because he can't respond the same way. If someone knows how to push buttons in your life and they push your buttons, and you end up in bit fights and all that kind of stuff, like relationships I had in the past. Well, if you change your mind, you change your thinking. You change.

Of course, you don't react and respond the same way to them and they don't know what to do with it. Cause they can't push your buttons. It just seems like when you change everyone around you changes too. Then you get a different perspective and then you realize how to take responsibility because you go, "Wow, now that my perspective is different, this isn't at all how I perceived it." Right? It goes all the way around in the cycle that you shared with us today.

So what are those three things again? If you can, pop them out for everybody just to check on their sheets.

Margie's response: *Basically, take responsibility, secondly, start paying attention to what you are thinking and thirdly, decide in your heart that you want to make a change. Then just do it.*

KM: Amen. Thank you. Ok, I'm just finishing writing that last sentence up here. Yeah, OK. Say I decide today that's what I'm going to do. I'm going to take what we talked about today and I'm going to take action – because that's what I recommend, when you are blessed with knowledge and wisdom that you know is true, you need to start taking action right way. So how could we go to that next level? What can we do to go to the next level? Have you got another piece there that we can talk about?

Margie's response: *Sure, sure. This is what a lot of people have a hard time with because they get this in their head that they think this is a great idea, but then when it comes to applying it, it's like aw, and do I really have to? But the truth is there are no short cuts. You do have to practice this. Once you know that you need to take responsibility, once you start paying attention to what you are thinking, and once you decide in your heart that you want to make a change, you have to practice that on a regular basis. You have to keep paying attention to what is going on in your head. You have to keep taking responsibility. You have to keep deciding in your heart that you are going to go forward in this new way of thinking. So, it's practice, practice, practice. It's a life change that takes practice, consistency and persistence. It's exciting to see the difference that comes about in your life as you change the way you naturally think to purposefully putting thoughts into your head and deciding to follow them in your heart. It is a new way of life and a never-ending journey into endless possibilities!*

KM: Awesome!

Margie's response: *So just do it!*

KM: Practice, practice, practice, practice, practice. Man, you give so much information here today. I keep saying and if they just take this one point, everything will be better, but the truth is, everything you just said is so vital to our life. I love that practice, practice, practice. I think for me in the next few days, what I'm going to take out of this is it's going to be my mantra. As a matter of fact, I'm going to print it out - practice, practice, practice and I'm going to put it up on my bulletin board so I can remember that it takes practice for anything I want to change.

Practice for my thoughts. Practice to recognize my thoughts. Practice to – oh my goodness – everything. You know everything, everything, everything gets all wrapped up in it. I really appreciate it.

What I'd like to talk about now is the next step. The fact is that you have written a book that's really a great reference guide to do this. Folks, you need to have this book in your success library. You absolutely do. When I talk about three copies, this is one of those books you want three copies of. One to give one to a friend, can you think of a friend or two who could really use this? I know I have. Of course, you need two for yourself – one for reading and one for you to write in. Highlight the book, really delve into it. Put the words that she's got in there into action. Because, really the only person that can help you outside of Jesus Christ is you, and he can't even help you if you don't decide to make changes. So it's really you who has to start to make those decisions. How can they get a copy or copies of your book Margie, or get a hold of you if they have any questions?

Margie's response: *Well, they can get a hold of me on my cell phone at 403-597-0216, or they can email me at* margiemcintyre2011@gmail.com.

KM: Do you have a website for people to go to?

Margie's response: *Yes, I do. Its* www.mindmattersseries.com

KM: Perfect. Just wrapping up our time together, would you give us a word of encouragement in regard to your message?

Margie's response: *Um, sure, I just want to help people understand that I know that there are so many people out there wanting constructive change in their lives, but it just doesn't happen! We have to go after it......but we don't always know how. I believe the varied experiences I have had in life and I have shared in my book will be a source of encouragement to anyone who wants to get started on their own "change your mind, change your life" journey. What goes on in your MIND really does MATTER! We need to think about that.*

KM: Thank you so much! You are such a blessing to so many people and I've watched how you have changed lives even around here, you know, and in my life, how much you have changed it. I really appreciate your taking time out of your schedule to share with us today. Thank you.

Margie's response: *You are sure welcome, and I appreciate you Kathleen. Thank you so much.*

Well, that ends our time together, that wraps up another Aurora Publishing learning centre moment for you to take this information and change your life. Don't forget to put some action in today, because life is about just doing it. Take care and until next time, be abundantly blessed.

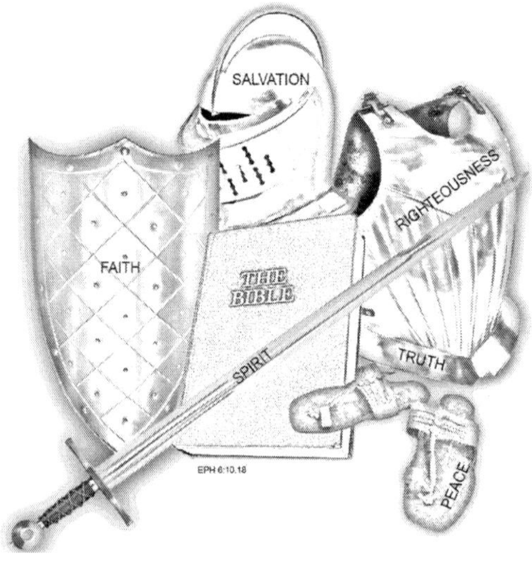

(c) 2014 Kathleen Mailer - KBO

LESLIE J. SMITH

Interview With An Expert From Aurora Publishing Learning Center

Welcome one and all! We are BACK here at the Aurora Publishing Learning Center, where we help turn Christian writers into published authors.

My name is Kathleen Mailer, as you know. I am your host and I come bearing gifts of wisdom for you. I love to connect people with Life Enhancers (Experts) from around the world in order to equip, educate and encourage you to walk in the fullness of your calling in business and in life.

For those of you who don't know me, I am a best-selling author and my latest book at the time of this call is ***'Prepare To Prosper, Taking Your Business to A Higher Level'.***

Many of you listening today have actually purchased your pre-launch copies… of my latest book and you are reading along with us today – as we interview one of my favourite people in the whole world. IF this is you…. BRAVO… turn to the interview page with Leslie J. Smith and get ready to highlight and mark up your working copy book.

For those of you, who are now just tuning in order to listen to this, make sure you have a pen and paper handy as we go through some really remarkable material today. You can also grab some pre-launch copies of my latest book (or bundles for your networking group or church) at www.PrepareToProsperBook.com

I always say that you should buy 3 copies of a life-changing book. **One for a friend** that really needs the information (a gift of wisdom tops everything else EXCEPT our salvation through Christ), and get two copies for you. One is for you to **'READ ONLY'**… and one that's a **"WORKING COPY"**… seriously, this is really the way to go. You will find that the information just SOAKS right in, when you **LISTEN** (like you are doing here in the interview), when you **WRITE** (when you're making notes) and when you **READ**…

All of those things incorporated will change your life.

That being said, I think you will want to get 3 copies of my next guest's book, too and do the same thing with it. With me today is Leslie J. Smith, owner of Leslie J. Smith Professional Corporation and author of '***Legal Ease – Essential Legal Strategies to Protect Canadian Non-Union Employees***'

Leslie is really a BRILLIANT woman who was called to the Ontario Bar in 1988.

Currently, she practices exclusively in the area of Employment Law. Leslie also has a Certificate in Mediation from the University of Windsor and sits part-time as a Small Claims Court Judge in Central West Region, Ontario. I just find that just so impressive!

Ever since 1997, Leslie has written a legal column for the Burlington Post Newspaper (Burlington, Ontario) on Employment Law issues. Leslie is a successful communicator and advocate in court or at the settlement table. Leslie enjoys an excellent reputation before the Bench and with her clients. She provides ethical and practical legal advice that is client-centric and in the client's best interests. Of course, because she is God-Centred, what else would she do?

What I particularly LOVE about this woman is her passion to do business God's way and that is why we have her on the call with us today. As business owners, we need to see our business through our employee's eyes. Truthfully, I think THIS interview will be an EYE OPENER!

Leslie J. Smith.... WELCOME to our Learning Center! THANK YOU, THANK YOU, THANK YOU for taking time out of your incredibly packed schedule to spend some time with us today!

Leslie responds: *Thank you my dear. Thank you Kathleen, it's always a pleasure to talk to you. I'm happy to be here.*

KM: You know, Leslie, I am so glad you took time today because I know with all of those things that are on your plate, you still have a heart to be able to share and teach and communicate with anyone who really has a need in their heart. That is a quality that is second to none – and very rare! So today, I really want to show that quality to all of our listeners here today.

I know that you are an advocate for justice in - the lives of employees… tell us a little more about that AND… when it comes to entrepreneurs, what would be your primary mission to help them grow?

Leslie responds: *Sure, ok, my primary mission in life, when I'm dealing with an employee is to make sure that they understand their basic legal strategies to assist them as they move into and through and out of their employment. And I also make it my business to give them practical knowledge that will empower them in the workplace which will inevitably give them peace of mind. At least that's what they keep telling me.*

And then, on the flip side, I am very impassioned to inform small businesses of their rights and obligations and also their employee's rights and obligations with the whole purpose of raising the ethical tenor of the work place.

KM: Absolutely mind-blowing. I mean, this is something that I think a lot of especially small business owners don't think that they have anything to contribute to this or worry about it. What you are saying is that we need to start now really thinking about how to build a great business that will house employees and our treasures, right? That's kind of what I got from that.

Leslie responds: *A lot of small businesses really don't know what to do, but they need to know because the laws are very complex and to be honest, they are a little bit slanted in favour of the employee.*

KM: So why exactly is it important for a business owner to really understand this in terms of doing business God's way?

Leslie responds: *Well, as Christians, we have a higher calling in my view to treat our employees properly. We have a calling and we are mandated to do so by the laws of this country, but over and above that, I feel that a Christian Business Owner has a higher duty to make sure that they treat their employees as they are instructed to in the Bible, which is to treat them properly, understanding that God is their master. Not only do we want to make sure small businesses understand their legal obligations, but also Christian business should understand their moral and ethical obligations.*

KM: I love that. Love that! I just want to interject right now because I'm going to ask you about giving us some advice today. If you don't have a pen and paper handy now is the time you should grab one. If you are reading along in the book, of course that's fantastic, get your highlighter ready. I am actually going to ask Leslie for at least three pieces of advice today that we can use as business owners to really make our business a house of God. So if you don't have a pen and paper handy - run and get it right now and I am going to just hand the floor over to Leslie.

OK... Leslie, if you could give us even just one piece of advice today, one piece first, what would that be coming from an employee stance first, then we will spin each one into enhancing our business as an entrepreneur. How about that?

Leslie responds: *OK, to an employee I would say if you are not sure about what's going on at the work place, if you're in trouble in some way,* ***do not take the advice of your friends and relatives*** *although they mean well, if they are not Employment Lawyers, they really do not know enough to give you the right strategies that are necessary. Get proper advice. Equally, if you are a business owner, it is the same advice from the flip side. If you are having problems with an employee and you don't know what to do, don't do anything until you have talked to an employment lawyer because there are sharks in the waters for the unwary.*

KM: Right, absolutely. You know it's like anything, a lot of times we take situations like this to our family and our friends and you know they are the wrong way for you to get advice because they don't know. They may think they know but they don't know. Really, in their mind's eye they are coming from I want to protect you, I want to love you and I'm going to fight anybody who comes against that. While that's good for that loyalty, it's not necessarily good for us to be going into that kind of a platform without having legal counsel. I really, really get that. You know, it's like people – and you and I have talked about this in the past, too. It's like people who go get marriage advice from someone who is divorced three times and they are not married and they have terrible trouble with relationships, right? And they end up going to them for advice about relationships. It's probably not a good place to go, unless those people have been healed from that, it's probably not a good idea, so I really love that and that's really good advice.

So what's another piece of advice you can give us today?

Leslie responds: *Ok, so to the employee, I would say that if you are experiencing a toxic work environment and you feel like you are going to melt down, don't tough it out and don't try to be a hero,* ***go to a doctor and get a stress leave if the doctor recommends it.*** *There are two reasons for this. One, no job is worth jeopardizing your health over. That's the first thing. Secondly, if your work performance is starting to suffer as a result of stress in the work place, you don't want to continue down that path because the next problem you are going to have is your performance is slipping. So not only are you under stress because of some toxicity in the work place, but now you are not performing well. Better to just extricate yourself from the situation, go get a stress leave for a time and then sort out what you are going to do later.*

For the employers, I would say don't be a toxic work environment, don't allow toxicity in your workplace. If its happening don't ignore it, it won't go away. Go to an employment lawyer and get some help on how to deal with it because we have the strategies.

KM: Awesome, you know how true that is. Can you give us some examples of toxicity in the work place?

Leslie responds: *Um yes, um... A classic example is an employee that is going along and suddenly new management comes in. They have a new manager who has probably been hired to clean house and all of a sudden, the screws are tightening and that boss is micromanaging and being uncivil,* *being snide, sarcastic, riding the tail of the employee, putting on too much work, criticizing, all sorts of things. So, essentially, our laws require the work place to be covered with the mantle of respect and stability. And where that doesn't happen – that's what we generally call a toxic work environment. That kind of environment can actually make people sick.*

KM: Absolutely, I can totally see that. My daughter just went through this very scenario. Her manager at this one place is actually very much a control freak, to the point that she's abusive. There are a lot of people that have obviously quit but, you know, I encouraged my daughter to talk first.

This kind of stuff, really, if you think about it in terms of how we are supposed to act as Christians, sometimes it's people who really need help and the way they are acting and bringing that toxic environment into the work place means that they need some help. So, if you put it in those terms it's not even about you, it's about getting them some help. Of course, going for legal counsel with that is the best way to do it, to make sure that it's done in a professional, loving kind way. Especially if your own legal counsel is a Christian, because then they get it on all avenues. That's what I would think too.

That's wonderful. How about one more piece of advice… what advice for employees would you give and then spin it for an employer.

Leslie responds: *Ok, so same advice on both sides – your work is a gift from God, Yes, and it's a means to an end and* *does not define who you are. Who we are is clearly laid out in God's words. We are not our jobs. We don't want to allow ourselves as employees to be swallowed up by our work at the expense of our talents and our self-esteem and our relationships in your lives. That's also good advice for entrepreneurs, solopreneurs, and people running mid-size and large-size companies. Work is a place to earn a living, a place to advance your skills, to develop social relationships and so on. It is not who you are. Don't allow it to become out of balance with the rest of your life. That really is advice for employees and employers.*

KM: Absolutely, because if you go out of alignment with who you are inside, because really the work we do is the vehicle of expressing who we are. The vehicle isn't who we are; it's the vehicle we use to express that. That is really good. So when one person, whether it's the employer or the employee, is out of alignment - it causes all sorts of trouble. As entrepreneurs, I mean that's one of the reasons I said to you that I am definitely getting a copy of your book because I want to kind of see things through the eyes of the employee and what kind of stuff is really out there. I'll get into that in a few minutes.

I think this is a really key piece – I think in every area – because you don't want to even have relationships outside of the work place that swallow you up either, so this piece of advice, Leslie, is vital to all of us in terms of everything we do. Did you get that folks? Did you get that written down? The three pieces of advice? I'm going to just ask you, Leslie, if you could just list those three things again so I can take a look at my list that I'm writing and make sure that I got them all in my notes.

Leslie responds: *Yes, so the first one is essentially to consult an employment lawyer when things are going wrong at the work place or at your company when you need to make a change or are thinking of doing something with an employee. Consult an employment lawyer before you do anything. Secondly, if you are an employee in a toxic work environment, step away from it, get some help. If you are an employer, don't allow a toxic work environment to take place on your premises. Get some advice from an employment lawyer right way. Thirdly, both employees and employers need to keep a healthy work/life balance.*

KM: That's awesome, got it down. I've just got to say it again, because I think it's absolutely imperative that we 'walk a mile in another's shoes'. That is why I think your book is a success book. It should be on every entrepreneur's success library. It should sit on our shelves as a reference guide. I know that you came to this calling NOT by accident but by design. There are a lot of companies out there NOT treating employees right and I love that about you, that you are making sure that we are treated with honour and respect. Personally, I think that reading this book will equip us with a greater understanding of how the 'world' does business. I think it will help us differentiate ourselves - and set up our business to be a HOUSE OF GOD. Wouldn't you agree with that?

Leslie responds: *Yes, oh absolutely. I think I've certainly acted for Christian Businesses, Christian Charities and so forth and they have the same difficulties as everyone else does in terms of how to behave and how to conduct their human resources policies and so on. So, it's nice to be Christian, but we also want to be teachable and understand that we have things to learn as well.*

KM: Absolutely, because as Christians, that's who we are, we're life learners. You sign up for salvation - it doesn't mean it's the beginning and the end. It's just a beginning folks - how many of you know that when you say yes to Jesus, it's just the beginning, it's not the beginning and the end.

Now, that being said, how can our listeners or readers connect with you and get some copies of your book? I bet there are many people right now, listening to this/reading this who can think of people who are NEEDING this information to give as gifts, but also for themselves. How can we get a hold of you?

Leslie responds: *Ok, so the best way is through my new website* www.legaleasecanada.com *All of my contact information is there if need be.*

KM: Awesome, so everybody go to that website and pick up some copies, because I know that there are people in your life that actually need it because they need that counsel right now, they are having trouble at work. I mean seriously, all of us probably know at least one person who is in that situation, but as entrepreneurs, pick up a copy to be part of your success library.

I thank you so much Leslie, I mean, you again are like a breath of fresh air. You really help put things into perspective and I just really appreciate you in every way.

Leslie responds: *Thank you. I just thank God that we met to be honest with you. My whole life went in an entirely better direction after I met you.*

KM: Thank you! That was a nice thing to say. You know, before we end our time together, could you give us a word of encouragement in regard to your message?

Leslie responds: *Yes, I mean would you like me to pray or what would you like me to do?*

KM: Well sure, if you have a word of encouragement or a prayer, that is always great, right everyone? We love prayers too. If that's what in your heart, then please do.

Leslie responds: *So Father, we just thank you so much for all of the gifting you have given us, the blessings that you give us. The ability to work and think. We ask Father that you would guide us in these endeavours, whether we are employees or employers and we pray a special blessing over Kathleen and her business. May it prosper and be extremely successful and wide-reaching in this year of 2014. I bless the listeners and pray that their lives will be enriched and blessed by your bounty this year. In Jesus' name I pray. Amen.*

KM: Amen and I agree. Thank you so much. Well folks, you know what to do now; you've been with me for a long time. It's time to put that word into action. Get out there and start making a difference. Sit down and think "How can I use this information to make my business a house of God." Until next time, I pray a million blessings over your life.

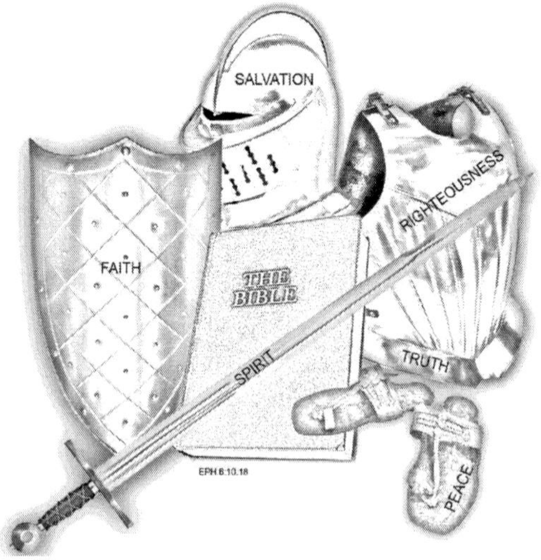

(c) 2014 Kathleen Mailer - KBO

MARY E. STEVENSON

Interview With An Expert From Aurora Publishing Learning Center

Hello and welcome to Aurora Publishing Learning Center, where we help turn Christian writers into published authors.

My name is Kathleen Mailer, and I am your host today as we bring you incredible experts that give you 'life enhancers'. They share life enhancers (or nuggets of wisdom) for your business and of course, that spills out everywhere in life.

I am a bestselling author and my book ***'Prepare To Prosper, Taking Your Business To A Higher Level'*** is my 37th published book.

I am ecstatic about our show today. I have author Mary E. Stevenson joining us from Whole Harmonized Healing. She is the author of, ***'Ready to Love, Fact or Fiction?'***

And that's not all! OH NO… wait until you hear this…

I found out that Mary has always had a passion for life, people and animals. She has been able to combine ALL three of these loves into a very special and unique platform that truly makes a difference in the world around her.

Over the past 17 years, she has melded a variety of healing modalities to assist people to become more empowered in their lives. And who doesn't need more empowerment, right?

Well, through this incredible unique ability to grow and change, the teacher in her is ready to share these techniques and her experiences to move people forward physically, mentally, emotionally and spiritually.

As a Certified Clinical Hypnotist, she has helped people to find their own answers in how to live their lives to the fullest! And I just love that because, you know, in healing, it's really about that partnership between the facilitator – between God, the facilitator and the person that needs healing, so she really helps them to live that life to the fullest.

What I just love about Mary is that she doesn't even stop there, and she has a unique gifting that is her ability to connect to animals. I've seen it, I mean, with the animals that she and her husband have, it's awesome to watch on Facebook. These furry kids are just amazing. She says that animals can tell you so much about their owners and it is through the ability to be an *Animal Communicator* – if they are sick or something is not right - she can actually connect to their owners and inspire change. Isn't that something?

Mary, welcome to the show. I am so THRILLED you could take time to join us.

Mary's response: *Well, thank you very much Kathleen. I'm very happy to be here today.*

KM: You know, since we are talking to my peeps today, who are Kingdom Business Owners; we have the K.B.O's on the call here today… I was wondering if you could share some of your passion and why you have a passion for Business Owners?

Mary's response: *I have a passion for Business Owners because I am one myself and I know to make your business a success, you must have support. People that are like-minded around you, people that understand all the challenges of being a business owner and what you need to have and to be in order to make it a success.*

KM: Awesome, what would be your primary mission to help entrepreneurs grow?

Mary's response: *We are all born with special gifts, talents, and abilities and we are meant to use these in our lives to serve others. In using these abilities, we will receive great reward on many different levels. What I help people to do is to shed any old beliefs or behaviors that may be blocking them from loving ourselves completely and fully, or acknowledging who they are at a deeper level, and then freeing ourselves to use these abilities. When we love ourselves unconditionally, as God loves us, we then can reach our full potential.*

KM: No Kidding! Is that not the truth or what? I know from my own life that I have struggled in the past about not loving myself and it just makes us shrink back. If we could just see ourselves through God's eyes, then you know what? The world would be a majorly different place, wouldn't it?

Mary's response: *Absolutely! That aspect of loving yourself unconditionally, I really do believe is the key.*

KM: That's just fabulous.... I'm going to start to talk to you about some things that you and I have discussed and that would be your TOP three pieces of advice you would have for us... I hope everyone out there has a pen and paper handy... because you will WANT to jot this down. So run and get a pen and paper really quick.

For those of you who have my book, '*Prepare To Prosper, Taking Your Business TO A HIGHER LEVEL'*- you are going to find these gems in the reference section of the book. Now, follow along, HIGHLIGHT – yes you have my permission to highlight and mark up your book - as it is imperative to learning. What I do with books that are just full of wisdom, like Prepare To Prosper – is I actually buy two books and I know many of you have done this already. One that I keep on my shelf to go back to and just read and enjoy, and the other is to write in and dog-ear and to highlight and mark up and I think it's really important to do that when you have a how-to book that really can inspire change. Wouldn't you agree with that Mary?

Mary's response: *Oh yes, absolutely, that is a wonderful idea!*

KM: I think they should do that. Yeah, I think they should do that with your book too. If you are going to pick up a copy of her book, buy at least two because there's so much in there. Anyway, I digress, Mary let's get started... Let's discuss the bit, your FIRST little nugget that you have for us.

Mary's response: *Ok, the first piece of advice that I would like to touch on is to look at yourself from all angles. This means looking at all the different parts of you. Are there parts of yourself you have been purposely ignoring for years? We have all done or said things at some point in time that we are not proud of. When we look at ourselves honestly, we can then start to change, IF we make that choice. We first have to have the courage, though, to look. Know that you can shift and change yourself whatever you want to change. Looking at different angles of yourself, you may even develop a better sense of humour than you have ever had before.*

This also applies not only to things that you may not particularly like – behaviors or beliefs, but it also applies to being honest with yourself about what you love! Sometimes we feel that we need to look or act a certain way, do a particular job, or acquire numerous things in life; but is that what we really what and what we love? Maybe we feel this way because of societal pressure or because other people in our lives want it. But do YOU honestly love and want these things? Check it out and see what you really love and what is important to you. When we identify what we love and what we are passionate about, we will then have the energy and the focus to pursue it. Life will then start to flow.

KM: Wow, that's fantastic. You know, it's so true, this is coming straight out of the bible where it talks about the fact that we need to take responsibility first and foremost. And a lot of people think that taking responsibility will be a hard thing and that it's for bad stuff, right? BUT it could also be for good stuff, good stuff as in – if I can't be living my life in the fullness of who I am in Christ, I can't really be the person, they guy or the gal, that can overflow to my family. So, I mean, this is really an important thing folks; write it down, look at yourself from all angles, the good, the bad and the ugly. If we really follow what Jesus taught us, loving one another is the greatest commandment. That's what he says, he says is the greatest commandment. I think that spills out to loving ourselves don't you?

Mary's response: *Yes, it starts with loving ourselves and when we look at ourselves and we understand why we are the way we are, and know that we can change things if we want to, we also develop more compassion for other people. As you said, it spills out into our families, and it most definitely affects our careers and other relationships in our lives.*

KM: Amen, that's awesome. Thank you. You have a second piece of advice that I want to hear more about... you had mentioned a little bit about intuition and I would like to hear what you have to say about that.

Mary's response: *I tell everyone to listen and to follow your intuition. I do believe we have the answers within ourselves of what is right and good for us in our lives. And that's all areas of our lives. When we are guided by God through our intuition life opens up for us. But we must take the time to be quiet and listen, so that we can receive those answers. I recommend to people, in your daily schedule, book time off for yourself to be silent. Quiet time is time well spent. When we do receive our answers in this way and we follow our intuition, whatever we are pursuing will fall into place.*

KM: That's AWESOME! And of course, everyone is recognizing that intuition is a very key element. God gave us intuition because it is our filter, if you will, from the Holy Spirit. You know that quiet, small voice of the Holy Spirit. Jesus went to be with our Heavenly Father and He sent the Holy Spirit to live IN us. So we have that God Power, that God Wisdom, that God Creative thought, the God Ideas within us from God himself. The Holy Spirit. The Holy Spirit will give us grace and grace really is about empowerment. It's the ability to do things you never thought you could do, ever. It's through this, you know, people use the word intuition because that's kind of what it is, it kind of feels like intuition. But it truly is from God. If you are a born-again believer and you believe that Jesus Christ is your Lord and Savior, then you get this power of the Holy Spirit. It's like a heightened intuition. It's something much deeper, stronger, broader and we've got it within us. Like you said, when God directs us through that, we need to pay attention, we need to be obedient to it and take action, because he has given us the grace to do whatever we need to do.

A good example, and I think it's really funny, is just recently – I've always tried not to say I can't do things, you know it's like people who come to me with their book and say well, I can't write a book, I'm not a writer, well I have been saying things, Mary, about how I can't play the piano and I can't, you know, write songs, but God proved those things wrong to me in the last couple of years. My children and my husband gave me a keyboard for Christmas and God gave me a song and I went on there at the beginning and I just played by one hand and now I've got the complete song that I've played on the piano. Now I don't know how to do that, but it's by God's grace, the intuition, the listening to Him and how He tells me to put my hands on the keys and asks me does that sound right, what would be different? You know, he guided me, I didn't do it, but I did through his grace. And those are the things you are talking about! We can have those kids of results, Right?! If we take this and we're quiet, and we take time to do it, Right?!

Mary's response*: Yes and if we get information like that, a desire to do something, it's because God wants us to do it.*

KM: Amen sister! That's true!

Mary's response: *Yes, when we are listening God will be with us and help us to make things come to fruition.*

KM: Exactly, because it says in the Bible that he puts the desires on your heart and I think that is so imperative. Thank you for that. Ok, so there is one more piece of advice you want to talk about and this one, I'm super excited about because I even have some real life experiences to give. So what would be the last piece of advice you want to give to us?

Mary's response: *The last piece of advice I would like to give today is to Express Gratitude! Again, it's something that you do daily. As you look at yourself and your life, see all the good things. Even if things feel like they are not going well in a day there are always some good things in every day. As you appreciate and acknowledge all those blessings in your life, you will find that more are coming to you. See what makes* *you special, acknowledge it in yourself and appreciate who you are. Having a 'gratitude journal' and writing it down, whatever you are aware of is most beneficial. As you acknowledge all that is good, you find that you are becoming stronger, more confident, and you will see your path more clearly. When we love ourselves unconditionally as we have talked about and we also grateful, we attract the right people and the right opportunities to us so that we are living our lives fully and in a way that God sees us living it. Using our abilities, our talents, and doing His work here.*

KM: Amen that is so true. So did you get that folks? It's, you know, you have got to start a – well, I call it a blessing journal or a gratitude journal. I have got to share this experience because one of the things my husband and I have put in our lives on a daily basis, one which we've made a very important piece in our Fasting and Prayer time with God, was to write our blessings down at the end of the day before we go to bed. We really look at, ok, what are the blessings today? We started writing this blessing journal and you know what I found out? How many blessings we have in a day. Those little things that just come in and at the time you are grateful, oh Thanks God, but you don't sustain that gratitude until you bring it up again and write it down. You take a look at it and go "Oh my gosh, this was one of the best blessed days of my life". It changes everything, doesn't it?

Mary's response: It absolutely does, because we could all have those days where things seem not to go right. If you sit down, and you really look at it like you said, you can find so many blessings in every day. It – it's just amazing and it fills your heart up.

KM: Right, and the joy of the Lord, you know, in the Bible, it talks about the joy of the Lord that is one of our promises from God. I believe it's because we are taking a look at these blessings that we can then receive this promise and you don't focus on the negative, you focus on the positive and it goes back to, you know, some of the things you have talked about, too.

I'm just thinking in terms of something the Lord said to me a long time ago: he said when worry and doubt come in; you can start focusing on them. What happens to most people, and you can correct me if I'm wrong, but what happens to most people is they think, let's talk about finances. They go "Oh, I don't have enough money to pay my bills". "Oh my gosh, the money is coming out and I have got nothing coming in," and their mind goes down that - what it's going to be like and how painful it's going to be and blah, blah, blah, blah, blah.

The Lord said, "I have given you imagination; you can use it for a blessing or a curse." Now use that same imagination, and the minute that imagination comes into your mind, change your story. Imagine that you have received the money and how good that's going to feel and how great it is and go down that way. It goes right back to what you are talking about with a blessing journal, you know if you don't write down the blessings, you can just think about all the crap that went on that day. And then you stay in that place.

Mary's response: *With finances, one thing I tell people to do is when you do have a bunch of bills, as you are paying the bills, think about what you are paying the money out for. Say you are paying your mortgage, or the heat, or the water. You are very grateful to have a roof over your head, you are grateful to have heat so you're warm at night. When you change your thought process around about that money going out, you will just be amazed at how more financial abundance starts to flow to you. Just by placing that gratitude...*

KM: By changing your mind about it.

Mary's response: *Yes, exactly.*

KM: That's great, I agree! I agree! He did a lot of work for us and died on the cross so we could live a life of abundance and that means finances, health, relationships, and a walk with God. It means everything! Everything! Everything!

That is awesome! So, did everyone get those lists? Mary could you list those three things again? Just to make sure that everybody's got them? Begin with the first one...

Mary's response: *Look at yourself from all angles. Listen and follow your intuition. And express gratitude.*

KM: AMEN. So, I hope you got all of those things down folks! Again, if you have my book Prepare to Prosper, just go to the reference section. This whole interview is typed out for you. You can highlight it. Start putting these things into action today. You know we're serious about putting the word in to action. Any KBO that has been working with me, Kingdom

Business Owners, they know that this is an imperative piece to changing your mind and changing your life.

So I guess I have another quick question for you, Mary. Could you tell us how we can help you go to the next level? Because I truly believe that when in the Bible talks about this – when God sends someone to bless us as you have done on this call, then we need to also pay attention to that and as we receive a blessing, we should give a blessing. So, I'm really mindful of that. What can we do to help you get to the next level?

Mary's response: *We I would say just in putting this advice into action and making yourself more happy and feeling good in your life, I really believe that that helps to heal the whole planet. It helps all of us. So that is one thing for sure. If you want to check out my website and perhaps look at what I have to offer and my book, Ready to Love, Fact or Fiction? And you could see what else I might be able to do for you.*

KM: That's awesome, so it's really a level of service. So, if you really felt connected to Mary today, like I have, go and check out her website. I'll have her give you that information in a moment. I would like to just sit for one second and really speak to your heart. Are you ready for those changes in life? Right now, I'm just asking the Holy Spirit to bless you. I'm asking the Holy Spirit to lift you in this moment. I lift, Lord God, Mary to you. I just thank you for her willingness to grow and change and learn. I ask Father God that you give her the grace she needs to go out and serve the multitudes, serve the masses that you have for her, Lord. I pray in this incredible place of the Holy Spirit that she will be equipped and that she will grow prosperous and productive so that she might do more for you Lord. And I pray for the people who are listening to this right now, or reading this. I pray that they take action, Holy Spirit, help them to take action. I pray that the bondage that holds them back from taking action is now gone. In the name of Jesus. And we ask for this incredible change to happen right now, even as we pray. Things are changing in everyone's heart right now in the name of Jesus. And we lift this time to you, Lord God, and are grateful, we are so grateful for this blessing of today. And so folks, in Jesus name I pray for all of this.

Go ahead. I'm going to have Mary give you her contact information. I will tell you she has a great ability to be able to talk to you and help break you free from these things that are binding your heart. So, Mary, could you give us your contact information so they can go to your website and buy your book.

Folks, buy her book, buy her book and did I say, buy her book? Buy 2, buy 3. Buy one for you to mark up and highlight, buy one for you to have on your shelf and also, buy one to give to a friend because the greatest gift you can give others is the gift of true knowledge. Go ahead Mary, what is your phone number and email address as well as your website?

Mary's response: *Ok, well thank you Kathleen.*
My email is info@maryestevenson.com *and my website is* www.maryestevenson.com

KM: Perfect, thank you! And so, just before the end of our time together, I'm so grateful that you took time for us, thank you. Could you give us a word of encouragement in regards to your message?

Mary's response: *Know that this life is a journey that we are meant to enjoy. The more you love and accept yourself fully, the more the world will open up and give you that joyful experience!*

KM: Amen, thank you so much! Thank you, thank you.

Mary's response: *It was my pleasure to be here with you and everyone today. God Bless.*

KM: Thank you. All right folks, we will be back with more experts and you know, I just pray that today is the day that you take action and change your life. In Jesus name. Amen.

See you soon.

JAN MOORE

Interview With An Expert From Aurora Publishing Learning Center

We're having a great day here Aurora Publishing Learning Center we're here to help turn Christian writers into published authors.

Hello, hello, hello! My name is Kathleen Mailer, and I am your host today as we bring you incredible experts – or… as I like to call them, 'life enhancers' to your business that of course, spills out into every area of life.

I am a bestselling author and my latest ***book 'Prepare To Prosper, Taking Your Business To A Higher Level"*** is my 37th published book. Many of you are listening to this, because you have bought a few pre-launch copies of the book OR you have actually bought some of our bulk bundles for your church, organization, or sales team.

I want to thank you so much that you have done that. Right here and right now and I know you have heart to make the world a better place. Buying one, giving one to friend – because the gift of knowledge is really the greatest gift outside and inside of our salvation with Christ.

I am ecstatic about our show today. I have author, Jan Moore joining us from Blooming Bloomers. I LOVE IT!

She is the author of ***"Work On Your Own Terms."***

That is incredible within itself but you know what? I can't wait for you to get prepared to hear this!

Jan Moore has been a career counsellor for 20 years. Can you believe it? 20 years! Some of us have children that old. I mean man, 20 years and she's on a mission to change the world of work for the better. What I love about her is that she is a thoughtful and passionate teacher that desperately wants to help those who have reached midlife (and are not yet working in their passion and joy), so she wants to help them to WALK in the abundant life God has called them to do.

She says all the time that you CAN make money. You can live and work on purpose, make a difference in others' lives, AND have the JOY of the Lord as he has promised.

I don't know about you, but we're in for a treat today as Jan comes forward to share. You know she has a MA in Leadership & Training, she is a qualified instructor with Myers-Briggs Type Indicator, and she is certified in THREE areas: Life Skills Coach, Senior Advisor and Retirement Coach. I mean, is she the right person to talk to, or what? It shows that she teaches from experience and you will soon realize how much she can bring her life forward into the hearts of all of us because her life is filled with music and laughter. Just watch how she oozes that out today as we visit. You know what? You'll find yourself anointed just listening to the sound of her voice. You will feel that joy pop right out. **Kathleen laughs.*

JAN! THANK YOU! THANK YOU! THANK YOU! for joining us all the way from California today (yes folks, she does live the life that she teaches)!

Jan's response: *Thank you so much Kathleen, I am so excited to be on the call with you today. And, yes, it is sunny here.*

KM: Yeah, you know right now at the time of this recording, I was just mentioning to Jan that we are experiencing snow, but I live in Canada, in the winter, what do I expect? But here she is in sunny California. You know I wouldn't put it past her to be sitting beside the pool and sunning herself as she shares. You know what? That's a good thing! I am so glad that you do that Jan.

Jan's Response: *Thank you Kathleen, it took me a long time to make one of my dreams come true.*

KM: Well, that's what this call is about today. Let's help other people do the same thing! Oh man, as you know, I have a really strong passion for K.B.O's - Kingdom Business Owners that are passionate for Christ. I KNOW you have the same heart as I do … Jan, what's the primary mission you have in regard to helping entrepreneurs grow?

Jan's response: *I am really on a mission to change the world of work for the better. I have read several studies that say seven out of ten people say they are only in their jobs for the money because they really don't enjoy it. I feel that if you have reached midlife and you are not yet working with passion and joy – you really need to make a change. My aim is to show you how to remove any fears that hold you back so* *you can live and work on purpose – while making both money and a difference.*

KM: That is AWESOME! I know from chatting with you I have just been so blessed because we've known each other for a few years now and I know from chatting with you that you have all these great nuggets of wisdom, and I love the fact that you have put most of that in your book, so folks, if you are like chomping at the bit for some more wisdom, definitely go – I'll have her give you her website. Go pick up a copy or you know my motto, pick up two or three copies. One for you, one to give to a friend and one as a working copy where you highlight, and you mark it up. Buy three copies – anytime you find something of value because you are going to need to do it. So go and get that. She's got all these nuggets of wisdom in there. But, I digress... you just have a passion to share and I want to make sure that our listeners run and get a pen and paper handy to jot this down.

Folks, also I know that some of you have my book Prepare To Prosper, this is that working copy where we highlight and dog-ear and write in the book. Grab that one out and follow along with our interview here because you will be reading the transcribed version in the book. Make sure you take notes inside. When God pops something up as she speaks today, write a little note in the side or highlight your book so you can walk along with us. OK? That sounds like a really good idea.

Jan, let's get back to you. What is your first piece of advice for us today?

Jan's response: *I strongly believe Kathleen, that work is love made visible.*

KM: Oh, stop for just a second, just stop for a second. Did you hear that you guys? Did you hear that? I hope that if you are not highlighting this, you are writing it down. Which I think you should do both. Say it again Jan, it was beautiful.

Jan's response: *Work is love made visible.*

KM: Wow. OK, I receive that for one.

Jan's response: *Love is service to others. So I want you to think about how can you best serve the world with your own gifts? I believe our culture has largely separated our passion from our work. Once you reach midlife, you will feel an urge to re-align your gifts and passion with the needs of the world. It is through our work that we are best able to evolve ourselves. It is who we become while we are on this journey that is our goal. Our work can be our best expression of our love made visible.*

I want you to own the power to create the work you love. It is the ultimate act of self-love and it is a pre-requisite to sharing your loving work with others. When work becomes your calling, there's no telling where that path will lead. That's what makes it so exciting.

If you heed the words of the Bible from Matthew: "For where your treasure is, there your heart will be also." Matthew 6:21 and from Ecclesiastes: "So I saw that there is nothing better for a person than to enjoy their work." Ecclesiastes 3:22

KM: AMEN! That was AWESOME! You know, you said this earlier on the call. Here you were talking about who we involve on the journey and who we become. That's just so awesome. I liken it to one of the things I always say is "if you are looking to ask God for miracles in your life, the thing is it's never about the miracle. God can produce the miracle in such a fraction of a second that we couldn't believe it, but it's who you become in the process, in receiving that miracle. Doing what you love, it's a miracle isn't it? I think of it every day. You and I, we talked about this so many times. It's like living a life filled with joy and living a life on purpose and doing what you are called to do. That in itself is a miracle and you gave staggering statistics that so many people are doing the job for the money. Man, you know, we gotta change those things. I really hope...

Jan's response: *It's not an impossible dream. That's what I want the people to really realize.*

KM: MMMhmm. You can do it too. I mean if I'm doing it and you're doing it, it obviously means there are a lot of people who can be doing it, right?

Jan's response: *Exactly, we all can.*

KM: Good. So she gave two bible scriptures there that I think we're really important. Matthew 6:21 and Ecclasiastes 3:22. Make note of that. Go back and study it. I just love the *"So I saw that there is nothing better for a person than to enjoy their wor*k." I mean, my goodness, if that doesn't describe your calling, I don't know what does!

Alright,

Jan's response: *That's everyone's calling!*

KM: It sure is, isn't it? Yeah, I guess I do that too, right? I really enjoy people who love their work and here we are today because of that. Well, that's awesome! Ok, what's your second piece of advice?

Jan's response: *Designing Your Future is half the Fun. So while retirement planning can be boring, I want people to realize that worth planning certainly isn't. It is definitely the journey not the destination Kathleen, as you have already pointed out.*

To do what you love first requires you to know yourself, though. This is something that many people just haven't had time to do. This is why a stress at midlife may be the best time to do your real work. It's also why seeking money first for its own sake fails to satisfy. So, who are you, and what do you really want to do with your life? I strongly believe our gifts are gifts from the Divine and we are born with them inside us.

KM: AMEN!

Jan's response: *If you are struggling to access who you are at the core and what your gifts are, I would like you to have a look at the Myers-Briggs Type Indicator. It's a personality assessment tool. It's the most widely used assessment tool in the world by career counsellors. It's been translated into about 13 different languages. It can really help you realize what your inborn gifts are in a relatively short period of time.*

You really should find a qualified instructor who can walk you through the results is my only caveat with this.

KM: Can I just stop you there for just a second? I don't mean to interrupt, but if you are talking about this, what I'm seeing is this would so valuable. I hear so many Christians and even business owners saying I just don't know if this is what I am called to do. I don't know what I'm good at. This is really going to bring out a new value of self-assessment and learning. Learning what you are, what your tools are and what your gifts are so that you can incorporate that into your work place? Is that part of why you would do this?

Jan's response: *Exactly. It helps people zero in on their inborn gifts that they have forgotten that they actually have.*

KM: Right, so brilliant, Jan, and now I understand what that means, so can people – I just need to interject for a second here – I really believe folks that understanding your gifts, your talents and your abilities, that is what you need to share with the world. God has given you those things.

What happens to many of us when we have a gift, we think, well doesn't everyone? You know, let me give an example: I just realized the other day, it was really funny, is that I have an ability to really see the potential in other people. so when I look at somebody, immediately God gives me their 'WOW' (their potential). WOW, where that person is going to go. WOW, who that person really is. Well, I think to myself, doesn't everybody do this?

But the other day someone said wow; you've got a real gift to see that. I said A GIFT? I have a gift? No gift, it's just what I do. I don't even think of it as a gift. Then I realized that not everybody has that.

So, in order for me to see that as a gift flourish, I need to continue to grow and evolve into what I am called to do. We all really need to find out what our gifts are. And Jan, you are a great person to have them come to in order to get this done, right?

Jan's response: *Yes, definitely.*

KM: Good and you will give them some information at the end of the day to help them with that? Perfect. I'm sorry to interrupt, but I just had to get that out there that that is so true. I'm in agreement with you. So when your work allows these inborn gifts that you talk about, what happens then?

Jan's response: *You will feel fulfilled, because at some level, we all hunger for our lives to have meaning. If you are working with your own inborn gifts, your purpose comes from using our skills to help others. If you think about people like Terry Fox, Mother Theresa, or former President Jimmy Carter, you can see what their gifts are. What is your work? What legacy do you want to leave behind?*

I want you to start thinking about how can you make a difference? It'll be based on something that you actually enjoy doing? What do you care deeply enough about that you could dedicate the rest of your life to? Anything that sparks your interest is a clue you can use to follow to see where it leads. So start taking notes about what sparks your interest if you are really not working on purpose already.

I would like you to ponder this message; this is actually in the original book that was written about the Myers-Briggs Type Indicator. The original creators of that work Quote from Romans 12: 4-7 "We have different gifts, according to the grace given to each of us. If your gift is prophesying, then prophesy in accordance with your faith; if it is serving, then serve; if it is teaching, then teach; if it is to encourage, then give encouragement; if it is giving, then give generously, if it is to lead, do it diligently; if it is to show mercy, do it cheerfully."

KM: Wow, and that's Romans 12:4-7 isn't it?

Jan's response: *Yes it is. It's actually quoted in the beginning of the Myers-Briggs Type Indicator book.*

KM: So the creators of that actually came from very clear faith based training. So that's what this is, it's really faith based. Find out what your gifts are in Christ so that you can share with the world what you are called to do.

Jan's response: *Yes.*

KM: That's awesome! That is AWESOME…ok, so folks a couple of things that you want to make sure that you have down is asking yourself those questions, you know that she asks. What legacy do I want to leave behind? How can I make a difference? Using my gifts, talents and abilities, how can that happen? According to Romans 12: 4-7, it says whatever your gift is, just do it already. Do it in small way, they don't have to go into great big huge ways of doing things. They can just do it small, right, in the beginning?

Jan's response: *Exactly! We're not here to cure, we're not all here to cure cancer or do brain surgery, really it's what your gift is.*

KM: What you do every day. So if you are a server, if you just love to serve, then just for heaven's sake, invite people over to your house and serve away, right? It's ok to serve. You know a lot of people have had others in their life kind of condemn their gifts and I think about people that want to be homemakers and they want to stay at home with their children. I hear this all the time. As a matter of fact, I remember being interviewed about it. You know, Kathleen you're a mother, you're a wife and you're a business owner and you're this and you're that and they asked me – what is your most fulfilling part? I said all of it. There's nothing wrong with – if your passion is to serve and you want to serve your husband and your children, go right ahead and do that. Do it right at home. Don't listen to other people. If you love to do it, just do it. Listen to what God says, not what man says, right?

Jan's response: *Mhmm! correct!*

KM: So, you're number one piece of advice that you want to give, and I know that you love this topic because we have talked about it and you've helped so many people and this is what holds people back like tremendously! Give us that last piece of advice.

Jan's response: *Kathleen, this is so important! I really want people to hear this: don't allow Fear to hold you back! It has been said that fear is mans and woman's greatest enemy. Fear can cause failure if it stops you from walking through it. However, fear is only a thought in your mind. So don't fear your own thoughts. Change them if they are not helping you get what you want.*

I really think we need to break free of the self-imposed prison that we have unwittingly placed ourselves in due to our beliefs, opinions, training and environmental influences. I think sometimes we fall into our habits and will stay there unless we deliberately decide to change them. Before deciding on a new career path, become aware of any self-limiting beliefs you have, so you can change them.

To live and work on your own terms, you can consciously overcome the six main fears that tend to hold people back from living the life of their dreams. The six main fears, Kathleen, are fear of poverty, fear of criticism, fear of poor health, fear of loss of love, fear of aging and fear of death.

KM: OK, I'm just getting these down on a piece of paper. I am writing furiously today too. Let me just – I think I missed one here. OK, I have fear of poverty, fear of criticism, loss of love, fear of poor health, fear of aging and fear of death. Again those are - poverty, criticism, poor health, loss of love, aging and death.

Jan's response: *Correct. Those are all of the biggies.*

KM: They sound big.

Jan's response: *They hold people back.*

KM: It's true, mhm. I see it in people I meet in my everyday life. So what does God have to say about that?

Jan's response: *Again Kathleen, you can look to the Bible to help you walk through any fear you might have. Here's another quote: "For I am the Lord, your God, who takes hold of your right hand and says to you, do not fear; I will help you." That s from Isaiah 41:13.*

KM: That's one of my favourites.

Jan's response: *And at the end of your days, you will be able to say: "I have brought you glory on earth by completing the work you gave me to do." That's from John 17:4*

KM: AMEN! That is Awesome! John 17:4 I have brought you glory on earth by completing the work you gave me to do. That is so imperative, folks that we can say that at the end of the day. You know by overcoming our fears, and God has given you the ability to do that because God is the God of peace, he's the God of order and he does not want you to live by fear. It doesn't say and man shall live by fear alone in the bible. That's not what the Bible says. It says that man shall not live by bread alone, but by the works of the father. So yeah, that is awesome. Thank you.

I hope everybody has written things down. Jan if you could just list those three things again in order just to make sure that everybody has that. The very first piece of advice was:

Jan's response: *Work is love made visible.*

KM: Cool the next…

Jan's response: *Designing your future is half the fun.*

KM: Perfect, and again

Jan's response: *Is don't allow fear to hold you back.*

KM: That's awesome, thank you! Thank you. Jan, we all know that, like, incorporating is a difficult task when we try to do it on our own – without someone walking it through with them. Can you tell us how you could help us go to the next level?

Jan's response: *Well, Kathleen, my book, '**Work On Your Own Terms**', I've written it in bite-size pieces so it is easy to read in small snippets of time. Because I know not everyone has time to sit down for an hour each day, but if you can read for ten or twenty minutes, this will help you overcome the six primary fears that can hold you back. It will encourage you to overcome those fears I mentioned earlier: Poverty, Criticism, Poor Health, Loss of Love, Aging or even Death.*

The book was written for midlife working women who want to love their work, travel in a meaningful way and recapture the idealism of their youth and use it then to make a difference in the world.

Kathleen, I also offer retreats to help women gather in community to support each other in transitioning to meaningful work in midlife and beyond if you want that extra support. Of course, laughter and music are always included. I love both.

KM: Of course, goes without saying when it comes to you. That's who you are. That's fantastic. How can they contact you? Can you give us some contact information?

Jan's response: *People can email me at* Jan@WorkOnYourOwnTerms.com, *or you can visit my website* www.WorkOnYourOwnTerms.com. *And while you are there you can download my free e-book called:* ***'Create Career Joy****!' That may be all you need to help launch your new career.*

KM: That's AWESOME, thank you SO much! I really appreciate it. So folks, go check out her website, get that free download; start checking into who you are and what you need to do because you know what? You are supposed to live the life you dream of. It's what we are called to do. You can do it.

Jan, I'm just so grateful that you took time in your schedule to come and see us. Before we end our time together, could you give us a word of encouragement in regard to your message?

Jan's response: *Of course Kathleen, we were each born with greatness inside us. Sometimes, we just need a little help uncovering it. Do you know why wild geese fly in a V-formation? As each bird flaps its wings, it creates an updraft for the bird immediately following. By flying in a V-formation,* *the whole flock can travel farther than if each bird flew alone. By travelling together in community, they can get where they are going more quickly and easily, because they take turns uplifting one another. Geese honk from behind to encourage those up front to keep going. This is also how the best groups work together. This is why I love group work so much Kathleen.*

KM: No kidding.

Jan's response: *This message is also found in the Bible.*

KM: Get out of here, really?

Jan's response: *Yes*

KM: Imagine that.

Jan's response: *"Therefore, encourage one another and build one another up, just as you are doing."*
1 Thessalonians 5:11

KM: So are you telling me that the Bible is really a manual for life?

Jan's response: *Yes, I am saying that Kathleen. The more I read it, the more that I realize that, you know, it's the book I really need to follow.*

KM: Thank you so much Jan, you have been such a pleasure as always to chat. I know I've got a whole gamut full of notes. I hope you on the call do as well and if you are reading this, make sure you put these plans into action. To start living the life you are meant to live right now.

It's Kathleen Mailer and it looks like we are running out of time so I want you to have a very blessed day and a very blessed life. *In the name of Jesus. Amen.*

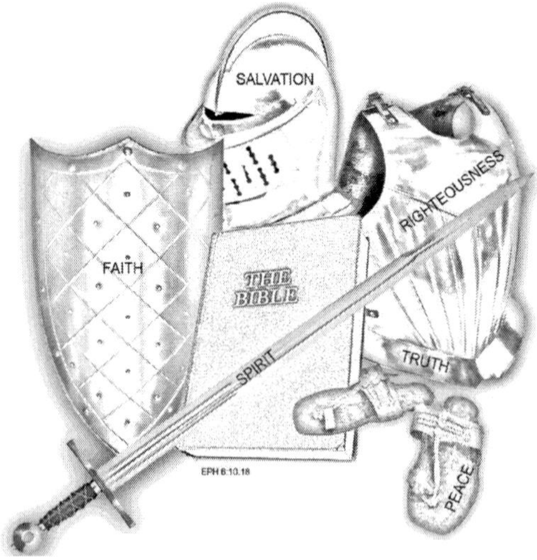

(c) 2014 Kathleen Mailer - KBO

CORALIE BRAUM

Interview With An Expert From Aurora Publishing Learning Center

WE are having a BLAST here at Aurora Publishing Learning Center, where we help turn Christian writers into published authors.

My name is Kathleen Mailer and as your host today, I come to bring you great treasures: an international treasure today.

If you have tuned into our show before, you know I am all about making sure you are connected with the right people who can lift you higher and higher in your business and in your life. My guest today is one of those people who can make you look good and position you to reach the platform that you need to be on. Putting God's best forward is what she is all about and I just really love her.

Joining me on our platform today is none other than Coralie Braum from Leaping Cowgirl Productions Ltd. & Braum Consulting.

I had such a hard time, Coralie, downsizing into a bite sized introduction for you because she, you guys, she has done so much for entrepreneurs.

CB response: *Well thank you!*

KM: She's just so wonderful! I'm gonna tell them a little bit about what you do. Um, let's see, how do you put this: FCMC a certified management consultant, you're an author, a speaker and an award-winning film director as well, right? You've worked in the realm of TV, video producer, with 20 years of experience. I don't know how you've done it, because, I mean, are you only 25 or something like that.

You taught entrepreneurship for many years at Mount Royal University. Folks, she has worked as a coach and strategist with dozens of growing and successful clients across Canada, and in SE Asia, South America and Cuba.

Isn't that incredible? AND the good news is… she is gets to be here today with you and me. Isn't that great?

Welcome, welcome to our show Coralie! Thank you SO much for taking time between video productions, marketing programs, coaching and just being such a good friend to join us today.

CB response: *Oh, thank you so much. What a lovely introduction Kathleen, it's a pleasure to be here.*

KM: Oh, I am so excited to share your wisdom, well, and just you with a growing, growing group of Kingdom Business Owners around the world. It's just such a privilege to have you here today. I know that everyone on this call or who is reading this particular interview will really, really want to connect with you, but what I want to do at this moment is kind of sum up how you see yourself in terms of partnering with entrepreneurs, what would that look like?

CB response: *Well, I use the term friendly co-pilot, Kathleen. I really see myself coming beside entrepreneurs and sort of helping them understand what their vision is and then I bring in the right team from around the country or around the world, if necessary to make sure that we are going to successfully help them bring that vision down into reality. And that's really my joy Kathleen, I'm really happy when I see someone I have worked with is even more successful because we've worked with them.*

KM: Isn't that Awesome!!!! I know what you mean. You and I have talked so much about that, that we just find the joy of the Lord in what we do because we get to go to work, like I say, I get to go to work with my Daddy today and see what he's doing and I know you feel the same way. I for one have to say how grateful I am that God brought you into my life and that we get to work side by side and in partnership together even now as we're going through this interview process. I mean I think you are busy working behind the scenes on my marketing platform too, right?

CB response: *That's right. And it's going very well.*

KM: You know we all need partnerships. We are in partnership with the Holy Spirit. We are in partnership with our clients, as I say explain in my book ***Prepare To Prosper,*** the truth is we just cannot function without partnerships. We need as K.B.Os very key partners to help us go to that next level. That's exactly how the Body of Christ is supposed to live.

***CB response:** I agree.*

KM: Coralie, I want to pick your brains for a few minutes. I am going to ask you to give us a few pieces of advice to help catapult us to the next level.

You know what, for those of you who have bought copies of my book, please turn to the interview with Coralie Braum and follow along with us a little bit. Make sure you take my advice to highlight the important points that come up and write the things right in your working copy all of the things you want to remember. Go ahead and highlight it, dog ear it do all those things you need to do in this particular book.

For those of you who don't have my book yet, you can go to: www.PreparetoProsperBook.com to pick it up. Some of you already know why I always say buy 3 copies of life changing books.

1 copy to give away… because giving is a lifestyle and it styles your life… and the other 2 are for your success library. One is for reading ONLY and the other is a WORKING copy. Again, highlight, dog-ear, write in it and make it a reference that you will refer to over and over again. I have those books in my library right now and I don't let anyone have them. The only time I ever share books is to buy them a copy or lend them from my read only library.

So, if you don't have a copy, get your pen and paper ready because you are going to want to write down everything this woman says, you won't want to miss anything, not one thing! Ready? …let's get started.

Coralie, what would you give to us as the number one piece of advice to help us change our business and change our lives?

CB response: *The first piece of advice I have is to pray continuously, not just for your own business but also for your partners, your clients and for finding a balance between your work and the other elements of your life. I just can't underline that enough, we have Jesus Christ, CEO in our company and if you go to him and ask him for strategy and for ideas, he will most graciously provide that for us. I think that that keeps us exactly on the path that we need to be on in our business, not turning to the left or the right, but going exactly where we are meant to go. That makes us all successful together.*

KM: Yeah, absolutely, I am in agreement. So hopefully you got that down, pray continuously for your business, your partners and your clients. It is a vital strategy. It is also the core of being a Kingdom Business Owner. Awesome thank you.

What else can you share with us to help position us as a Kingdom Business Owner?

CB response: *Well, I think one of the things I have learned in the over 30 years of business experience I have had with many different industries and people, and frankly, many cultures is that it's critical that you choose the team that you work with extreme care. You need to understand, of course, the skills you need and that sort of thing, but skills can be learned. Attitudes, however, are really hard to change and so,* *especially in earlier stages, you want to find people that are going to partner with you, support you, that are going to buy into your mission and that aren't just going to be an overhead drain or bring negative things into your business. I can't emphasize that enough – hire very, very wisely because those people that you start with, that you bring together, are going to be the ones that make your business a long-term sustainable success.*

KM: Amen. I totally concur with you. You know, I think that goes over into one of the things it talks about in the book is about partnership with your clients. You know, I no longer call clients, clients. I partner with people, so if I am helping them with their book, they're not clients of mine, I actually partner with them to get their book out there. And so, even in that place, when you are choosing clients or partnership, think about partnership in that because that's important and in your experience, is it ok to say no to people who want your services? I talk at great lengths in the Prepare To Prosper book about this.

***CB response**: Absolutely, as a matter of fact, I recommend it. This was a real learning for me Kathleen, when I started out, I had the feeling I had to do each piece of work that came along, or somehow I wouldn't have enough work. I found over the years that in fact that is now true, that you need to be selective in terms of the work that you engaged in and the people that you choose to partner with, because you're right, it's not just the sort of traditional relationship clients and service provider, it's really developing a long term relationship where you are looking to make your partner* *successful over the long term. So, when you pick out characteristics that are not going to make a good partner, and I have my own list of those, and you will develop a list of them as well, you need to listen to that and feel free to say "mmm, this isn't the right match, let me refer you elsewhere, you know maybe you need to rethink some things, maybe it's not the right timing.*

This is again going back to point one where we really need to pray for clear discernment on who the Lord wants us to work with. That won't just be Christians, and it might be people that have lifestyles and issues that we may not subscribe to because the Lord wants to work with them as a way of demonstrating his grace and who he is to us. That's ok, however; there are certain characteristics which don't make for good clients and so we want to understand what those are and try and avoid them. You know an obvious one would be somebody who doesn't pay. So if you discover early on that they are really difficult to collect from, well then maybe you are not dealing with the right partner. People need to understand they have to invest in you the same way you are investing in them. It's a two-way street. I find real pressure on fees and things like that where people are unwilling to pay for quality, they are probably not a good partner then.

KM: Right, and that again, I love what you said... I want everyone to write that down too, we're getting extra advice from her, about writing down a list of characteristics of what you want in your partner – and partner meaning people that you partner with to move your business forward and your clients. So yeah, write it down, get really, really clearly.

One of the things that sort of changed my life in the past was to really nail down: you know, God, who is it that you want me to touch, who is it you want me to reach? One of the biggest things that changed my life is that they are ready, willing and able to move forward.

So I ask for partners that are ready, willing and able to move forward. I find that that really changed things for me. It made it really clear who I want to work with and who I do not want to work with.

Awesome, this is great stuff! I know, I can't get enough, I won't bug you too much longer, but maybe we could get just one more piece of advice?

CB response: *Yeah, I have a piece of advice that is particularly for smaller business owners who may not invest in this area yet. Do invest in building the right image.*

These days that's not just good business cards and a logo but also a good website that is fully functional and works that makes you look like a real business.

Your average consumer attention span has reduced from 2000 seconds down to eight seconds. People will make a decision whether or not to stay on your website basically in the blink of an eye. They're that fast, so if you want to capture customers and their information and get them engaged with you electronically, which is really important these days, you need a website that works well that loads quickly, that is visually appealing, that has the right buttons and calls for action, etc.

The other thing you need is a very positive and a very targeted social media presence, but in addition to that, 96% of companies – I just read a big study in the US – have added video into their marketing strategy for 2014 and in fact, the web crawlers and search engines are going to be favouring video. I just read another piece on that. So you need to think about adding that kind of component into your marketing strategy as well. Let me encourage you to have a really professional quality in all of these things. It's worth the investment.

With good video, you'll get four times the conversion rate of customers coming, even if they don't look at the video incidentally. So it's really key to start...

KM: Isn't that odd? What a great piece of advice. Four times.

***CB response**: Yeah, we have to be really careful what we put online though Kathleen, because it will live for a long time.*

KM: You know we all need to think about that too, even in terms of doing the little videos that we do at home, printings on Facebook. We are leaving an imprint and so um, as Christian Business Owners, we have to really be careful of that kind of quality. You are not saying there is anything wrong (me either) with doing a video and uploading to Facebook if you are going to some event. If you are helping to entice people into your business and all that kind of stuff it is good. But you need to have the framework, the foundation of some high quality videos, especially if you are marketing something at the end, that's the key is to get the high quality video in that direction and yes, by all means do video blog here and there on your own that's an added bonus to it. You need that foundation.

CB response: *Well, we can train people, Kathleen, and have, how to do blogging, but even then you need really good lighting and really good sound or people will step away very quickly from you.*

There is an equation that high quality will bring a sense of high value. People are frankly more willing to pay for the products and services that are presented as high quality, so you know, that's how it fits together.

KM: Awesome advice! Love it! Again, I'm getting more and more stuff every time we talk. So I am writing these things down furiously here. Can you just sum up again the three pieces of advice so we can check our list? Please?

CB response: *Yes, the three pieces of advice in brief are:*

1. *Pray continuously;*

2. *Choose your team most carefully; and*

3. *Invest in building the right image, including video.*

KM: Perfect, thank you.

CB response: *No thank you, it's a pleasure. I get so excited when I think about the possibilities and I see people reaching their dreams and it is just my absolute joy.*

KM: Thank you, thank you! I'm just finishing writing that down because I got more out of our time together as well. I just really appreciate you being here today and sharing with everyone. I was wondering because I know that... I can just feel it and I can sense how many people are chomping at the bit to get going and to connect to you. Can you tell us how you could actually help us get to our next level, what it is that Leaping Cowgirl productions can do to get us there?

CB response: *Well, as you know I'm a management consultant by background, so we look at marketing strategy and tactics, and then we create very high quality and professional videos, including animation and other things that are targeted specifically to the right customer. We tell stories that are interesting and that are targeted to sell.*

KM: Awesome. How can they get a hold of you if they want to touch base?

CB response: *Well, they could email me at cbraum@telus.net; they can go on our website and reach me there, that's* www.leapingcowgirl.com *or I'm on Twitter or LinkedIn under my name. Coralie Braum*

KM: Thank you so much for our time together today. It seems like we are actually coming to the end of our time, but before we actually close, would you mind just giving us maybe a word of encouragement or something in regards to your message today?

CB response*: Well, Kathleen as I mentioned, you know I have really joyfully helped hundreds of people to achieve success* *over my career and I have seen over all of those decades – mind you, I am still very young of course - that the best predictor of success isn't what many people would think. It isn't your sex, nationality, age, or your background, or your education level. The best predictor of your success in business is your persistence, your optimism, your dogged dedication and your faith.*

KM: Wow, thank you. I just pray that God blesses you and multiplies you and takes care of you as you continue in your business today. I am just so very grateful and honoured for this time together. Thank you!

CB response: *Thank you so much Kathleen, the honour is mine. It's just a great pleasure. I hope that my few small words will be of help to those out there that are listening and I look forward to talking to you. No obligation, but give me a call if you want to find out more about what we do, or get a piece of quick advice.*

KM: That sounds awesome. And for you out there, I hope you have actually written down some of this information for people who are hearing this. Write it down. For people who are reading this, make sure you make notes and highlight it.

I thank you for joining us on this call today. I thank you for partnering with me to make a success for the glory of God, in Jesus' name. Until next time, have a fabulous blessed day.

KATHLEEN D. MAILER

I Was Born An Entrepreneur

I had the privilege of being born in a family of leaders. Thanks to Dad, the ability to dream and hope for a better future was installed at a young age. My father was a hard-working, loyal, dedicated family man and would stop at nothing to make sure we knew that all he did, he did for us.

As a water-well driller with his own business, he taught me you had to believe in your mission in life. His mission was one of good, clean drinking water. I think his purpose may have surfaced in his childhood as he survived through the dirty thirties when water was as scarce as everything else.

While I inherited many valuable lessons of character and integrity from my Dad, I also saw the flip side of entrepreneurship. I watched Mom and Dad struggle to make ends meet with a growing family to feed. Dad worked day in and day out. No one worked harder than Dad did. As a result, he wasn't home very much. I saw the stress of all of these things take its toll on their marriage, family life, and health.

This launched me on a path to discover my own gifts, examine my inequities, study the issues of the heart, and find out the unequivocally truth – that one can do nothing without or aside from Jesus Christ. I realized that my thoughts and belief system (the B.S. in my life!) manifest our current reality – and the Bible had the answers that could change it.

Being a K.B.O. (Kingdom Business Owner) is my destiny. It is a ministry and a platform to share God's Honest Truth about wealth and abundance in all areas of life.

My path has led me to be blessed by God, as he created a platform for my purpose. I praise God for the world renowned boot camp: A Book Is Never A Book, How To Write, Publish & Market Your OWN How To Book; Today's Businesswoman Magazine providing quality, AFFORDABLE Mentorship; Breaking Chains Radio Show, and the KBO Monthly Mentorship program.

Won't you link arms with me and become one with a powerful army of God?

Together we CAN make a difference!

Here is to our SUCCESS!

Kathleen Mailer

The International Business Evangelist, Founder/Editor-In-Chief of Today's Businesswoman Magazine, Founder/ Facilitator of "A Book Is NEVER A Book Boot Camp", Co-Founder of C.C.K.B.O (Christian Collation of Kingdom Business Owners), Author/Speaker/Trainer.

RESOURCES & BLESSINGS

Ready, Set, Go Higher!

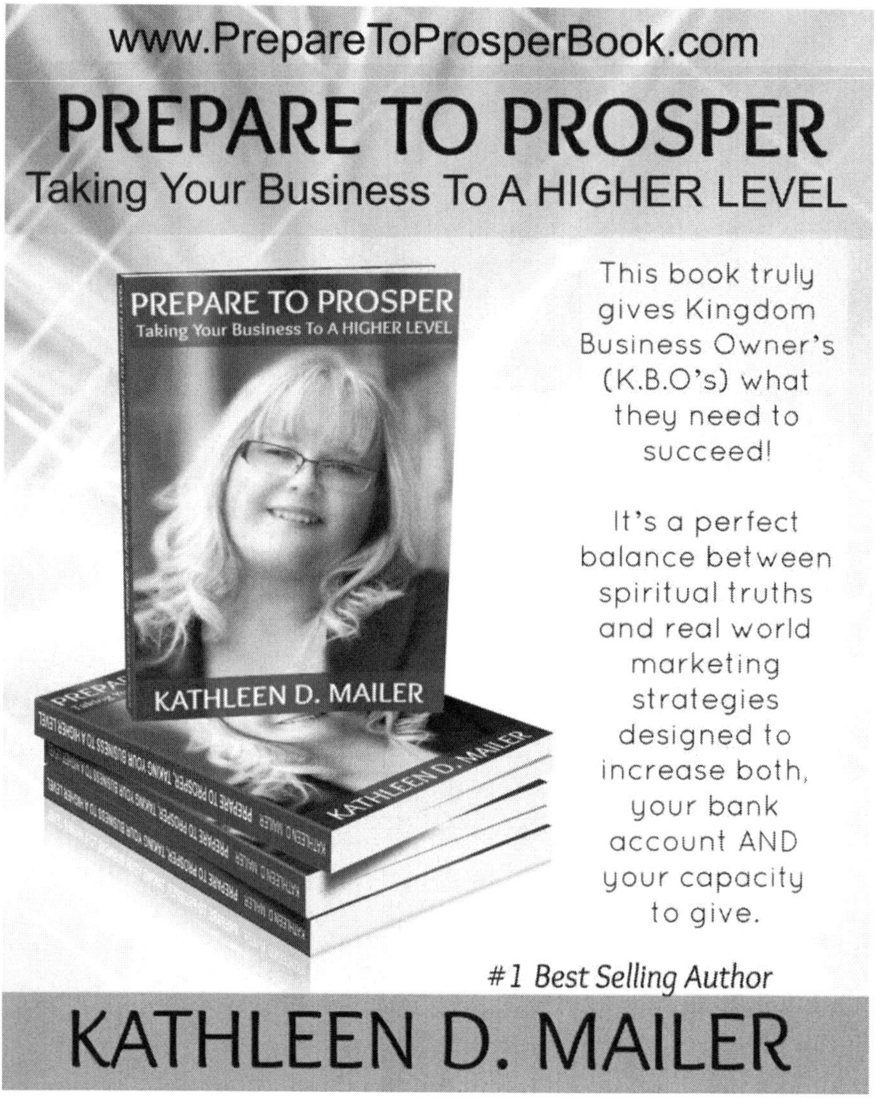
www.PrepareToProsperBook.com
PREPARE TO PROSPER
Taking Your Business To A HIGHER LEVEL
PREPARE TO PROSPER
Taking Your Business To A HIGHER LEVEL
KATHLEEN D. MAILER
This book truly gives Kingdom Business Owner's (K.B.O's) what they need to succeed!
It's a perfect balance between spiritual truths and real world marketing strategies designed to increase both, your bank account AND your capacity to give.
#1 Best Selling Author
KATHLEEN D. MAILER

19738137R10283

Made in the USA
San Bernardino, CA
12 March 2015